The Information Technology REVOLUTION in Financial Services

Using **IT** to Create, Manage and Market Financial

William S. Sachs and Frank Elston

A BANKLINE PUBLICATION
PROBUS PUBLISHING COMPANY
Chicago, Illinois
Cambridge, England

BANKLINE
A BankLine Publication

Table of Contents

Preface

Like many industries, financial services are experiencing an increasing reliance on information for decisionmaking, fueled largely by new technologies that are transforming our ways of doing business and creating new businesses.

Computer systems are hardly new to finance. For decades, banks, credit card issuers, insurance companies, brokerages, and mutual fund houses have always used internal databases to maintain customer accounts and records. For the most part, however, the work consisted of crunching numbers and reducing record-keeping costs.

Today's information networks are far more sophisticated and encompass a vast array of applications. Recent developments include systems to perform the following functions:

- match bids and offers during execution of trades in securities and financial instruments;
- permit commodity traders to post margins in a matter of minutes at any time from any place in the world;
- use artificial intelligence techniques in financial models to evaluate loans, underwrite insurance policies, and plan investment portfolios;
- target both institutional and private investors with sophisticated databases;
- allow bank customers to buy, sell or exchange their funds through teller machines;
- buy and sell securities directly from home computers and "smart" telephones;

- establish interactive networks which hook up instantaneously to a wide array of informational databases; and
- update financial markets with portable computers and pagers, and use such transient microchips to trade from wherever a person happens to be.

This book is written for professionals engaged in the management of financial services. It focuses on the use of information in creating, carrying out, and marketing a broad spectrum of financial services. Though the book addresses financial managers, it is also written to appeal to secondary audiences—those of you who might be concerned with software and computer science and their uses in business and academia.

Our approach is a functional one which emphasizes business applications rather than technical arrangements. Our concern is not technical operations which involve skills such as programing, engineering, systems design, and maintenance. Rather, our emphasis is on the uses of computer outputs in business decisions. However, we recognize that technical forms and applications are linked to each other. For example, a software program that is difficult to use results in poor performance. On the other hand, computer illiteracy on the part of business managers can lead to inefficient mechanical systems.

The rationale for a user approach is that information provides a means of accomplishing company tasks, and the use of information is a user responsibility. From an operating perspective, what is important is the way computer information is employed in managing financial services. Company personnel do not have to understand how a computer works in order to use it effectively. After all, we drive cars without knowing how an internal combustion engine works. We can enter information into a computer and retrieve desired data without knowing COBOL or any other language that instructs electronic machines.

Desiring to produce something more than a "how-to" book that mimicks current practices, we evaluate those practices. We analyze why things are done.

In accordance with this approach, the book is divided into four parts:

Part I
The Context of Financial Services (Chapters 1–2)

This section discusses the environment in which the financial services industry must operate. Topics include: classification of databases; their potential uses; suppliers of information; legal constraints; and current issues regarding privacy.

Part II
New Product Strategies (Chapters 3–5)

The main theme of this section is the creation of new financial services, showing that innovative behavior can create competitive advantages. The chapters raise such issues as:

- why process innovation must be married to managerial innovation;
- when technological services should be outsourced or done in–house;
- how to get the most out of development spending at each stage of the new product process;
- how companies can use existing assets to create new sources of revenue and profits;
- which methods of generating ideas for new financial services work and which don't; and
- when market tests pay off and when they don't.

Part III
Marketing Strategies (Chapters 6–9)

These chapters deal primarily with marketing and distributing financial services, with particular emphasis on using databases. This section covers primary marketing issues as they relate to financial services. These include: database marketing, geodemographic segmentation, lifetime value of customers, strategies of countersegmentation, response tests.

Part IV
Managing for Superior Performance (Chapters 10–12)

This section covers: a model of service quality; forecasting techniques and their uses; mathematical models and how they get fractured; trends that will guide financial services into the 21st century.

Acknowledgments

We wish to acknowledge the fine editorial work of Joyce M. Sachs, who made our text infinitely more readable. We owe a debt of gratitude to Stephen Kerns, who read the text and made many initial suggestions. We also thank Devesh Chatuverdi and Bin Zou, graduate students at Eastern New Mexico University, for their library research and assistance.

Part I

The Context of Financial Services

1

The Scope of Financial Services: An Overview

Financial services are vital to any advanced economy. According to the Department of Commerce, the financial services industry, excluding real estate, accounts for $5\frac{1}{2}$ percent of our Gross Domestic Product (GDP). These government statistics, however, greatly underestimate the GDP contribution of the financial sector.

Probing into the different aspects of financial services, this chapter presents in broad terms the context in which financial firms operate. Specifically, main subjects covered in this chapter are:

- Major components of the financial services industry
- The emergence of hybrid financial companies
- Shifts in market share from banking to funds management
- Productivity issues in the financial services industry
- The handling of information technology
- The distinction between data and information
- The types and uses of databases

The Financial Service Industry

As an industry, the financial services industry lacks cohesion. There are no well-defined forms to characterize them. There is no focus or central tendency to bind these services together. These services extend into many nooks and crannies of our economy: from warranting shoppers' credit card payments to financing home mortgages; from protecting against loss from property damage to insuring against loss from death; from making personal loans to underwriting huge sums to organizations and governments.

The common thread that runs through financial services is that each segment of the industry deals with money. Since money has diverse uses, services cater to a wide mixture of needs for individuals and institutions.

According to government statistics tracking broad categories, the main components of the financial industry include banks, insurance companies, brokerage houses, and bond and equity funds. The industry has also sprouted numerous specialty firms operating in narrow niches, such as purveyors of electronic data, financial planners, and real estate trusts. (Leading financial institutions are listed in the appendix at the end of this chapter.)

Official figures of our nation's product accounts, separated by industries, provide continuous data of output and change. The oldest and best known series for financial services is the category known as "finance, insurance, and real estate," often called the FIRE industries. Some two-thirds of total product value originating in this classification arises from real estate, an industry not completely inside the generally-accepted boundaries of financial services. For example, the buying and selling of real property does not involve financial services per se. But, real estate brokers have close ties with financial institutions, since loan underwriting secured by property often accompanies the consummation of a sale. Many banks, mutual funds and financial houses also deal in mortgage securities in various forms.

According to the Department of Commerce, the major components or subgroups which make up the total class, other than real estate, are shown in Table 1–1.

As a whole, the so-called "FIRE" industries contribute about $5\frac{1}{2}$ percent to our gross domestic product (GDP). GDP is a crude measure of all goods and services produced within our national borders. As a barometer of our economy, the Commerce Department in 1991 substituted GDP for gross national product (GNP). The latter figure includes U.S. operations abroad and excludes foreign production within the U.S.

Table 1-1. Gross National Product by Industry Segments, 1989

Segment	GNP in $ bils.	Percent
Banking	119.4	41%
Nonbank credit agencies	20.5	7
Security, commodity brokers	43.8	15
Insurance carriers	60.4	21
Insurance agents and brokers	37.4	13
Holding, investment companies	8.1	3
Total	289.6	100%

Source: Survey of Current Business (April 1991).

Both of these statistics grossly understate the contribution of the financial sector. The national income accounts are based on the government's Standard Industrial Classification (SIC). Leakage in SIC categories occurs in many ways. It takes place when nonfinancial companies perform financial services. The reason this leakage occurs is that government agencies classify firms in accordance with their major activity, and this often ignores related financial services. For example, when a retail store extends credit to finance customers' purchases the activity is listed under "retail" services. Multinational corporations that deal in currency exchange have their trading categorized under their primary source of revenue. Profits or losses from currency translations of oil companies are reported as part of the petroleum industry operations.

Even among those organizations or business units classified as "financial," there can be considerable ambiguity. The government classifies separate financial units of large corporations under the "financial" label. GE's financial subsidiary would be classified as a financial firm. But Ford's credit card would be credited to Citibank, the organization that manages the card operation.

Not-for-profit organizations such as Teachers Insurance and Annuity Association (TIAA) fall under "other" regulated investment companies. But government agencies are not included in the class of "finance, insurance, and real estate." These excluded organizations provide a veritable host of financial services. Among them are the huge government pension funds and health insurance agencies. State and local activities are also part of government operations rather than part of the financial sector. Quasi-government agencies have an ambiguous standing. Fannie Mae operations are assigned to the "FIRE" designation, but Ginnie Mae's activities are not.

Such anomalies may be adequate for analyzing broad, macroeconomic tendencies. But they frequently present difficulties in making analyses and comparisons with respect to narrow industrial segments and task-related financial functions.

Hybrid Organizations

Another difficulty in developing a cohesive database technology is the fact that the financial service industry itself is becoming increasingly hybridized. Like retailers who display scattered merchandise, each segment of the financial service industry displays an often bewildering assortment of diverse offerings. Firms in each segment engage in a wide variety of services that cross segment boundaries, corrupting the once uniform segment definitions.

While firms still concentrate on a set of core businesses, their operations often spill over casually into other fields. Savings banks run checking accounts and commercial banks offer various retail accounts. Insurance companies, security brokers, and banks compete with mutual fund sponsors for investor dollars. Chase Manhattan's family of Vista mutual funds hold more than $1.5 billion of assets. Large brokerages and insurance organizations are major players in the area of mutual funds management.

As of December 1993, the 25 largest mutual fund management firms controlled assets worth $1.6 trillion. That figure represents almost 62 percent of the mutual fund market. These top fund managers include financial firms from many fields. Banks are represented by such firms as Goldman, Sachs, insurance companies by such organizations as Kemper and Prudential Insurance, and brokerage houses by such stalwarts as Dean Witter, Merrill Lynch, and Shearson. In fact, these three brokerage firms are three of the top eleven mutual funds managers in the country.

On the other hand, mutual funds have made their presence felt in fields of traditional banking, brokerage, and insurance. Fidelity Investments and T. Rowe Price operate thriving brokerage businesses. Vanguard, the third largest mutual funds management firm, competes with insurance companies by offering variable annuities. Mutual funds companies also vie with banks and financial consultants in offering financial planning services.

Though insurance companies still dominate the pension management field, they are experiencing increasing competition from mutual funds in managing 401(k) plans. The ease with which firms enter new lines of business obscures traditional boundaries between financial segments, and provides financial service firms a broad variety of financial options in planning for products and markets.

The top 25 funds managers are listed in Table 1–2, together with the amounts of assets under management.

Although top 25 mutual fund management companies controlled an aggregate of more than $1.6 trillion as of December 1993, market share figures suggest a competitive environment. Industry concentration is relatively low as compared with that of other industries. The share of the largest four firms amounted to 27.5 percent, with Fidelity enjoying a 10.2 percent slice. The next four largest firms held a combined market share of 14.7 percent, making an eight-firm concentration ratio of 42.2 percent. This compares with a ratio of more than 60 percent for all manufacturing industries.

The ability of financial firms to enter into other segments of their industry implies a certain degree of resource mobility. It also suggests industry segments with different growth rates, and money flowing more rapidly into segments that promise higher monetary returns. Successful corporate strategy today depends heavily on product development. For example, banks must compete with mutual funds for depositors' money. Similarly, money placed in pen-

Table 1-2. Leading Fund Management Companies

COMPLEX	TOTAL ASSETS
Fidelity Investments	$237.1
Vanguard Group (The)	130.4
Merrill Lynch Asset Mgmt	117.4
Capital Research & Management	100.7
Franklin Group/Templeton	91.8
Dreyfus Corporation (The)	73.4
Federated Investors	68.3
Dean Witter InterCapital Inc.	58.9
Putnam Funds	58.8
Prudential Mutual Funds	51.8
Smith Barney Shearson	44.4
IDS Mutual Fund Group	44.0
Kemper	43.9
T. Rowe Price	35.8
Scudder	34.1
SEI Financial Services	27.2
Oppenheimer/Centennial	25.8
Massachusetts Financial Service	25.0
Twentieth Century	24.2
AIM Group	24.1
Alliance Capital Management	23.4
PaineWebber	22.7
Goldman Sachs & Co.	19.8
PNC Financial Services Group	18.6
Janus Funds	17.0
American Capital	16.1
Schwab Funds	15.6
Colonial Group, Inc. (The)	14.4
USAA	13.7
Keystone Group, Inc.	13.1
NationsBank	13.1
Lord Abbett	12.8
Concord Financial Group, Inc.	12.8
United Funds	11.8
Winsbury Company	11.5

Table 1-2. Leading Fund Management Companies (continued)

COMPLEX	TOTAL ASSETS
Benham Group (The)	10.8
INVESCO Group	10.1
Phoenix	10.1
Smith Barney Funds	9.8
Boston Company (The)	9.8
Pioneer	9.8
Eaton Vance	9.7
Van Kampen Merritt Companies	9.6
Delaware Group	9.5
G.T. Global Funds	8.2
Wells Fargo	7.7

Source: Investment Company Institute, December 31, 1993.

sion funds decreases the amount that goes into investments and bank deposits.

An article in the January 18, 1993 issue of *Business Week* dramatizes changes in the financial services industry. According to that article, the market share of mutual funds and pension funds rose from 15.9 percent to 32.5 percent of a much larger market in 1992. Meanwhile, our venerable institutions of thrifts and commercial banks registered a declining market share.[1] Savings went into 401(k) plans, IRAs, and mutual funds rather than into bank accounts. The funds could also buy commercial paper at lower rates than banks charged for short-term loans, and so competed more vigorously for the business of the banks' biggest customers.

In this sort of environment, competition comes not merely from companies offering the same product. Different services from different industry segments compete for the same uses. Economists call this phenomenon "cross-elasticity" of demand. For many individuals mutual funds appear as a viable substitute for CDs, savings

---

1   "The Power of Mutual Funds," *Business Week* (January 18, 1993), pp. 64-65.

accounts, or purchases of individual stocks. Fluid markets and mobile capital mean competition comes from outside an industry. This kind of competition puts a premium on product development. To be successful, you must find new ways to combat different financial services that offer superior results—in this case, better returns on money. If you cannot fight competitors from outside your industry, join them in another industry.

Sometimes competitors emerge from nonfinancial sectors rather than from another segment of the financial service industry. A prime example is AT&T's move into the credit card business in 1990. Within two years, this AT&T unit became the second-largest credit card issuer in the U.S., outranked only by Citicorp.

In this particular case, AT&T's foray into a financial field succeeded with a highly innovative offer to consumers, but one which might have been matched by any competitor. In contrast, the new General Motors credit card would be difficult to imitate. Banks and financial companies do not produce motor vehicles on which they can offer discounts based on credit card purchase volume. Nevertheless, some credit card issuers have linked products with credit cards through alliances. For example, Citicorp entered into a partnership with Ford to offer a card similar to that of GM. Other issuers have for some time been offering bonus points with card usage that, like the old green stamps, can be applied to purchases of appliances, video recorders, airplane trips, and so forth. American Express goes so far as to offer guarantees for products bought with its card.

Growth Via Productivity

Like other service industries, financial services are labor-intensive. That is, their operations require a large amount of human effort in relation to output. In 1991 the financial service industry paid out some $182 billion in wages and salaries. According to the Department of Commerce, the major components or subgroups of the financial service industry are shown in Table 1–3.

The high labor content of financial service industries has often been criticized as a symptom of a tired and ailing economy. This

Table 1-3. Gross National Product by Industry Segment, 1989

Segment	Wages Paid*	Percent of Industry
Banking	119.4	41%
Nonbank credit agencies	20.5	7
Security, commodity brokers	43.8	15
Insurance carriers	60.4	21
Insurance agents & brokers	37.4	13
Holding, investment companies	8.1	3
Total	289.6	100%

*in billions

Source: *Survey of Current Business* (April 1991).

disparaging verdict is based on the industry's historically low level of employee productivity. An inordinate amount of manpower is needed to render essential services.

Increasing productivity has become the hallmark of a good society. Our president annually presents to Congress a lengthy report on national progress with respect to gross domestic product, employment, wages, prices, and business profits. This report implicitly presents a picture of national productivity. Employment statistics tell us how much human effort it takes Americans to produce the goods and services of our economy. Wages indicate how much this effort costs. Prices reveal what consumers pay for products, and what producers receive for selling them. Profit is defined as an accounting concept that calculates the difference between the money firms take in and the money they spend to generate the intake.

There are several ways of measuring productivity. The most popular measure is "labor productivity," calculated as output divided by the amount of labor it takes to produce our goods or services. Economists and politicians use this method most often to describe national efficiency because it provides a clear indication of per capita income. The labor productivity method thus emerges as a key component in rises and declines in our standard of living.

Productivity for service providers is infinitely more difficult to measure than for manufacturers. Nevertheless, this difficulty has not deterred attempts to assess productivity in service industries. After all, service industries account for between two-thirds and three-quarters of employment and job compensation in practically all advanced economies.

By all estimates, financial services are seen as productivity laggards when compared with manufacturing, farming, and transportation. While financial services firms have made massive investments in computers and telecommunication devices, these attempts brought no cheers from economists and industrial engineers. In an article in the September-October 1991 issue of the *Harvard Business Review*,[2] Stephen S. Roach, partner and senior economist at Morgan Stanley, maintains that technology has done little to improve productivity in financial services companies. Roach claims that the technological overdose moved financial firms "from a variable-cost to a fixed-cost regime, thereby sacrificing flexibility without gaining any concomitant productivity benefits."

Roach's severe judgment contains a great deal of truth about technology disappointments. From a national point of view, however, our financial services are not all bad. They must be judged not merely in relation to other domestic industries, but also against foreign financial services companies. As with other industries, financial services are immersed in the global economy. The United States is no longer self-contained as in the past, when it grew its own food, possessed most of the raw materials it needed, and made almost all the finished goods its citizens consumed.

Auto manufacturers may be more productive than banks. But if Detroit cannot produce cars cheaper and better than Japanese firms, its failure can jeopardize our standard of living. Similarly, if our banks service customers better and cheaper than foreign banks, our citizens benefit. Relativism rules national growth rates in a global economy.

---

2   Stephens S. Roach, "Services Under Siege—The Restructuring Imparitive," *Harvard Business Review* (September-October 1991), pp. 82-91.

A recent study by McKinsey & Co., a leading management firm, exudes optimism with respect to our financial service industries. This survey estimates that U.S. bank employees are almost 50 percent more productive than German and English bank workers. McKinsey attributes the American advantage mostly to automation.

Increasing productivity is the greatest challenge facing the financial service industry. Success in this effort will figure prominently in a company's competitive performance.

For all intents and purposes, the productivity agenda boils down to how firms handle information.

Information Technology

The most popular way of increasing productivity still follows the time-honored method used in industries that produce and transport goods. This calls for changes in the factors of production, or tilting the production mix away from labor toward capital. When machines can produce more physical units cheaper and better than humans, the substitution of capital for labor increases productivity.

A number of outputs in financial industries are analogous to those of goods-producing firms. These are essentially products of back office operations. Bank account summaries, for example, are nearly identical in form from one bank to another, and computers have long ago replaced manual methods in churning them out. Credit card bills, brokerage and mutual funds summary statements fall into the same category. These represent simple, routine tasks which require unskilled "production work," such as inputting data, operating computers, and mailing out standard forms.

But financial services companies today rely increasingly on knowledge. In turn, knowledge calls for information at all levels of operation. Banks and brokerage houses must know the status of current accounts. Financial firms must be aware of changing conditions in their external markets. Insurance companies must have information about risks of insurance policies they underwrite and of securities in which they invest. All firms must keep abreast of competitors activities. Information is the bloodstream of financial operations.

Yet, all too often, managers confuse information with data. The two are not alike. Data are raw, unrelated facts. Information is refined data, transformed so it can be applied to particular tasks. Understanding the distinction between data and information is vital to making financial services more productive.

If information is task related, productivity depends on how information is handled. For example, financial houses spend more than $1 billion a year on both hardware and software to process mountains of transmitted data. A process called "programmability" converts data to information. A single computer chip no larger than your thumbnail can hold masses of data. It can combine these data in almost limitless arrangements, perform various functions, and produce various outputs. In "production work" the task is given, or does not involve wide options. In "knowledge work," as used by Peter Drucker,[3] tasks are indistinct and ill-defined. It is interesting to note that programs can spew out data in many forms. But we must ask ourselves: what arrangements are important and what can be ignored? What form of data is relevant to improve our operations today and tomorrow and the day after that? A key idea of any knowledge-based system is to minimize data and maximize information.

But how? The arrangement and conveyance of data must relate to tasks and their purposes. By themselves, data are devoid of sense without human reasoning, judgment, and experience. Even a cybernetic age cannot make computers think like humans, though some systems analysts and business school professors think people should emulate machines.

The arrangements and uses of data are most contentious in operations that demand higher levels of knowledge. For example, this antagonism emerges plainly with respect to decisions about equity investments. The writings of Peter Lynch, probably the most

---

3   Peter Drucker, "The New Productivity Challenge," *Harvard Business Review* (November-December, 1991), pp. 69-79.

successful money manager of the 1980s, form a conspicuous example of this dichotomy. In his *One Up On Wall Street*, Lynch tells us that in college, he avoided "science, math, and accounting—all the normal preparations for business." At Wharton graduate school, he writes, "most of what I learned . . . could only help you fail."[4]

As manager of Fidelity's Magellan Fund, the largest mutual fund in the U.S., Lynch emphasized personal contact with companies in which his fund invests. The personal-visit approach is followed by most large brokerages and equity funds. This conventional wisdom regards these face-to-face meetings with managers, competitors, and industry insiders as basic to decision-making. These, Lynch insists, produces the "ten-baggers"—stocks that appreciate tenfold. In fact, Lynch attributes his success to his ability to "think like an amateur," and insists that the average investor can outdo the expert.

On the other hand, many researchers deplore this "know-nothing" attitude. Bart Zehren, laments the wide failure of financial service firms to "recognize the full potential of marketing research." This will only come to pass, he writes in Stephen Kerns' book, *Marketing Financial Products & Services*, "when researchers bring to the corporate table their own plans for action."[5]

This view strongly implies a world in which hands-on experience follows research as the bridesmaid in decision-making. This situation is best exemplified in the operation of index funds, where computers select stocks in accordance with a set of predetermined rules. But the rules are formulated by humans, not computers. Computers have made routine the rather limited applications of trading. Some firms are currently working on computer programs where machines learn and make decisions, but they have yet to demonstrate superiority compared to human judgment.

---

4   Peter Lynch, *One Up On Wall Street* (New York: Simon and Schuster, 1989).

5   Bart D. Zehren, "Marketing Research in the Financial Services Sector," in *Marketing Financial Products and Services*, ed. Stephen Kerns (Chicago: Probus, 1988), p. 17.

The fact is that "thinking" and "doing" complement each other. Increasingly, this combination is being built around databases, which have virtually become the centerpiece in the rendition of financial services.

Firms have two prime functions: to make products and to distribute them. Unlike goods-making industries, financial service firms produce intangible products. Some are goods-related, such as credit cards which are used to buy chips and shoes and sealing wax. Other services are "pure," completely unrelated to tangible objects. These include bank accounts, insurance policies, and mutual funds. In either case, there is no physical distribution of financial services in a literal sense. Intangibles cannot be shipped like oil or wheat or autos. They are not inventoried. Rather, their distribution assumes a different form, which is called performance.

Role of Databases

What is a database? And why can it play so important a role in a financial services company?

There is no exact agreement on the definition of a database. Generally speaking, it is a collection of data held in a computer. In the simplest case, this collection can be a "list," or a set of records. These lists can comprise people, things, organizations, events, or any combination of these four elements.

The basic database in financial services is an operational one used in the performance of a service. Banks must keep records of each customer's deposits, withdrawals, and current balances. Brokerage houses must keep track of purchases and sales of securities, send confirmation notices of transactions, and collect or disburse monies due. Similarly, credit card issuers must account for purchases, payments, and credit limits of each client. Insurance companies must have ready access to such information as relevant personal data, terms of coverage, and premium payments.

All transactional databases have two elements in common. First, they must have a "list" of customers with information on how to get in touch with them. At minimum, each record shows a name, address, and often a telephone number. Entries can refer to individuals or organizations.

Second, each record itemizes customer transactions, such as orders, payments, disbursements. This sort of database forms the basis of day-to-day operations. Its main purpose is carrying out the routine tasks of ongoing business. It is therefore organized to effect transactions and after-sales services.

The exact organization of a customer database is company-specific. For example, customer information files of financial houses serving businesses may contain lengthy records of each corporation, updated monthly or quarterly. Firms with wide product lines may track customers' inquiries for purposes of cross-selling. Large files of retail customers may be enhanced by computer overlays using information generated by suppliers outside the corporation.

Databases also are used widely for purposes other than those of performing current transactions. Product development often entails careful analysis of customer characteristics and outside databases. Marketing frequently relies on segmentation techniques to target customers and prospects, and uses both internal and external databases to do so. In short, databases should be designed to meet the various goals of a business.

Types of Databases

Like the disharmony in definition, no one can say precisely how many databases exist. According to Martha E. Williams, a researcher at the University of Illinois, some 5,600 databases were commercially available in 1990. This number had grown from only 300 in 1975. Carlos Cuadra, a long-time gatherer of such information, reports similar figures of database growth.

To make sense out of this gigantic accumulation of computer-stored information, databases are defined by type. Broad-based types can be depicted as bibliographic, directories, numeric, and transactional, with each category containing many possible subclasses. Following is a brief description of each major type:

Bibliographic. This type of database acts as a reference for articles, news releases, and various publications. Content often is described by key words, such as demographics, population, company earnings, markets, forecasts. Most of such databases provide abstracts or summaries of the material. They also cover a specific time period, current or past. However, most databases do not date back earlier than the 1970s.

Directories. These databases list names and addresses of individuals and companies. Examples are D&B Electronic Yellow Pages, Marquis Who's Who, and Standard and Poor's compilation of corporations and executives. Mailing lists in computer-readable form also qualify as directory databases.

Numeric. These databases provide statistical and time series data. Government bureaus are major compilers of numeric data. The Bureau of the Census, for example, produces continuing statistics regarding population and industries, including those of financial services. The Bureau of Labor Statistics puts out a continuous series of data on prices, employment, and income.

Many statistical series are produced by private research firms, such as Standard & Poor's Marketscope's updated stock prices. Trade associations, such as the American Council of Life Insurance, the American Bankers Association, and Bank Administration Institute, produce inexhaustible mines of statistical data.

Transactional. As previously described, these data are usually generated from company transactions, and regarded as proprietary. However, there are several transactional databases available to financial service companies. One form deals with credit checks. Dun and Bradstreet is the best known outfit for checking the creditworthiness of companies. TRW and Equifax are the leading compilers of financial information about consumers. They provide lending institutions with credit data regarding individuals, which are widely used for making personal loans, issuing credit cards, and approving mortgage applications. A number of list purveyors and list compilers make transactional data available. For example, R.L. Polk sells car registration data.

There are various sources of database information. The major ones are *Directory of Online Databases*[6] and the semi-annual *Directory of Portable Databases*[7] published jointly by Cuadra Associates and Elsevier; *Computer-Readable Databases: The Directory and Sourcebook*[8] issued by Gale Research.

Database publishers and producers commonly make their information available in printed and electronic form. These data can be obtained from libraries and system vendors. Among the most popular purveyors of on-line services are Business Research Corporation, DIALOG Information Services, Dow Jones News Retrieval, Reuters, EasyNet, Mead Data Central, and Vu/Text Information Services.

The number of commercially-available databases is bound to increase at a rapid pace, and new competitors will emerge. Chicago-based Online Access Publishing Group updates business managers regarding new and existing information services. Though new firms and services will multiply, older leaders will likely continue to be favored.

Databases and Productivity

Onward and upward! These words best describe the ongoing database revolution that has taken place in financial services during the past two decades. Incessant cries for more information and quicker delivery spurred an almost insatiable demand for larger computer memories, faster data processing, and cheaper machines.

Computer technology has made great strides in those directions. Today, personal computers (PCs) can be linked to larger machines, or servers, which store considerable amounts of data and programs. These servers themselves are often PCs enhanced with data-storage capacity. PC makers herald this sort of arrangement as a viable substitute for the expensive mainframes.

6   *Directory of Online Databases*, (New York, NY: Cuadra Associates and Elsevier Science Publishing Co).

7   *Directory of Portable Databases*, (New York, NY: Cuadra Associates and Elsevier Science Publishing Co).

8   *Computer-Readable Databases: A Directory and Sourcebook*, (Detroit, MI: Gale Research, Inc).

There is no doubt that smaller machines have made inroads into data processing once dominated by the heavyweights. There is also a high probability that the smaller, more flexible machines will play a dominant role in the future.

Yet mainframe computers run most large financial databases, and often act as servers for smaller machines. The big computers are more cost effective. They process data faster, contain more storage capacity, and have the advantage of greater flexibility. These qualities assume particular importance for on-line information systems. For example, brokers can execute trades and give customers their results in seconds, during a single phone call.

Databases used for marketing call for less volume, more batch processing, and simpler applications as compared to operations. Because marketing involves different patterns of usage, marketing databases often are separated from the larger operating and corporate management information systems. Many companies find it cheaper to fill their needs by hiring service bureaus, especially when they rent mailing lists from outside sources. The list rental business is frequently run by list management specialists, who combine data processing with selling activities. In any event, data maintenance costs are reduced because many small lists are thrown together and processed on larger machines. By sharing expenses this way, small list owners gain the advantage of scale economies.

Financial databases have prolonged the twilight of mainframes owing to three factors: customer increases, product proliferation, and market expansion.

The United States boasts the most advanced consumer economy in the world. The consumer segment accounts for about two-thirds of gross domestic income. Consumer spending on financial services has more than kept pace with purchases of goods.

The credit card, one of the first services to appeal to mass tastes, has become as much a part of American tradition as baseball, hot dogs, and apple pie. As of 1991, there were more than one billion credit cards in circulation, the number having grown better than 3 percent a year during the decade. With the number and amount of transactions continuously rising, computers must track and store ever-increasing quantities of credit card data.

Mutual funds constitute another financial service witnessing a massive influx of customers. At the end of 1992 roughly one out of every four households—some 26 million owned a mutual fund. Since two or more people in a home may own a fund, individual accounts exceed the number of fundowning households. If market share is roughly indicative of the number of customers, a fund with as little as a one percent share would have to keep and update transactions for more than 250,000 records.

As we have already observed, financial companies have moved strongly to broaden product lines. Many firms have also provided for monetary exchanges between accounts. For example, brokerage houses offer clients the convenience of having their dividends and sales proceeds swept into money market accounts. Likewise, equity purchases are paid by automatic paper transactions whereby computers shift funds from individuals' money market to brokerage accounts.

Mutual funds permit customers to transfer money at will from one fund to another, though some impose limitations on frequent trading. And all funds have increased the number of client choices. Today, the number of mutual funds exceeds the number of stocks listed on the New York Stock Exchange.

As buyer options increase, computers inherit an ever-increasing workload.

Databases and the Global Economy

After the World War II, American economic might dominated the globe. The United States was the world's banker, and American industry was second to none. But those halcyon days are past. Many foreign economies have grown at far higher rates than the U.S. economy. At the same time, electronic and communication technologies have made the world a smaller place, globalizing financial services and creating new opportunities for American firms to participate in growing economies beyond our borders.

This overseas expansion of financial transactions means more extensive data processing and communications. To handle the expanding volume of global transactions, the financial industry turned to automated trading systems. The new technology links many organized exchanges throughout the world in 24-hour-a-day trading in securities. The automated systems encompass not merely common stock, but a host of derivatives, such as futures and option contracts.

Promises, Promises

Technology still holds out intriguing prospects of greater productivity. Each new generation of computers has more processing power than its predecessors, and sells at lower prices. Unit processing costs have fallen steadily, and are still on a downward spiral. Each new wave of software displays more sophisticated features, and boasts the ability to do more things. Yet the promised benefits of technology have been fulfilled only partially—here and there, erratically and haphazardly.

Firms that invested heavily in information technology have not vaulted into market leadership as a consequence of that action. Rather, they are like men on the proverbial treadmill, running faster but staying in one place. Every benefit they gain seems to be offset by additional costs, so that productivity edges forward at a snail's pace.

As firms transferred more work to computers, overhead expanded at a heady pace. Staffs were added to customer service departments on the assumption that business growth depends on satisfied customers. Often, managers never asked the correct question: "What makes customers satisfied?"

As systems became more extensive and complicated, specialists were added to technical staffs. Larger customer databases called for more highly-paid market researchers, programmers, systems analysts, and model builders. Greater amounts of data from the outside increased demands for more "knowledge workers" such as economists, social scientists, research librarians, and statisticians.

Fidelity Investments, for example, employs more programmers and technicians than funds managers and security traders.

The newly-created armies of specialists encouraged the expansion of administrative staffs. The administrators were needed to integrate the diverse specialties which knowledge workers offered. Trained in the "science" of human relations and social behavior, the administrators devised programs of boring meetings and endless busywork. In the meantime, secretaries, typists, and clerical workers bloated payrolls. These workers were necessary to feed the machines with data, prepare masses of reports, and circulate them to employees who had absolutely no connection with the subject matter. Instead of reducing paper, computers generated more paper than ever before.

Perhaps this portrayal of technology usage is exaggerated. But it is also obvious that technology has all too often prevented companies in the financial industry from rendering their services in the most productive manner. Why? Because technology in financial services plays a different role from that in the production of goods. It is frequently subordinant rather than dominant as an agent of productivity. Whether technology can increase productivity depends on its relationship to specific tasks, and whether it is employed intelligently. The remaining chapters of this book address this theme. They discuss the various tasks of financial services and the issues of rendering these services productively in order to advance a firm's competitive performance.

Summary

Financial services embrace a wide area of diverse tasks. Excluding real estate, banking comprises the major portion of the financial services industry. Banking's share of market, however, has diminished as funds management companies have garnered a larger share.

Since different financial products often can be used for the same purpose, financial firms are increasingly becoming hybrid organizations. Similarly, non-financial firms find few barriers in entering the financial services area.

The financial industry is often regarded as a productivity laggard. This judgment is based on comparing financial firms with other domestic industries. When compared with global competitors, however, U.S. financial services are far more productive.

Financial services have spend billions of dollars on technical investments for handling information, wherein databases form the centerpiece. A major challenge for financial services firms is to translate those technical investments into growth and profitability.

Appendix 1

Table A1-1. Leading U.S. Banks

Company	Assets (in $mils.)
Citicorp	217,000*
Chemical Banking	139,700
NationsBank	118,100
BankAmerica	115,500
J.P. Morgan	102,900
Chase Manhattan	95,900
Bankers Trust New York	72,450
Banc One	61,420
Wells Fargo	52,540
PNC Bank	51,380
First Union	51,327
First Interstate	50,860*
First Chicago	49,280
Fleet Financial	46,940
Norwest	44,557
NBD Bancorp	40,937
Bank of New York	40,910
Barnett Banks	39,460
Republic New York	37,150
SunTrust Banks	36,650

Note: Assets are for 1992 fiscal year. When followed by an asterisk, assets refer to 1991. All subsequent tables in the appendix of this chapter follow the same format.

Source: Based on "Global 1000," *Business Week*, (July 12, 1993).

Table A1-2. Leading U.S. Financial Service Companies

Company	Assets (in $mils.)
Fannie Mae	181,000
American Express	175,800
Salomon	159,000
Merrill Lynch	107,020
Morgan Stanley	80,350
Sally Mae	46,620
Bear Stearns	45,768
Transamerica	32,300
Household International	31,130
Dean Witter, Discover	23,822
Primerica	21,560

Source: Based on "Global 1000," *Business Week*, (July 12, 1993).

Table A1-3. Leading U.S. Insurance Companies

Company	Assets (in $mils.)
Aetna Life & Casualty	89,930
American International Group	79,835
Equitable	78,869
CIGNA	66,740
Travelers	53,600
American General	39,740
Lincoln National	39,720
CNA Financial	36,680
Capital Holding	20,590
Chubb	15,020

Source: Based on "Global 1000," *Business Week*, (July 12, 1993).

2

Financial Regulation

Financial services, like utilities, are deemed to be clothed in the public interest. As such, the financial services remain among the most regulated of American industries. Yet, state and federal governments made concessions to technological and competitive pressures, relaxing many restrictions on financial institutions.

This chapter deals with the following government actions that affect financial services:

- Federal laws which lessened restrictions on interest rates, deposits, and lending practices
- Consumerism legislation
- Privacy issues raised by firms marketing personal information in databases
- Issues of "nonbank" banks
- Expansion of permissible nonbanking activities through Regulation Y

A System of Regulation

Regulatory issues affecting banks and financial services abound. Despite the deregulation of the late 1970s and the early 1980s, financial services are among the most regulated industries.

Banks must adhere to a chartering process, lending limits, geographical restrictions, regulations as to permissible activities, especially in regard to insurance and securities, and various anti-discrimination laws.

Financial institutions are subject to a plethora of regulatory bodies: the Federal Reserve, the Comptroller of the Currency, the

Office of Thrift Supervision, the Federal Deposit Insurance Corporation, the Resolution Trust Corporation, as well as state banking authorities.

Banking and the delivery of financial services is also a severely fragmented industry. The trend toward integration of financial services, accelerated by a period of deregulation, can only be properly viewed in the context of an outmoded and cumbersome regulatory system.

This system of regulation can be examined in four broad areas: the rationale for regulation, the trend toward breaking down regulatory barriers among "banks," consumer legislation that affects the delivery of financial services, and how regulation organizes the banking industry.

Regulation in Brief

The impetus for regulation comes from both legitimate concerns about the public interest and from special interests seeking legislated competitive advantages. The public interest concerns emanate from two broad areas. One is bank safety and soundness. The other is bank efficiency. Why should government intervene to promote safety and soundness in financial services? One traditional argument is the existence of externalities, or "spillover effects." Weak financial companies, particularly those whose liabilities may be part of the payments system, may inject the virus of loss of confidence into soundly run institutions. Federal Deposit Insurance Corporation (FDIC), created during the Great Depression, was instituted to take care of this confidence problem.

Similarly one might wish to question the wisdom of governmental regulation to promote efficiency. After all, don't firms—financial or otherwise—already have an incentive to be efficient? The answer could be no. Consider that some regulations or institutional arrangements may provide incentives for under- or over-pricing of services. This certainly occurs with deposit insurance that results in underpricing of insurance for deposits in risky banks. This fundamental problem of governmental mispricing was one of a number of causes of the savings and loan crisis. Regulation, such as capital requirements, may then be designed to try to overcome or offset the effect of current regulations for excessive risk taking.

Various other issues can be related to one or the other of the aforementioned rationales for governmental intervention: safety/soundness and efficiency. For instance, conflicts of interest may impair the soundness of a bank. Sometimes banks are prohibited from engaging in a particular activity; other times the bank may be authorized to engage in the activity, say trust banking, but be required to do so with "firewalls." This firewall exists to prevent the trust officers from pawning off commercial bank investments onto trusts administered by the bank.

Another cited reason for bank regulation is concentration of resources. This rationale could relate to efficiency. The economic argument for antitrust intervention is that a monopoly will not produce at the socially optimal output point when its incentive for profit maximization leads it to increase prices and restrict outputs. Yet, clearly the thrust of financial regulation, such as entry restrictions, is often aimed at reducing competition rather than increasing it. Thus, the practice of regulating the concentration of resources appears to favor special interests, for instance, protecting the financial interest of small banks, rather than encouraging efficiency in the public interest.

Deregulation and Convergence

One of the basic themes of the regulatory changes wrought in the last 15 years is that financial institutions are appearing more alike. Competitive pressures, technology, and deregulation have broken down barriers among financial firms. The result is that commercial banks and thrift institutions both will accept transaction deposits and make some commercial loans. Indeed, insurance companies and banks as well as securities firms and banks will offer increasingly similar products. The modern financial company often will provide a great array of financial products.

Consider Merrill Lynch that offers traditional securities transaction services, foreign currency hedging, investment banking, mutual funds, insurance, and loans. Merrill Lynch has become a banker for an increasing and surprising number of firms. Similarly, commercial banks have been promoting their securities-oriented services to their banking customers. They are selling securities, mutual funds, and financial planning. This trend toward less compartmentalization of financial institutions accelerated after the passage of the following two laws: The Depository Institutions Deregulation and Monetary Control Act of 1980 (DIDMCA) and the St. Germain–Garn Act of 1982.

The DIDMCA consists of two parts. Under the Monetary Control portion of the law, the Federal Reserve was able to impose reserve requirements on all transaction accounts regardless of whether the institution belonged to the Federal Reserve Bank system. The Federal Reserve was prompted to seek this legislation because it perceived a lack of monetary control occurring from erosion of its membership. Indeed Member Banks had to keep non-interest earning reserves in the form of balances at the Federal Reserve or in vault cash. Under the Monetary Control Act Congress extended this "tax" to all depository institutions.

The deregulation part of the Act was concerned largely with loosening interest rate and deposit restrictions. The legislation began the phaseout of the infamous Regulation Q, under which the Federal Reserve had set maximum interest rate caps on consumer accounts at member banks and (indirectly) at non-member banks and thrift institutions. With the dissolution of Regulation Q these financial firms could compete on price to attract deposits. Normally this is a fine idea. But when S&Ls are deposit-insurance subsidized, the end result is often excessive risk taking by these financial firms.

The DIDMCA also relaxed rules that tied the thrift industry to the housing business and excluded it from ordinary commerce. The DIDMCA allowed all thrift firms to offer transaction accounts that paid interest; these were called Negotiable Orders of Withdrawal (NOW accounts). The S&Ls were given trust powers and the right to make more consumer loans and issue credit cards. Mutual Savings Banks were empowered to make business loans and accept business deposits. Thus, the thrifts began to look a lot more like commercial banks and could compete accordingly.

Two years after the DIDMCA, the St. Germain–Garn Act continued the deregulation of the thrift industry. This Act allowed for increased commercial and consumer lending. It also authorized new types of deposit accounts, notably money market deposit accounts. These provisions permitted thrifts to open higher interest accounts to compete with the money market mutual funds that had been prying consumers away from banks and thrifts by paying attractive rates of interest.

Consumer Legislation

Consumer legislation has hit the banking industry as it has many other industries. The consumer concerns range from interest on credit cards and disclosure of loan terms to various privacy interests. One relatively early legislative effort was the Truth in Lending Act of 1968, which specified disclosure of credit terms and promoted some standardization of the computation of the "interest rate." Another problem area for both lenders and consumers has been the accuracy of credit reports. Stories abound as to how creditors have denied credit to individuals on the basis of an erroneous credit report. Richard Bryan, Senator and former Governor of Nevada, found that his credit report included a list of various lawsuits against him, the actions naming him in his official capacity as governor.

A number of states have sued TRW, the leading credit-rating agency, for reporting excessive amounts of inaccurate data. These suits were settled in 1992 with TRW agreeing to certain procedures tightening operations, correcting errors promptly, and setting up a more responsive system for handling complaints. When an applicant tries to correct erroneous information credit-rating agencies are reluctant to make a change. Agency personnel often cite the computer as a source of authority as though the computer's databank must be unassailable.

Databases, Accuracy and Privacy

The problem of inaccurate credit information is partly addressed by the Fair Credit Reporting Act of 1970. Applicants are given access to reports generated by credit rating agencies. There are three principal credit agencies: Equifax, Trans Union, and TRW. If individuals are denied credit they can get a free report, provided they request the report within 30 days. (Generally the credit agencies extend the period of free reports beyond the mandated 30 days to 60 days.) Applicants have the right to present new, more accurate, information. The credit rating agency does not have to change its information, but may be liable for damages if it acts negligently.

Consumers who disagree with the finding of the credit agency have the right to include a statement in their credit report. Legal action can be pursued for any damages due to negligence by the credit agency so long as suit is filed within two years. Interestingly, the law provides for recovery of actual and punitive damages, as well as attorneys' fees.

In addition to issues of database accuracy and resulting damages, legislators have raised those of privacy. These concerns arise because credit rating agencies had been selling database names to marketers. Equifax, TRW, and Trans Union have sold lists of affluent consumers. The Fair Credit Reporting Act of 1970 does not directly address the issue of selling information to junk mailers. Although credit agencies do not sell credit histories as such, they identify people as "upscale" or as having incomes of more than $100,000. Consequently, the agencies claim they are not issuing unauthorized credit reports, whereas the Federal Trade Commission has interpreted the Act more broadly to prohibit the liberal release of credit-database information. New legislation may address this issue.

In the meantime, growing consumer objections against usage of personal data for marketing purposes have deterred some software houses from selling names. Lotus Development Corp., for example, ended plans for its Marketplace Households. The project would have created a database of 80 million households, containing addresses and demographic information, including salaries provided by Equifax. Likewise, New England Telephone & Telegraph ditched its plans to sell names of its 4.7 million customers to direct marketers. New York Telephone, which planned to join the New England venture, had earlier withdrawn from the project when public reaction turned negative.

Financial institutions are also under fire for allegedly turning down applicants of certain racial or ethnic minorities or not lending in various neighborhoods inhabited by minority populations.

One result of these concerns was passage of the Community Reinvestment Act during the Carter administration. This Act has made redlining illegal. Redlining refers to the practice of under-serving customers who live in a particular geographical area. At one time the term redlining referred chiefly to the insurance industry practice of avoiding policyholders in areas that have been at least metaphorically marked with a red pen on a map. Now the term often refers to the banking industry practice of discriminating against loan applicants living in certain neighborhoods.

It is not really clear how pervasive the discrimination problem actually is. Banks defend themselves against the charge of discrimination by citing reasons other than race for their denial of credit. Essentially we have a multivariate statistical problem. Few academic studies shed much light on whether racial minorities are denied credit for financial reasons or racial reasons. Some non-academic studies have tried to show discrimination, but they suffer from severe methodological biases—notably the omission of relevant variables that may explain the disparate results of banks granting more credit to Caucasians than to minorities (other than Asians). Both the Federal Reserve Board and Federal Reserve Bank of Boston in the early 1990s tried to improve upon the previous studies of race and home mortgage lending. Their research concluded that there is a higher rejection rate for minority applicants for loans that could not be explained by any other factor than race.

Under the Community Reinvestment Act, banks are supposed to provide service commensurate with the deposits locally generated. Service should be judged in terms of numerous variables such as hours of operation. However, the issues of mortgage lending and redlining have been of particular public concern. Federal regulators, namely the Federal Reserve, the Federal Deposit Insurance Corporation, the Office of Thrift Supervision, and the Office of the Comptroller of the Currency rate the banks' Community Reinvestment Act performance as "outstanding," "satisfactory," "needs to improve," and "substantial noncompliance."

When banks apply for mergers, acquisitions, or deposit insurance, Federal regulators are supposed to consider the history of compliance with the Community Reinvestment Act. Regulators might grant the request, deny the request, or grant the request conditional upon compliance with the Act.

In March of 1993 Banc One of Columbus, Ohio, acquired Valley National Bank of Arizona. The Federal Reserve noted that the Comptroller of the Currency had rated Banc One's Cleveland Bank as needing to improve its service under the Community Reinvestment Act. Many commentators considered the Fed's appraisal a light slap on the wrist—perhaps only a slap, but also a warning that Banc One had better satisfy Cleveland's activists lest future acquisitions be held up.

However, there also is evidence that the Act has perverse impacts. Banks may find that particular communities generate more deposits than good loans. As a consequence, banks find themselves vulnerable to the charge of failing to reinvest in the local community. To avoid potential penalties for failure to comply with the Act, as well as adverse publicity, banks may make more risky local loans. As a result deposits carry an implicit "tax" equal to the expected negative net profits the "extra" loans cause. With a "tax" imposed on each deposit made in a low income area, banks are loathe to build up such deposit accounts. The predicted result is that banks will avoid branching into low income areas, further reducing the lending services available in those communities.

Apparently the cost of the Act is not just bad loans, but also paperwork (documentation) and bank funding (payoffs) of community activists and their groups. In fact, the Financial Institutions Reform, Recovery, and Enforcement Act of 1989, known as FIRREA, aided these community groups by giving them the right to know the regulators' assessments and ratings of banks. A 1992 American Bankers Association study indicated that the Community Reinvestment Act was the single biggest regulatory headache for bankers. Will the notion of redlining be expanded to include other financial institutions not promoting services to certain low income groups? There is some signs of minority advocates voicing complaints that low income recipients are not offered financial services made available to others.

As a consequence of the Community Reinvestment Act providing disincentives to operate in officially designated low income areas, the structure of the lending business could be marginally—if not significantly—altered by banks trying to avoid the sting of this law. Commercial banks might avoid the origination of home mortgages and instead purchase mortgages in the open market for investment purposes. This process of "outsourcing" allows financial companies to purchase assets at market driven prices instead of being forced to create or "purchase internally" the loans at subsidized prices. Not to be outdone by the limitations of the market and the Community Reinvestment Act, the Clinton administration has proposed government funding of community development banks to funnel funds to the low-income areas. Predictably, these new banks will be political operations.

Another anti-discrimination law is the Fair Housing Act of 1968. It currently protects not only racial minorities, but also the physically handicapped and families with children. The Equal Credit Opportunity Act of 1974 and the Home Mortgage Disclosure Act of 1975 also are designed to fight discrimination in banking services. The latter law requires banks to disclose the location of real estate loans, which essentially provides a database for community activists. Until 1990 this data did not contain sufficient individual information.

What Are Banks?

The banking industry is organized along functional lines. What is a bank, what constitutes a branch location, and what activities may a bank engage in?

A bank is widely considered to be an institution that accepts deposits and makes loans. The combination of these two functions created an inherent legal ambiguity. A financial institution doing only one of these functions would not be a bank. Thus commercial enterprises exploited this loophole to acquire a "nonbank" bank. Many large industrial companies such as Ford Motor Company, Sears, and AT&T set up their own "nonbank" banks. Section 901 of the Financial Institutions Reform, Recovery, and Enforcement Act of 1989, an Act largely known for dealing with the Savings and Loan crisis, removed this nonbank loophole.

State laws restricting branching location increased importance on the technical definition of just what a branch is. The pervasiveness of branch banking regulation is apparent when the courts must determine whether an automated teller machine constitutes a branch. One important case in New York state involved the large Buffalo-based bank, Marine Midland National Bank (currently owned by the Hongkong and Shanghai Bank), and a grocery store chain, Wegmans. In Canandaigua, New York, Wegmans had an ATM, not a point of sale machine, with Wegmans' logo on it. The ATM was shared, that is it could be used by a variety of financial institutions. The shared ATM network, known as HarMoney, used a central electronic facility owned by Marine Midland. Marine customers could use the ATM in Wegmans to make deposits, to withdraw cash, obtain cash advances with a credit card, transfer funds between bank accounts, obtain bank account information, and pay certain bills.

A Bankers Association, which included the Canandaigua National Bank, brought suit under the McFadden Act, claiming that the ATMs were branches.

The McFadden Act of 1927 is known for outlawing branch banking by national banks. Actually it subjects nationally chartered banks to state branch banking laws, which can be very restrictive. Thus, section 36 of the McFadden Act makes Marine Midland National Bank subject to New York Banking Law section 105. Under this state law, a bank may not open a branch in a city smaller than 50,000 that has the principal office of another bank. The population of Canandaigua is 11,000, and Canandaigua National Bank is headquartered in Canandaigua.

Marine's legal argument was that Wegmans was the owner and operator of the shared ATM and, thus, Marine was not establishing a branch in Canandaigua. The courts deciding this case had to apply the McFadden Act's definition of a branch, a definition written well before electronic banking. The complexity and arbitrariness of defining a branch in the electronic age was noted by the Second Circuit Court of Appeals: "If Wegmans' supermarket cashes a check and at the same time telephones the bank to guard against insufficiency of funds in the customers' account, apparently there is no branch; if the same functions are instantly performed by an automated teller, plaintiffs claim that there is a branch."

In the end the Court of Appeals adopted the Comptroller of the Currency's interpretation in 1982 that an ATM must be "owned or rented" for the ATM to constitute a branch. Wegmans owned the ATM and charged a per customer transaction fee to Marine. The Appeals Court ruled that the latter arrangement was not "rent." This position was the opposite of the District Court, which had ruled in favor of the Bankers Association. The Second Court of Appeals thus reversed the District Court and ruled in favor of Marine Midland.

What Banks May Do

Besides the original Federal Reserve Act, the two most important pieces of legislation governing bank entry into "nonbank" activities are the Glass-Steagall Act and the Bank Holding Company Act.

The legislative history of the Bank Holding Company Act discloses Congressional concern about the undue concentration of banking activities as well as the soundness of banks. In regard to the latter, a bank holding company might imperil the soundness of one or more of its banks by borrowing from one of its banks, discounting risky commercial paper at the bank, making the bank pay large dividends, or otherwise upstreaming funds from the bank to the bank holding company.

Even before Congress enacted the Bank Holding Company Act, banks could not enter the investment banking business due to the Glass-Steagall Act. This act was suppose to instill confidence into a banking system devastated by the Great Depression. The idea was to prevent the errors of the investment banking system, especially those of too aggressive security promotion, from contaminating commercial banking. More broadly stated, Congress did not want the faults of any non-commercial banking business to harm the public's confidence in depository institutions.

To some, the reform was not just a matter of cleaning up some troublespots, but of removing the most incredible abuses. Frank Pecora, a future SEC commissioner, described what he considered a "shocking corruption in our banking system, a widespread repudiation of old-fashioned standards of honesty and fair dealing with creation and sale of securities, and a merciless exploitation of the vicious possibilities of intricate corporate chicanery."

In contrast to the Pecora's assessment of the banking system, economists such as George Benston of Emory University claim the Glass-Steagall Act resulted from the investment bankers' attempt to preclude bank competition. From this point of view, the Act was essentially a turf battle won by the investment bankers through their influence on Congress.

The Bank Holding Act and the Glass-Steagall Act are similar in that they restrain bank entry into various activities. The latter pertains to securities, while the former pertains to nearly everything involving commerce.

The Glass-Steagall Act bars commercial banks from investment banking, that is primarily the underwriting of new securities. The Act attacks the combination of investment and commercial banking, known as universal banking. This means it is illegal for any person or company to accept deposits while issuing, underwriting, selling, or distributing securities. The Act cements this divorce of investment and commercial banking by prohibiting interlocking management of banks and security firms.

Notwithstanding the Glass-Steagall Act, commercial banks may participate in the security business in certain respects. The Glass-Steagall Act left banks the power to purchase and sell securities upon the order and for the account of customers. Discount brokers conduct business this way. The banks may purchase debt instruments, such as bonds, notes, or debentures, for their own account. They may even underwrite U.S. government obligations and general obligations of state and local governments. And so, banks can promote government bonds and hold them for the banks' account. Furthermore, banks may hold a small amount of voting stock of a company. Thus, banks are afforded several loopholes to the general prohibition of engaging in the securities business.

Language in the Glass-Steagall Act can be read so as to create a substantial presence of commercial banks in investment banks. Commercial banks are prevented from being "principally engaged" in the marketing of securities. A sympathetic Federal Reserve Board has interpreted the Act so that subsidiaries of a bank are allowed to engage in investment banking on a limited basis. This had made a commercial bank like the camel trying to get into the tent. Congress won't let it in, but, the Greenspan Federal Reserve Board is helping a bit.

In essence, the bank holding company mechanism offered a gigantic loophole seeking to market securities. Partly in response,

Congress passed the Bank Holding Company Act in 1956 to maintain the Glass-Steagall divorce of commercial and investment banking. The Bank Holding Company Act attacked the practice of holding companies engaging in nonbanking activities. Generally a bank holding company and a bank are allowed to engage in the same activities. Under Section 4 of the Act, a bank holding company can only control a company whose activity is "so closely related to banking or managing or controlling banks as to be a proper incident thereto." This special clause bears repeating: "closely related to banking and proper incident thereto."

The law charges the Federal Reserve Board with making the determination of closely related and proper incident. The Board utilizes a framework laid down by a circuit court of appeals for analyzing the closely related criterion. The court specified a three part test for closely related:

1. Banks generally have in fact provided the proposed services.

2. Banks generally provide services that are operationally or functionally so similar to the proposed services as to equip them particularly well to provide the proposed service.

3. Banks generally provide services that are so integrally related to the proposed services as to require their provision in a specialized form.

The Federal Reserve Board pronounces its interpretation of "closely related" in several forms. The first is in adjudicatory proceedings that examine applications of individual companies to engage in particular nonbank activities. A second method is the Federal Reserve Board's promulgation of regulations under Regulation Y, setting forth a list of closely related activities. Among the listed activities are operating a trust company, selling data processing services, underwriting certain types of insurance, providing courier services, and offering management consulting. Normally, the Federal Reserve Board utilizes this rulemaking procedure only after it has already decided a number of cases about the same proposed nonbanking activity. A third method of shaping the meaning of "closely related" is writing official interpretations of the regulations.

In deciding the issue of "proper incident to banking," the public benefits must outweigh the costs of a proposed activity. Congress enumerate the factors that the Board should examine in its cost/benefit analysis:

Benefits include,

- greater convenience
- increased competition
- and gains in efficiency

Costs include,

- undue concentration of resources
- decreased or unfair competition
- conflicts of interest
- and unsound banking practices.

In adjudicating the proper incident standard the Federal Reserve Board invariably finds an applicant offers some type of public benefit. Providing a good to the public can be considered a public benefit in itself. Alternatively, the availability of a good can be a pertinent factor for increasing competition. In either case, increased availability produces public benefits in the judgment of the Board. For instance, in amending Regulation Y and expanding the permissible activities of management consulting services, the Federal Reserve cited the increased availability benefit exists even where there is a takeover of a going concern. Typically, this occurs when the takeover candidate is a failing or weakened firm. Numerous S&Ls were acquired under this rationale. Citicorp, in particular, gained access to the California market by acquiring a failed thrift institution.

Although the Bank Holding Company Act limited bank entry through the holding company, it established a mechanism of regu-

lation by which the Federal Reserve could allow increasing integration of bank factors of production with new products. To the extent
the Federal Reserve authorizes such mergers, a socially useful exploitation of potential economies may result. While the Bank Holding Company Act does restrict bank acquisitions, the Federal
Reserve has shown a willingness to expand the permissible activities. It may do this subtly by deciding a greater number of the cases
favorable to applicants. The Federal Reserve also can increase the
scope of permissible activities by adding to the closely related list
or by amending the scope of items already on the list. The Chairman
of the Federal Reserve may very well affect the liberalization trend.
Certainly Chairman Alan Greenspan has steered the Federal Reserve toward allowing increased bank integration with nonbank
activities. This tendency is in step with the Chairman's long standing libertarian philosophy, as exemplified by his one time association with Ayn Rand.

Yet, besides the role of the Chairman, the process and logic of
the Act leads to greater liberalization. Once a great number of banks
engage in an activity, the activity becomes closely related to banking. This event could occur before the Federal Reserve has adjudi-
cated the issue of permissibility. Typically, the achievement of the
state of prevalence occurs during the process of adjudication. Banks,
whose applications are approved, augment the number of banks
engaged in the specific nonbank practice. When an activity becomes
sufficiently prevalent, the Federal Reserve approves it in a rule. This
process results in a slow but sure expansion of permissible activities.

The provision allowing banks to engage in consulting activities
also illustrates this regulatory process which inexorably increases
the breadth of permissible activities. Originally bank holding companies could not offer management consulting services. Later, the
Board allowed management consulting to unaffiliated commercial
banks. Subsequently, the Board amended Regulation Y to allow
bank holding companies to offer management consulting advice to
thrift institutions. The Federal Reserve liberalized its rule for service

Table 2-1. Regulation Y List
of Permissible Nonbanking Activities

1. Making and servicing loans
2. Industrial banking
3. Trust company functions
4. Investment or financial advice
5. Leasing
6. Community development
7. Data processing
8. Insurance agency and underwriting
9. Operating savings association
10. Courier services
11. Management consulting to depository institutions
12. Money orders, savings bonds, and travelers checks
13. Real estate and personal property appraising
14. Arranging commercial real estate equity financing
15. Securities brokerage
16. Underwriting and dealing in government obligations and money market instruments.
17. Foreign exchange advisory and transactional services
18. Futures commission merchant
19. Investment advice on financial futures and options on futures
20. Consumer financial counseling
21. Tax planning and preparation
22. Check guaranty services
23. Operating collection agency
24. Operating credit bureau

Source: Table prepared by authors from 12 C.F.R. section 225.25.

offered to non-affiliated nonbank depository institutions insofar as the consulting services relate to "bank operations and marketing, bank personnel operations, and consumer financial information." And so, the Board liberalized the list of permissible activities according to whom the service could be offered and widened the permissible scope of the service.

On occasion, the Board enlarges the scope of the activity by a liberal interpretation rather than by a revised rule. The rule permitting bankholding companies to offer management consulting does not mention audit services. But in an interpretation subsequent to the promulgation of the rule, the Board named audit services, inter alia, as an activity contemplated by management consulting.

The main thrust of this regulatory scheme is to inevitably expand the affiliation of banks with nonbanking activities. As this occurs, the process will reinforce itself. The fact that banks are seen as being involved in more activities justifies that involvement. Such involvement also expands upon the activities that may bear a resemblance to present bank activities. Furthermore, competition places banks in the position that compels them to offer a service to stay competitive. An example is the sale of excess computer time. Bank operation of computer facilities will be inefficient and too costly, if banks are not allowed to sell excess computer time.

In some areas the expansion of permissible activities that efficiency would seem to dictate can run up against the closely related banking requirement. Regulation allows for bank transportation services in regard to checks and other financial materials, but not non-financial materials. Arguably the transportation network of personnel and equipment constitutes a factor of production that might economically add non-financial commodities to its product line. The integration of the bank-owned input with another transportation activity would exploit an economy of scope and arguably rectify an inefficient and too costly bank operated courier service.

In the information age, the shared inputs to the production process that need to be exploited are not principally finite things but information and other intangibles. A modern approach to regulation must wrestle with restrictions against bank or bank holding company participation in various nonbanking activities. These restrictions may cause valuable information to go unused. Banks possess useful information about particular firms, their management, and certain industries. This information could be used in a variety of ways. For instance it might potentially aid a bank in a profitable takeover. Generally, a bank's equity in corporations allows a bank to discipline management. German banks typically take considerable equity interests in industrial companies and have placed numerous bankers on boards of directors, who presumably could use their superior information in making decisions. Because banks may have a comparative advantage in raising funds quickly, they may be able to attempt these takeovers efficiently.

Bank information also would be useful in offering other products. In particular, knowledge about a specific firm gathered for the purpose of making commercial loans may be useful for underwriting new issues. The Glass-Steagall Act specifically forbids U.S. banks from achieving this economy of scope. German universal banks, on the other hand, enjoy the advantage of pooling information, that is sharing the information between the commercial and investment banking divisions. Commercial banks' ability to achieve economies by integrating some security business into their banking business has spurred the Securities Industry Association to enlist its friends in Congress to block bank entry into the securities business. The Association lost the battle against allowing banks to enter the discount securities business; the pivotal event in this regard was the Federal Reserve Board's approval of Bank of America's acquisition of Schwab. The investment bankers' continued defense of the Glass-Steagall Act is the biggest battle of the war between the investment bankers and the commercial bankers.

The advantage of universal banking is found not only on the supply side, but on the demand side too. Bank customers may desire one-stop banking. At stake for customers is not mere convenience, but also confidentiality of information.

Summary

Two laws govern bank acquisition of nonbanking entities and thus the financial services that can be offered by banks. The Glass-Steagall Act prevents bank involvement in the underwriting of securities. The Bank Holding Company Act restricts bank acquisition of all nonbank entities, except those that are closely related to banking and a proper incident thereto. An activity is closely related if banks historically have been engaged in the same or similar activities. An activity is a proper incident of banking if the net benefits to the public are positive. Typically, the Federal Reserve makes these determinations under the facts of a specific application.

Eventually the Board may hold that a certain proposed activity as a general matter is closely related to banking. If the Federal Reserve also decides that the activity as a general matter is a proper incident to banking the Reserve will make a rule, adding the nonbank activity to the permissible list. Even then, the Board can make the rule more liberal by amendment or by broad interpretations. The clear tendency of regulation under the Bank Holding Company Act is to allow greater affiliation of commercial banking with other financial business.

Appendix 2

Vox populi

As computers and databases have accumulated and stored more and more information about the ordinary citizen, public concerns broadened to privacy violations in the uses of computer-stored information.

In a 1992 Consumer Privacy Survey, sponsored by Equifax, a leading credit rating agency, examined public opinion on business uses of databases. The survey, conducted by Louis Harris & Associates, questioned 1,254 people from throughout the continental United States. Following are the questions and answers.

A Clear and Present Danger

According to the survey results, most people are not computer Luddites. They have no desire to swing sledge hammers at machines. The vast majority readily acknowledge the beneficial effects of computers.

Q. *Computers have improved the quality of life in our society.*

Agree............................	79%
Disagree........................	18%
Not sure........................	2%

Yet Americans also see computer usage as posing a clear and present danger to personal privacy. Overwhelmingly, 76 percent agree that consumers lost all control over the way information about them is circulated and used by companies. The public concern with privacy issues has grown steadily over the years as computers and

---

databases are used more and more. The next table compares opinions from Harris-Equifax surveys for select years.

Q. *The present uses of computers are an actual threat to personal privacy in this country.*

	1974	*1977*	*1983*	*1992*
Agree	38%	41%	51%	68%
Disagree	41%	44%	42%	28%
Not sure	21%	15%	6%	3%

When Is Personal Privacy "Private?"

Even the most ardent libertarian does not consider all individual actions as private. Then when should personal matters remain private? This query raises an ethical question which cannot be answered by rational analysis. The public seems to accept open access to personal information when applying for credit, insurance, or other benefits from the rendition of a financial service. For example, 77 percent of respondents thought it proper for a car insurance company to check an applicant's driving and accident record before issuing a policy.

Q. *Many government records such as drivers' licenses, court records, and property tax information are legally treated as "public information" and are open to anyone who wants to examine them. In the following situations, how do you feel about individual consumer data . . . being available for the following . . .*

Situation	*Approve*	*Disapprove*	*Not Sure*
Auto insurance companies checking accident and driving record for a policy	77%	21%	1%
Business checking bankruptcy and other financial records for credit application	71%	27%	2%
Firms obtaining public record lists for direct mail about products/services	32%	67%	1%

The survey question refers to public records, many of which have legal restrictions on their use. Several states have limited access to addresses of auto owners and drivers. Federal and state laws restrict access to such sensitive data as individual income tax returns.

Many private databases are in fact quasi-public records, and consumers probably hold the same attitudes about them as they do about public records. For example, giant credit card companies keep purchasing records about many millions of individuals.

Consumers evidently support open access to their personal records when they initiate an action like applying for loans or credit. They do not support access to their personal files without their approval. One of the greatest negatives is use of personal information for marketing purposes. Many companies that sell responder lists ask customers' permission to make their names available for marketing purposes.

Two issues are paramount with respect to marketing. One is fraud. Although the vast majority of direct marketers conduct business honestly, the industry attracts significant numbers of scam artists and swindlers. Though list vendors cannot prevent fraud, should they unwittingly contribute to it by selling names without customers' permission? For example, investments in securities, art, and other collectibles have been notable for recent telemarketing scams. Customers can always say "No." The question is: should they be hassled by telemarketers?

The second issue concerns marketing practices that are annoying, distasteful, or devious. Most complaints to consumer protection agencies concern themselves with telemarketing. Obviously, what is private or distasteful to one person may not be regarded as such by another. One solution is the approach American Express advocates to the direct marketing industry:

- A person should be made aware of the information a company makes available to others.

- An individual should have the option of preventing personal data from being sold or rented against his or her wishes.
- A consumer should have the right to be excluded from any and all lists (sold to third parties).
- It is unethical for a firm to collect data for one purpose and rent or sell it for another against the customer's wishes.

Divided Opinion

When a transaction that requires access to personal information is initiated by a consumer, the public generally supports the business practices. Yet, there are substantial minorities holding contradictory views. Dr. Alan F. Westin of Columbia University, a consultant to the Harris-Equifax Survey, examined characteristics of groups with diverse opinions. In general, his analysis found that those who most supported business rights to personal information were socially upscale. The most negative feelings were held by the less-educated, poorer, Black and Hispanic segments of the population. Apparently, these groups have been considered high credit risks and are most likely to be denied credit.

Under these circumstances, the alienation of underprivileged segments is understandable. While instances of discrimination exist, many such charges are the result of pressure by advocacy groups and political figures. To avoid public controversy, should financial institutions embark upon "social" programs?

The truth is that financial firms have created neither poverty nor income inequality. Business firms are incapable of solving social ills; responsibility clearly rests with government. To avoid public controversy, many financial firms might be willing to lower credit standards. But this policy is a no-win course of action. It helps neither the borrower who cannot meet the obligations nor the firm that overextends credit. It also opens the door to charges of favoritism. How can a bank defend giving credit to one bad-risk individual and denying it to another? The most defensible policy is to set an explicit credit policy in accordance with law, and strictly enforce it with no regard to "whom an applicant knows."

Part II

New Product Strategies

3

Business Strategies

Business strategy is a hotly disputed subject among management experts. This book sees it as giving direction to business development at all organizational levels—corporate, divisional, and operational. These directions apply primarily to both products and markets. This chapter covers the following aspects of strategy as they apply to financial services:

- Single-product strategies
- Strategies for mature products
- Differentiating "standardized" financial services
- Line extension strategies
- Potential uses of substitutable and complementary services
- Potential cannibalization of products in "stretched" lines
- Ways of melding different product lines to achieve effective diversification programs

Strategy in Corporate Planning

The term "strategic planning" came to business from the military. "Strategy" is from a Greek word meaning generalship, concerned with the broad issues involved in winning a war. In business, strategy means pursuing long-term and substantive objectives. While the time-span of corporate strategy varies, the most common long-term plans run from three to five years.

Development of business strategies goes on at all levels of a company—from the CEO's staff, to divisional executives, to product line managers. Regardless of level, traditional thinking sees strategies as implemented by tactics. Tactical plans are of relatively short duration, with budgets allocated for no more than a year.

This view was strongly challenged by Thomas J. Peters, co-author of the best seller, *In Search of Excellence*. Peters inverts the conventional wisdom, arguing that strategy is execution. "Strategy," writes Peters, "is the dependent variable, operable at a lower level of business."

This bottom-up approach gained adherents as corporate America down-sized. Thick documents coming down from ivory-tower decision makers did not work; plans needed input from people who could execute them. Disenchantment with a "knowledge-but-no-experience" philosophy led many firms in the 1980s to reduce or eliminate staffs of corporate planners that had grown like weeds in the previous decade. Strategy now flows in both directions, top-down and bottom-up, though not always evenly.

A strategic plan should never be regarded as etched in stone. It must have flexibility. It must enable its managers to act rapidly when new opportunities arise. It must be continually evaluated, so that it might be changed as conditions change. In the '80s, financial houses were falling over each other to put money into leveraged buyouts. By the early '90s smart players were gobbling up leveraged buyout obligations at a fraction of their dollar value. Similarly, banks in the 1980s saw opportunities in funding the real estate boom. Several years later money could be made by purchasing troubled property cheaply from banks, thrifts, and insurance companies.

GE Capital Services exemplifies the driving spirit and keen alertness that is so necessary to make plans work. The company's assets in 1992 reached $155 billion, and its earnings surged to $1.5 billion. Though only one of thirteen major business segments of General Electric Company, the financial unit contributed fully one-third the earnings of its parent.

GE Capital operates nearly two dozen different businesses on a global scale. It issues retailer credit cards, engages in reinsurance, leases autos and oceangoing shipping containers, insures mortgages, conducts business in annuities and mutual funds, and finances commercial real estate projects.

Planners are part of various business unit teams, thus uniting thinking and number crunching with "doing." Every three months, unit business managers meet with top executives of the company to review both operating and strategic plans. These reviews include not only evaluations of monitored results, but ideas for changing plans in the light of new events. The system encourages a continuing search for new opportunities and new ways of doing things.

Many ideas thrown out at these meetings sprout from the bottom, especially the salesforce. Every call on a customer or prospect is a potential source of information. A perceptive salesperson should be able to sort out the kernel of good ideas when taking orders, listening to complaints, or even when receiving curt refusals to order. Companies selling goods and services to businesses obtain roughly a third of all new product ideas from customers' suggestions.

Keeping on top of events and having a willingness to entertain change does not prevent bad decisions. Bad debts at GE Capital in 1991 and 1992 mounted to more than $1.25 billion each year. The company posted $800 million in write-offs for bad credit during 1990—not an inconsequential sum. But successful dealings far outweighed the unprofitable ones.

Products and Markets

If the two main goals of corporations are to devise and distribute offerings, then the primary elements of strategy pertain to products and markets. This rule holds equally for services as well as goods, and applies to every level where strategy is formulated. This type of planning is "generic." It gives direction to business development.

Products define a firm's outputs. They determine in part the facilities and technologies required for performance. For example, a decision to start a mutual fund necessitates at minimum an incoming telephone operation, a database recording and summarizing transactions, and a staff trading in securities.

Markets determine to whom the outputs are directed. Markets define the company's vital links to the outside world—the customers who are the end of a distribution chain and the middlemen who help in reaching that final destination. For example, in 1989 Morgan Stanley began managing mutual funds for institutions. It then defined its markets as pension funds and wealthy individuals. The minimum investment Morgan Stanley accepted was $250,000 to $500,000. Later, the firm recognized the small investor as a potential source of growth.

In 1993 the company formed three "retail" funds, with minimum investment requirements of $1,000. Its markets changed from institutional investors to the larger public and Morgan Stanley had to communicate differently with its retail prospects. Without a strong image among the general public, or expertise in the use of mass media, Morgan Stanley chose to sell its funds through brokers. It charged a 4.75 percent commission, known as a load, and a 1 percent annual fee tacked on to fund expenses.

Neither products nor markets ever stand alone. They are two sides of the same coin. A product policy implies a marketing policy; the firm must adjust its marketing plans to fit an appropriate distribution system. Conversely, marketing policy affects a product policy; a firm must devise financial services that fit the needs of a defined customer base.

Product-Market Options

From a purely conceptual point of view, a firm has several options for producing products and choosing markets. Once a market is chosen, a firm can provide customers with one or many products. For example, traditional employee retirement plans at one time swept all participants into a fund managed in the same way for every investor. These "defined benefit" plans allowed for few options. Some plans gave employees a choice between bond funds, equities, or some combination of the two, but choices were limited. In the 1980s defined benefit plans gave way to company-sponsored "defined contribution" plans, commonly known as 401(k) plans. The new law permitted employees to contribute a portion of their salaries, tax free, toward their retirement. Companies responded to greater employee participation in decision making, with an increased number of investment choices. Financial services catering to the retirement marketplace went from single to multiple products.

Yes, the market did expand. Yes, the nature of the market changed. Markets always do. But the customers that compose the market remained pretty much the same—company employees. Now these same customers are serviced with many options regarding investment preferences.

However, to compete successfully, providers of defined contribution plans must increase their services in ways other than offering more choices of investment vehicles. Giant mutual funds and insurance companies in the defined contribution business conduct educational programs for employees. Once provided as perks to executives, knowledge of financial planning has come down to broad groups of employees. To make investment decisions, employees need to know about asset allocation, risk-reward tradeoffs, and tax benefits. Continuing workshops have become standard in the retirement-service industry.

Given a product policy, a company can sell its service in one or more markets. For example, before Morgan Stanley decided to enter retail markets, it serviced organizations and a narrow niche of wealthy executives with essentially the same products. Individuals who could plunk down a half-million dollars were treated in the same way as institutional investors. For practical purposes, the only difference was the size of an account. Likewise, many open-end mutual funds sell through various distribution channels in order to reach diverse market segments. For example, they sell through brokers, banks, advertising, and direct mail.

The Single-Minded Approach

A one-product policy implies highly limited services. This strategy is usually referred to as undifferentiated. The firm sees the same service as satisfying all customers.

This single-minded strategy arises under varying circumstances. Small businesses, for example, are constricted by limited resources no matter where they operate. Small insurance companies might confine their operations to one type of risk in order not to spread resources too thin. Similarly, market size and composition may act as a constraining force. Small local brokers deal in securities and little else, because a limited number of customers cannot support the increased overhead of peripheral operations. In like manner, agricultural communities may offer opportunities for leasing tractors and other farm equipment, but not for leasing automobiles.

Large growing markets may also encourage single-product strategies in varying circumstances. An expanding market fosters specialization, which in turn has spawned a host of narrow specialists.

Among them are financial planners—lawyers, accountants, insurance company retirees, college professors, systems analysts and other technicians. Some work for organizations. Other professionals work alone; they are still able to hang up a shingle and hustle for business. Many small businesses thrive in markets dominated by large, well-staffed organizations. Professors do consulting to augment their teaching income, and the better-known academics teach to augment their consulting income. Accountants moonlight in preparing tax returns, and work after hours during the tax season on a temporary basis for H & R Block.

Another large group of specialists are made up of newsletter writers and publishers of special investment reports. One of the best known writers is Louis Rukeyser, host of TV show Wall Street Week. *Louis Rukeyser's Wall Street* became the largest investment newsletter soon after it was launched in 1993. Some newsletters restrict themselves to certain investment vehicles, such as Jay Schabacker's *Mutual Fund Investing* and Don Phillips' *Morningstar Mutual Funds*. The category of specialties includes a number of financial research services, such as well-regarded Lipper's Analytical Service, Valueline, and Standard & Poor's. These reports go to both financial service companies and individuals.

Data processing is yet another form of specialization in the financial service industry. Computer service bureaus have become important vehicles of outsourcing, a practice of doing work on the outside. Automatic Data Processing has grown steadily by doing payrolls for business clients, competing with banks and companies' internal computer centers. State Street Boston Corporation, a venerable New England bank, derives most of its earnings from processing more than $1 trillion of securities for trusts and financial houses. Lending is no longer the bank's core business. The vast size of its data processing accounts gives State Street economies of scale; it can spread a technological-intensive service over a larger asset base than can rivals. This cost advantage induces companies to "farm out" their data processing instead of doing it themselves; outsourcing costs are lower than do-it-yourself costs.

In all these instances, a single-minded focus is essentially a small business strategy. The company directs its efforts toward a narrow market segment or niche.

The advantages of "niching" are several. First, it presents a less competitive environment. Large providers of financial services might not deem small markets worth their efforts. The sales potentials would not make a material difference to their net earnings. This is particularly so when the customized service deviates from their main lines of business. In that event, the small operator benefits from the "benign neglect" of the large firms.

A second advantage of "niching" is that once a small firm deeply penetrates a market segment, even giant corporations might find it difficult to dislodge them. The pygmy business may have developed preemptive skills that sheer size cannot overcome. Moreover, low volume by itself does not always lead to inefficiency. In part, productivity depends on human capital, and the niche player may have developed some special knowledge, competence, or other advantage over rivals. In instances of geographic differentials, local firms might service nearby customers better than larger companies operating at a distance. The practice of branch banking, for example, postulates local advantages accruing to on-site business dealings.

The greatest disadvantage to a niche strategy is that all a firm's eggs are in the proverbial "one basket." If that basket is exposed to danger, there may be no way to secure its safety.

So far, all examples of business single-mindedness have dealt with limited service functions and small, narrow markets. A one-product focus, however, may come in large, mass markets where services of various providers are very much alike. An outstanding example of a commodity-like service is the credit card, which is fairly standardized. Most credit card issuers perform other services, as do banks, financial houses, and even manufacturing and utility companies. But most "plastic money" issuers compete with look-alike products. Different firms may define their markets differently. For example, a regional bank may see its market as bounded by geographic borders, while large money center banks, such as Chase Manhattan or Citicorp, may regard the entire country as its marketing area. Regardless of geographic area, no credit card is so unique that it cannot be substituted for another.

Since credit cards bear a marked resemblance to each other, product development plays a decidedly minor role in maintaining or acquiring customers. Rather, credit card companies compete using advertising, price promotion, and market development programs. Many companies use tactics similar to the frenzied marketing tactics of packaged goods manufacturers.

Advertising is a way of differentiating product or service features that set yours apart from competitors'. In the case of advertising, however, the difference usually exists not in the performance of the service but in the eye of the beholder. People perceive attributes in a service that may be imagined, and have no basis in reality. The advertising profession refers to such attempts at persuasion as psychological differentiation or "positioning." Ads strive to create a "position" in the collective psyche of buyers. Advertisers define these "images" in nebulous terms, such as "share of mind."

As a service becomes standardized, image-creating advertising has less effect. The many millions of dollars that American Express poured into advertising to create an image of prestige for its card did not shield the company from the onslaught of competitors hawking special deals, discounts, rebates, and a variety of other price promotions.

The surge of competitive activity, particularly the rise of price deals, cut deeply into AmEx's market share and profitability. The firm reported in 1991 that its credit card division took a third-quarter write-off of $265 against earnings. The downturn accelerated in 1992. The third quarter of that year witnessed a $205 million loss, owing mainly to restructuring its flagship Travel Related Service Unit. The number of active credit cards fell from just under 37 million to close to 35 million in the course of a year.

What was AmEx's reaction to its declining fortunes? Its first move was to dismiss its long-time ad agency, Ogilvy & Mather, International, on the assumption that the upscale image the agency had created over the years had worn out. Or were the copywriters burned out? The new agency, Chiat/Day/Mojo Inc., was dumped within a year, criticized for producing images that were "confusing and uninspired." Several months later, AmEx's chairman, James D. Robinson III, under pressure from company directors, bid farewell with a golden handshake, though he did not get quite all the gold he had arrogantly demanded.

Perhaps AmEx's new ad agency *should* have been dismissed if it did not deliver memorable messages. Perhaps AmEx's chairman *should* have been pushed out since he received big pay bonuses when the company did well, and often when it did not. But neither a fresh company "image" nor a new chairman could solve the travails of the deeply-troubled company.

Fact: credit cards have reached market maturity. The top 100 credit card issuers in 1992 tracked more than 139 million of their cards in circulation. As a market approaches maturity, products tend to become similar to each other. Major players have had years to see what works and what doesn't, and to adapt to their markets. Why should a person pay four times the price of an average credit card for "ambiance" when other cards provide the same or better service for less money? Most credit cards extend credit. The AmEx green card does not. AmEx was able to stop its business decline, not by "positioning" new images in consumer minds, but by old-fashioned promotions to consumers and horse trading with retailers on commissions.

Even a cursory review of recent trends points to price, not image, as the driving force in a slow growth environment. Card issuers who were successful used price and merchandising strategies to build their business. Sears scored a major breakthrough in 1986 when it introduced its Discover card, with a no-fee charge and cash-back rebates. This offer gained cardholders by the droves, and in a half dozen years Sears' database held 41 million cardholder records.

Ironically, the 1992 Annual Survey of Brittain Associates, a highly regarded industry research outfit, reported a 15 percent drop in usage of Discover cards. The decline was attributed to Sears' refusal to lower interest rates from a lofty 19.8 percent, although its major competitors slashed their rates. Evidently, Sears forgot what brought it success initially. Eventually, the Discover Card was forced to drop its rates, and by March 1993 it charged a more competitive rate of 14.5 percent. But the move to a lower rate level was not indicative of a market leader. It was defensive, generated to keep existing customers rather than to attract new ones.

While financial services supposedly have inelastic demands, customers were not as insensitive to rates as Sears' managers assumed. Similarly, AmEx customers were not willing to pay much for snob appeal.

An entourage of other nonbank issuers adopted the same tactics as Sears to pry open the door to the credit card business. The crowning achievement was scored by AT&T, which started signing up customers with a promise of "no fees for life." In a little more than two years its Universal Card passed the break-even point and began turning out profits. GE, Ford Motor, and General Motors are other firms that solicit credit card accounts with discounts, low interest charges on outstanding balances, rebates, and promotional incentives.

GM's no fee MasterCard gives rebates equal to 5 percent of charges, totalling $700 a year, that can be applied to the purchase or lease of any new GM car or truck. In contrast, the GE card carries an annual fee, but beckons customers with rebates and discounts on retail purchases. A few months before the arrival of GM's card, Ford launched its Visa and MasterCard through its financial unit, The Associates. Ford's main selling point was a cash rebate of up to 1.5 percent of total charges. In early 1993 Ford and Citibank brought out a credit card that mimicked the GM card, giving customers earned rebates on purchases that they can use to buy Ford vehicles.

Strategies for Mature Markets

What strategies are available to financial services that have become commonplace in a mature market? Using credit cards as a prototype, the most important options are as follows:

Repositioning the Service

This calls for changing customers' perceptions or mental images. It strives to create a new "position" in customers' collective minds that would set the service apart from its competitors. Ad agencies and advertising mavens prescribe this as a favorite tonic when a radical alteration occurs with respect to business context. But it seldom works, unless the service itself really conforms to the new image and really offers a difference that is meaningful to users.

Selling with Price Deals and Incentives

Financial service companies are not alone in embracing price-off deals and promotional incentives in order to sell their products. Rather, they are part of a larger trend in a maturing consumer economy. Early in the 1980s producers of packaged goods, appliances, household supplies, and transportation services shifted their marketing budgets from general advertising to sales promotion. The era of building brand loyalty by advertising is over. Rebates, cents-off coupons, sweepstakes, and premiums are the new engines for driving sales. Savings banks were early adopters of these tactics, attracting depositors with free dishes, throw-rugs, and kitchen utensils. Today, about two-thirds of all consumer marketing expenditures flow toward sales promotion, while general advertising receives only a third.

Price promotion has become a way of life in the credit card business. As interest rates plummeted, many banks in 1992 changed over to floating interest rates which were pegged to the prime rate. Some banks in 1992 even dropped interest charges to 11.9 percent while credit cards were averaging interest rates of 18 percent.

The steep decline in interest rates in 1992 led to sharp disparities in bank charges. By mid-year, interest payments on credit cards ranged between slightly less than 12–19 percent.

This created opportunities for low-priced issuers, such as Bank of New York, Nationsbank, and Bank One Corporation, which began promoting "balance transfer" accounts with well-supported campaigns in direct mail and newspapers. These ads invited new customers to transfer outstanding balances that bore high interest rates. A person keeping an average monthly balance of $1,400 at 18 percent could save $85 a year by transferring that debt to an 11.9 percent card. In saturated markets with low growth, the best way to gain customers is to steal them away from others.

Marketing or creating attractive price deals in themselves do not provide a competitive advantage. The key to price competition is low operating costs. Price cuts erode margins without corresponding reductions in costs. Despite public pronouncements, one of the first steps AmEx took to meet the challenge of lower-priced competitors was to reduce its bloated work force, including its corps of middle managers. Company spokespersons were reported as saying that the massive layoffs would create "elbow room" to strengthen business. This would be true if lower overhead did not cut into necessary services. Low cost operations can best pursue low price policies under any circumstances, and the lowest cost issuer always holds the upper hand over competitors.

Incentive programs also need low operating costs to be productive. While price cuts attack profit margins from the revenue side, incentive programs attack margins from the cost side. Premiums and rebates give buyers something extra, but they also create extra marketing costs.

Most of the credit card incentives represent continuity programs. The "extras" depend on the length and degree of buyer involvement. Those who buy more frequently are credited with more bonus points. These promotions have only marginal value in expanding the credit card base, because they seldom lure non-customers into becoming cardholders. At most, they may push people who are "probable" customers into filling out an application for actual membership. The greatest value of these programs is to influence multiple cardholders, coaxing them to use one card as opposed to another.

Changing the Product

When performance is standardized, product changes are minor. In what ways can you really change the basic function of a credit card? No matter what you do, a card is a card is a card. Similarly, bank deposits and checking accounts resemble each other to a remarkable degree. Car and home insurance policies are basically the same, though they may differ on several options.

As time passes, incremental changes always take place, such as adding convenience-in-usage, enhancing value, or installing on-line credit checks. In many instances, such changes in the service are necessary in order to compete. For example, toll-free 800 numbers take calls 24 hours a day concerning lost, misplaced, or stolen cards. Undoubtedly, they have reduced the volume of fraud. Similarly, ATM machines lengthened banking hours and increased customer convenience without significant increases in labor costs. But all credit card companies have 800 numbers, and practically all banks offer ATM services. Since these amenities are industry wide, they are necessary for conducting business. Customers have learned to expect them. But they do not give credit card companies or banks special advantages. When something is common, possessed by everyone, it does not generate a differential advantage.

Stretching the Market

A "market-stretching" or market development strategy seeks to expand the markets for current products. In practice, market-stretching often goes hand-in-hand with product changes or modifications.

There are several ways of expanding markets using essentially the same service. Here are some of the ways:

Add new distribution channels

In the autumn of 1992 American Express lowered transaction fees paid by merchants who carried its card. By wheeling and dealing, it also signed up mass merchandisers to accept its card, such as Kmart. It seems that AmEx retreated from its upscale image in favor of getting more retailers to accept its card. After all, snobs shop at discount stores as well as Neiman Marcus.

Market-stretching by other credit card companies included aggressive moves into supermarkets. In 1989 only 17 percent of U.S. supermarkets accepted credit cards. By the end of 1992 that figure had jumped to about 39 percent. Both Visa and MasterCard made special efforts to that extent.

The same market-stretching tactics are employed by mutual funds sponsors. Many fund companies have added banks and brokerage houses to their channels of distribution.

Develop affinity services

Affinity services are being offered in greater numbers. For example, mutual funds sold at retail might, with only minor modifications, fit the pension funds market. Corporate credit cards are given to executives, but the firm pays discounted fees for the privilege. Insurance policies and mutual funds might be offered under a "co-brand," such as Scudder funds for AARP members.

Expand the market area

One way is geographic expansion, especially when locations close to customers brings new business. Branch banking is a case in point; the bank increases the number of sites. Brokerage houses have also expanded their offices geographically in order to provide better service to local customers. This strategy works best when customers transact business on the premises of the service provider. In that event, site location becomes an important influence on profitable operations.

Multiple Product Strategies

Sooner or later, a single product must approach the growth-resistance barrier. Consequently, in their normal course of business, most financial service companies tend to take on more than one product. These products reflect market and product orientations.

At the risk of oversimplifying the subject, we can describe the most important multiple product strategies as market segmentation, line extensions, and diversification. For purposes of illustration, we will discuss each strategy as though it existed by itself. In reality, however, firms pursue each of them at the same time.

Market Segmentation

As the term implies, market segmentation works from the demand side of the market. The strategy rests on a highly abstract concept, but one that forms the mainstream of marketing theory. It visualizes a market composed of segments, or groups of users, whose wants and needs differ from each other. For example, customers who enroll in a hedge fund have distinctly different goals from those who buy popular mutual funds. Hedge funds are exclusive investment clubs made up of 100 or so wealthy individuals who are willing to take high risks for potentially high rewards. Without having to register with the Securities and Exchange Commission, these funds employ tactics that conventional funds cannot, such as leveraging their investments with loans.

Segmentation theory assumes that demand arises independently from buyers' needs. Granted that heroic assumption,
supply obsequiously follows demand. Companies must therefore
"read" the market, the theory holds, so as to create the services that
buyers need.

Many have questioned the basic assumption of "buyer sover-
eignty." Did junk bonds come about because buyers raised their
voices and said, "Give us junk bonds"? Or were they a product of
Michael Milken's creative mind? Did Merrill Lynch hear a loud
clamor for a Cash Management Account or did someone in the
company create the idea? If buyers really did voice a need for cash
management, why didn't anyone else in the industry except Merrill
hear the call?

Other difficulties with the segmentation concept pertain to
implementation. The concept enjoins a company to divide a market
and offer each division a separate product to fill its particular needs.
But how do you define a market? Do you describe it in terms of
potential customers or actual ones? Ask the same question of a
dozen different fund managers and you are apt to get twelve different answers. Markets expand and contract, and companies are
apt to define the same market in different ways.

To make matters worse, financial markets are often devoid of
well-defined segments. While databases have improved the process
of segment selection, vague, subjective segment boundaries continue to exist. Because marketers hold the segmentation concept
almost as dearly as an Article of Faith, Chapter 6 discusses the topic
in greater detail.

In the meantime, we can only say that the concept works under
certain conditions. But it is not generally applicable.

Line Extensions

As in goods-producing industries, financial service firms offer product lines. These are comprised of closely related intangibles that
have similar functions. Most such services are offered to the same
group of customers. Like product lines of goods, those of services

tend to lengthen as the customer base grows and the market matures. Firms add more services to their lines.

Financial services that make up a line act as product substitutes, product complements, or both. For example, a bank with several types of checking accounts proffers substitute services to customers. One kind may require a minimum balance and impose no charge for checks. Another account may have no minimum on average balances, but charge a small fee for each check written. A depositor will pick one or the other account, but rarely both. The same holds true for insurance. A customer will normally take out one car and home insurance policy, but not two.

When services imply an either-or choice, the product line is usually small. Increasing the number of options would only add complexity to operations, while bringing in few new accounts. Profits of substitutable services depend importantly on customer service, marketing, and cost control.

For example, large credit card companies have expanded buyer options, but only moderately so. American Express added Optima to its line in 1987, but unlike its traditional green card, Optima has a revolving credit feature and a lower annual fee. Other bank cards offer other options. Choice, one of several Citicorp credit cards, offers customers an either-or selection of fees versus interest rates. A cardholder can opt for paying no fee with a higher interest rate on outstanding balances or paying an annual fee with a lower interest rate. Many issuers have brought out varieties of the basic cards, with such designations as "gold" and "platinum," but as yet no "lead." Since business occurs at a distance, and customer service is fairly standard, operating units of card firms emphasize promotion and cost control.

In contrast, complementary services encourage long product lines. Fidelity offers more than 200 funds under its management, spanning all 23 fund categories of Lipper Analytical Services. More than three dozen Fidelity funds make up the "Select Portfolios." These invest in single industries, which specialize in such fields as biotech, American gold, air transportation, and precious metal.

Other fund managers also offer large varieties of investment options. In March 1993, *The Wall Street Journal* listed 83 funds by Merrill Lynch, 64 by Prudential, and 57 by Vanguard. The funds invested in bonds as well as stock, in domestic companies as well as foreign, and in geographic regions as well as in specific countries. Newspaper listings are not complete. They do not include many small and newly created funds.

Line extension strategies are best illustrated by mutual funds management companies. They launch new funds like packaged goods' manufacturers produce brand extensions—and for the same reasons. They seek a competitive edge. Here's how:

- Firms gain efficiency through "economies of scope." These economies arise when one or more products employ the same assets, such as human and capital resources. A funds management company, for example, employs for each fund the same customer database, trading facilities, research reports, forecasting models, and computer processing. By the use of joint assets, the firm lowers the costs of marketing and operating each unit in the "family of funds."
- At the same time, these firms increase variety to fill gaps in their product line or to extend it. The use of joint assets reduces per-unit operating costs in general, and minimizes marketing expenses in particular. A large base of potential buyers already exists in the customer database, and promotional material for the new fund can be included with monthly or quarterly summary statements.
- A customer database also provides a receptive audience for other products, such as brokerage services, credit cards, and trust accounts.
- Customers own more than one mutual fund, and often switch assets from one to another. Funds often go through cycles of "the best of times and the worst of times." They experience years in which they take in more money than they pay out and *vice versa*. Foreign stock and short-term

investment funds had a particularly dismal year in 1992, showing low or negative returns. When a company portfolio contains a large variety of funds, redemptions need not mean the loss of customers. Redeemers can switch from a cold fund into a hot one.

- Stretching a product line increases customer choices, and so appeals to larger and more varied groups of potential customers. The fund manager might have something a competitor does not.
- Since funds are complementary, increasing the number of funds is likely to enlarge assets per customer. By combining various investments under one manager, cash management accounts and "wrap" funds are designed to enlarge the portfolios of existing customers.

When products are complementary, the firm tends to choose the path of a multiple-product strategy. The extent of the product line depends upon resources. Perhaps the granddaddy of all multiple-product strategies is Merrill Lynch, the company that introduced the Cash Management Account (CMA) in 1978. By the end of 1992 Merrill's CMA accounts grew to $255 billion in assets—more than half the firm's total. Success breeds imitators, and over the years other brokerage and financial firms copied Merrill's innovation. Now asset management accounts are commonplace, offered with only minor variations by most of Merrill's competitors.

The CMA's multiple-product strategies have lately encountered new competition from "wrap accounts." These were logical outgrowths of the cash management idea, basically a plan to increase service usage per customer. For an annual fee, usually 3 percent, financial planners promise overall money management that includes a variety of investment options.

Merrill's response to this competitive threat has been a plethora of new add-ons to cash management and more "wraps" of its own. The new competition for a customer's "whole ball of wax" resulted in large product line extensions, and customer choices of more "varied product combinations."

Proliferating options narrow differences in financial service. For example, some mutual funds companies may offer several kinds of money market funds, with only minor variations among them. Or, they may offer several types of "balanced funds," which invest in some combination of stocks, bonds, and cash instruments. While the investment mix differs, such funds tend to be influenced by the same market forces and to move in the same directions. To that extent, funds of the same type are more "substitutable" than complementary.

When financial products are clearly substitutable, such as insurance policies, bank accounts, and mortgages, firms extend their product lines by adding complementary products which provide economy-of-scope benefits. For example, insurance companies can extend protection to life, casualty, health, and property. They benefit greatly from synergies in marketing, especially if they already possess a large customer database. Customers have higher probabilities of buying financial products from companies with which they currently deal. Offering new products to existing customers also lowers marketing costs. But extending lines of complementary products may involve costs of getting into what is essentially a new line of business.

This sort of business extension is represented by brokerages and mutual-fund companies that have lately devised free consulting services to encourage larger investments per customer. These programs help investors decide how to allocate their assets. Shearson Lehman's Strategic Asset Allocator, for example, gives customers a questionnaire to fill out about their assets and financial goals. The answers are then fed into a computer and clients get elaborate printouts projecting financial results for various bundles of assets.

Some firms, such as T. Rowe Price and Fidelity Investments, send workbooks that let clients do their own calculations. For example, the Fidelity work sheet contains 12 questions, with a maxi-

Table 3-1. Types of Portfolios

	Capital Preservation Portfolio	Moderate Portfolio	Wealthbuilding Portfolio
Short-term	50%	20%	5%
Stocks	20%	40%	65%
Bonds	30%	40%	30%
Total	100%	100%	100%

Source: Fidelity Investments.

mum of 199 points. Depending on an individual's score, Fidelity suggests the customer consider the portfolio types in Table 3.1.

Clients can take a number of possible actions. They can choose a do-it-yourself approach by creating their own portfolio from a wide range of Fidelity funds. If they prefer, they can choose one of three asset management funds to diversify a single investment. Each fund contains a different mix of stocks, bonds, and short-term investments. Lastly, clients can consult with Fidelity's Advisory Services to allocate and manage their portfolios for them.

The advice all consulting programs give is generic. Each program also contains certain assumptions and company biases. For example, Fidelity's workbook program gives a weight of 50 percent to the investment time frame an individual chooses. Nevertheless, these programs are helpful to customers of financial services as well as to their providers.

Mutual funds are complementary only up to a point. They may cannibalize each other when a product line is long and contains several close substitutes. One asset allocation fund, for instance, is liable to siphon off revenue from another in the same family. This substitution effect is likely to leave some funds with low revenues and profits. Academicians insist that sales and cost analysis can identify the deadwood that should be pruned. But pruning is not as easy as it sounds. Any analyst would have spotted depressed profits in real estate funds in 1990 and 1991, when property values plummeted throughout the country. But statistical analysis does not tell whether such funds should be kept or discontinued. In 1992 these funds exhibited some of the best results in families of company-managed portfolios. Management is still an art, not a science.

Diversification

A diversification strategy refers to developing new products lines. Usually these lines are developed for new markets, resulting in a new business. For example, the same company can involve itself with both mutual funds and life insurance. New opportunities motivate the quest for new lines of business.

In effect, a new business translates into an additional product line. It may be related or unrelated to existing product-markets of the company. The greater the similarity between the old and new businesses, the greater the probability of success. Similar businesses succeed because a company can use existing assets to develop the new product line, thereby benefiting from economies of scope. This is especially true of financial services where a firm already possesses the prime ingredients to compete successfully—internal skills and organizational synergies.

When a brokerage house sets up a mutual fund, it is only a small step from what it is doing already, buying and selling securities. Similarly, when a mutual fund company sets up a brokerage operation, it integrates operations. The brokerage would act like a line extension if the firm offers it to current mutual fund customers.

The synergy in financial services between old and new businesses probably reduces the chances for success of new market entrants. For example, Sears' expertise in merchandising did not prove successful in selling financial services in department stores. Xerox Corporation decided to sell-off its insurance, investment, and real estate businesses after experiencing a decade of frustration. In contrast, virtually every success at developing new lines of financial services came from companies that were already operating in a closely-related business.

Firms with deep pockets may buy a business. But success, like love, cannot be bought with money alone. The skills to manage the relationship must be there in the beginning.

Summary

Strategy is usually thought of as top-down, emanating from a company's CEO. In recent years, this business philosophy has been severely challenged. This chapter sees strategy flowing in both directions—from the top down and from the bottom up.

Regardless of how it flows, strategy concerns itself primarily with long-term development of products and markets. Single-product strategies are essentially small business operations. However, mature financial services often become standardized and look very much alike even when operating in mass markets. To differentiate such products, financial houses may use repositioning, deals and incentives, product modifications, and "market stretching."

Multiple product strategies are more common in the financial services industry. One form is line extensions. When commercial services are substitutes for each other, firms have short product lines. At some point, services might cannibalize each other. When financial services complement each other, companies benefit from long product lines.

Diversification occurs when firms operate in different lines of business. When these product lines use the same assets, firms benefit from economies of scope.

4

Innovation in the Financial Sector

No financial service can remain unchanged indefinitely. It therefore behooves companies to work constantly at modifying existing financial services or developing new ones. This process of innovation is often referred to as "creative destruction." Firms create new offerings to replace older ones.

This chapter examines the innovative process, focusing on such topics as:

- The economic theory of innovation
- Risk considerations in development of new financial services
- Size of firm as a competitive advantage
- Objectives of product and process innovations
- Considerations of efficiency and effectiveness
- The necessity of coupling technology with managerial innovation
- Advantages of pioneering new services and following the leader

Managing Change

The only constant is change. Though this idea has become a cliché, it still speaks a basic truth. Over time, nothing can be maintained intact.

If a firm's operations remain unchanged, sooner or later gains in sales and profits slow down. Increased expenditures result in diminishing returns. As standard operating procedure, a company must do things differently to preserve its upward momentum. It must constantly pursue new approaches in systematic and purposeful ways.

Confronting change is not the crucial issue. Change is inevitable, and must therefore be confronted. There is no choice. The crux of the matter is how this confrontation is executed.

"How-to" lies imbedded in management theories. But these theories, like change itself, have exploded into fragments propelled in many directions. "Learning organizations," "re-engineering," "organizational architecture," "time-based competition," and "the virtual corporation" have emerged as the latest catchwords. Many of these are recycled concepts, converted into new forms with new terminologies. They may turn out as fads, like many Christmas toys that last for a season, for they have not yet passed the stringent tests of time.

Regardless of management style or philosophy, change implies something different happening, something that departs from what already is. From this standpoint, innovation emerges as the key to managing business in a changing world.

The Theory of Innovation

The basic theories of innovation were first promulgated by economist Joseph Schumpeter. He used the term innovation in a broad sense, defining it as applied to products, markets, and organizations. The organizational aspect refers to administrative actions, sometimes called "managerial innovations." Examples are management information systems, self-managed work teams, and job "time compression." Though the literature emphasizes goods-producing industries, Schumpeter's definition admirably embraces innovation in financial services.

Schumpeter did not describe innovation as a bright idea or an invention. New ideas are necessary, but not sufficient. They are commonplace. Rather, innovation revolves around application. Deeds, not words, are what bring change. Unless an idea is carried out in a practical way, it has no value. Schumpeter called the deed— the implementation of a new idea—"entrepreneurship." It is the entrepreneur who plays the critical role in economic development by bringing to fruition new ways of doing things.

Entrepreneurship means different things to different people. In popular usage, an "entrepreneur" connotes a business person who defied great odds, who rose to wealth and power from humble beginnings. The word conjures up images of someone who puts up all his or her own money—or even goes deeply into debt—to start a business. Many people think of an entrepreneur as a modern P.T. Barnum who scours the oceans for the iceberg that sank the Titanic so that he can put it on display . . . for a price, of course.

The economic interpretation of entrepreneurship has less colorful connotations. It does not connote inventing something, owning a business, or taking risks. As Israel Kurzner, a noted economist puts it, "the pure entrepreneur owns nothing." His or her main asset, holds Kurzner, is an "alertness" to opportunities. To that end, the entrepreneur arranges the factors of production in a new way.

Small Is Ugly

If innovation thrives on action, then, small business is the most backward segment of our economy. It lacks the resources to exploit opportunities. What small bank rose to challenge the dominance of a J.P. Morgan, a Citicorp, a Chase Manhattan? What small upstart intruded on the exclusive circle of leading securities dealers? What insurance company in recent memory opened as a store-front business and now competes with the agencies like State Farm, Allstate, or Prudential?

Many new products entail high risks, and are undertaken by firms that can afford the gamble. Product development activity is often beyond the limited means of small companies that have neither the expertise nor capital to succeed in a high-stakes game.

The financial sector does contain small innovative firms. For example, ten years ago Charles Schwab & Company was a struggling brokerage firm housed in a two-room office. Today, the company is the largest discount broker in the United States, with one million customers and 92 offices nationwide. But Schwab had lots of help. Its major growth occurred after the 1983 buyout by BankAmerica Corporation, which no doubt, provided the main source of capital so necessary for expansion. Though Schwab & Company operates independently of its family member, BankAmerica, the two subsidiaries share branch offices and offer services to each other's customers.

Regardless of the ways small-time startups grow, Horatio Alger stories are the exception, not the rule. Small enterprises have the highest proportions of bankruptcies. They operate on shoestrings, and commonly have trouble just keeping their heads above water, let alone introducing innovative products or striking out in new directions.

New product failures, however, are also not uncommon among large, well-financed companies. Failures hurt, but seldom prove fatal. In contrast, small firms are not cushioned by retained earnings. One mistake, one wrong turn of events, and the misstep is enough to plunge frail businesses over the edge into liquidation. Although the public might idolize fools who chase impossible dreams, probabilities of success do not improve just because there are many fools.

Large banks like Citicorp, Wells Fargo, Chase Manhattan, and Bankers Trust reported disturbing amounts of nonperforming assets when real estate values plummeted in 1989. Yet, these banks survived and continued to prosper. At the same time, the smaller savings and loans were devastated. Many of them closed their doors, and the ensuing government bailout cost American taxpayers more than $150 billion.

Unless a small business possesses some specialty, or finds some neglected market niche, it must eke out its profits from a contentious, dog-eat-dog environment. An innovation, however, suggests some unique product that other businesses do not have. It implies some form of monopoly, at least for the short-term. This line of reasoning makes innovation incompatible with competition, where many companies offer services that can hardly be distinguished from each other. There is no incentive to innovate when everyone can imitate at once.

Then under what conditions does innovation thrive? After reviewing masses of empirical studies, Morton Kamien and Nancy Schwartz concluded that settings lying between "pure" forms of competition and monopoly have the highest rates of innovation. This "in-between area" spans a wide range in which large firms typically divide among themselves the lion's share of all transactions.

Many writers have prescribed "small-is-beautiful" tonics to revive American competitiveness in world markets. They have taken Silicon Valley firms such as Apple, Intel, and Microsoft as prototypes to show how superior knowledge can elevate small companies into industry leaders. But that model does not apply to financial services. Companies in the financial sector do not compete on R&D. They are buyers, not purveyors, of information and technological research.

The banks, insurance companies, brokerage, and financial houses that compete in the international arena are all large. When Mitsui and Taiyo Kobe agreed to merge in 1989, forming the second largest bank in the world, the head of Mitsui, Kenichi Suematsu, gave the following explanation for the creation of the new $340 billion enterprise. "In today's world, you have to have a certain quantity in order to have quality," he told a news conference. "For us to survive as a universal bank, we have to have a certain size."

Survival or dominance? Similar explanations were given when Primerica bought Shearson brokerage from American Express in 1993. By merging Shearson with Smith Barney, Primerica created a new colossus on Wall Street.

Observers estimated that two big firms, Smith Barney Shearson and Merrill Lynch, would employ one out of every four brokers in America. Most industry commentators opined that economies of scale accruing to these two mega-firms would force competitors either to find merger partners of their own or lapse into niche players. William Donaldson, chairman of the New York Stock Exchange, said: "You'll have these big guys, Merrill and Smith Barney Shearson, and a couple of others, and then have smaller specialty people." Frank Zarb, CEO of Primerica's new brokerage unit, had a similar assessment. He saw the industry made up of a few large firms selling stocks, bonds, and mutual funds to the mass consumer market, and all others who must be "highly focused and work one part of the market."

The small-is-beautiful thesis is flawed. Why does every small firm strive to become large? The answer is obvious. Size is the greatest competitive advantage a business can have. It cannot be readily imitated. Small is not beautiful. It's ugly.

The Many Sides of Innovation

Innovation is many-sided, and takes various forms. It also can be viewed from many perspectives:

- Does the innovation take the form of a product or process?
- How much newness or novelty must an entrepreneur initiate before performance qualifies as innovative?
- Is innovation compatible with imitation?

Products and Processes

Whether an innovation is a product or a process depends on the way in which an innovation is used. Different uses imply different purposes.

A "product innovation" is a service that a firm offers to customers. These new services abound in large numbers. Recent examples are new "wrap" funds, debit cards and newly offered point-of-purchase systems, and interactive systems that permit consumers to do banking out of their home.

A "process innovation" is a product that its user installs for purposes of rendering a service. For example, when a software house sells a computer program, it effects an exchange. It sells a product for a certain price. But if the company buying the item is not a reseller, like an agent or wholesaler, and derives no direct revenue from the purchase. When a firm employs the computer program as a device to perform a service, the program is a process.

For example, a bank might purchase an imaging system for check processing. The system is a "process." It is a back office operation. Most customers do not know how their checks are processed, nor do they care. The imaging system is something the bank uses to render another service, usually an end product.

This distinction between product and process innovations clearly indicates the different objectives of each form. Product innovations aim at creating transactions directly. Their objective is to develop a new service that can be sold on the market. Its immediate objective is revenue creation.

Process innovations are meant to improve internal operations so that a service can be rendered more efficiently or effectively. They seek to enhance profits, primarily by decreasing costs.

Revenue enhancement is not mutually exclusive with cost reduction, but it is not the main thrust of process innovations. For example, a low cost producer might increase revenue by lowering prices of a service, if demand is elastic. But lower prices are options management can effect as a result of the lowered costs of the new process. In the long-run, process-type innovations tend to raise labor productivity. A company does more with fewer employees.

Considerations of Efficiency

Adoption of process innovations involves both expensing and capitalizing costs, depending upon accounting conventions. Either way, managers must be able to figure out the effects of a new process.

Many process innovations cannot be justified on the basis of cost-benefit analysis, whose theme relates to efficiency. For example, a firm considering an investment in cordless telephones for the sales staff might assess costs in terms of present value. That calculation concerns itself strictly with how much savings the innovation would bring and whether those benefits would exceed costs, discounted by the time value of money.

But suppose that cellular phones help the sales staff in dealing with clients more effectively. Suppose that, with the aid of cellular phones, itineraries can be rerouted so that sales calls are made at more opportune times. Should analysis ignore the revenue potential resulting from better timing of sales calls?

Similarly, the installation of new work stations might increase computer processing power. Even with outlays for new equipment, the new system may be cost effective. For example, it may result in more free computer time, which can be sold to smaller and non-competitive firms.

Efficiency calculations often ignore possibilities of effectiveness, particularly when expenditures involve large sums that are amortized. In many such situations, controllers may be correct in avoiding "soft" and "iffy" assumptions about future streams of revenue. Estimates of savings based on present value contain enough uncertainty when they are projected over a number of years. Surely, there are good reasons for viewing sales projections with skepticism. Sales people are hopelessly addicted to optimism by virtue of their occupation, and are prone to overpromise. But it is also true that ignoring potential revenue in cost-benefit analysis might forego opportunities. It therefore might be more prudent to alter cut-off points by considering the consequences of incremental sales and possible overestimations.

Considerations of Effectiveness

Not all process innovations are adopted to gain efficiency. Some have effectiveness as their main objective. For example, an insurance company planning to start a mutual fund business may have to develop software to process a set of new transactions. The same company may also have to build a toll-free incoming telephone system that gives customers the latest fund quotes and market values of their investments. New lines of business may often require new processes to support their performance. In such instances, product and process innovations are complementary.

In other instances, a process innovation may be undertaken as a reaction to competition. Many small banks adopted ATMs because competitors had them, and for no other reason. ATMs did not reduce costs nor bring in more business, so perhaps bank officers regarded addition of this service as the better part of discretion.

At one time, financial firms sent out separate summary statements for each account. Then someone developed a computer program to show all household account information on a single statement. These "all-in-one" forms reduced mailing costs and increased customer convenience, and soon were widely copied. These formats were process innovations, and the new business they brought in, if any, during their initial offering stages may not have warranted the additional costs. However, their usage became commonplace and created an expectation in customers' minds. Today, they are considered part of the cost of doing business.

Similar developments took place in securities trading. A customer would call in an order, and, at the end of the day, the broker would call back with the results of the trade. Improvements in communication technology were leveraged by a few larger brokerage houses, forcing others to obtain equipment that enabled them to report trades and prices to their customers in a matter of seconds.

Applications of Technology

Throughout the 1980s, U.S. business reportedly spent some $1 trillion on information technology. Of that total, perhaps as much as four-fifths came from the service sector, with financial services in the forefront of the spending spree. Yet these vast expenditures rendered disappointing productivity gains. Surprisingly, productivity increased the least in industries where investments in technology were highest.

Beginning in 1991, service-related sectors began flashing signs of a business turnaround. One sign was measured productivity gains that matched those of manufacturing in the 1980s. A second indication was rising profits at financial corporations. Though lower interest rates provided the main drive to better profits, productivity probably made a contribution.

What is working now that did not work before? The new element is a better coupling of technological innovation and managerial innovation.

Writing in the November-December 1991 issue of the *Harvard Business Review*, Peter Drucker drew a sharp distinction between factors and tools of production. He argues that technology and capital in the manufacturing and transportation industries are *factors* of production. A factor can be substituted for labor. In financial services Drucker asserts, technology is a *tool* of production. A tool may or may not replace labor, depending on how it is used.

Regardless of whatever one chooses to call them, factors or tools, investments in information systems are increasingly combined with managerial innovations. The employment of technology is task related. In turn, labor content varies in accordance with the tasks to which a given technology is applied.

Financial services firms employ many workers performing tasks similar to those in manufacturing companies, such as data entry, clerical jobs, telephone and mailroom operations. Machines can replace these types of production work, though they may generate other kinds of new jobs, such as programmers, electronic engineers, and maintenance employees. The only criterion for investment in these labor-saving machines is comparative costs.

For example, ATMs can replace people who perform identical functions. From 1990 to 1992, banks and thrifts closed some 4,000 branches and replaced them with ATMs. Booz, Allen & Hamilton, Inc. estimates that by the turn of the century banks will have more ATM facilities, but 15,000 fewer branches. At Grand Central Station in New York City, Citibank has a branch with 20 ATM machines, but not a single teller.

Similarly, Interactive Voice Response Units can do a better job of handling simple inquiries than human phone operators. A mutual fund's automated system can give callers fund quotes, calculate investors' balances, and make exchanges and redemptions. Callers need only punch in personal ID numbers and designate the information desired. Complex, nonroutine queries are usually routed to the proper service reps.

A "technology-structural" mix is exemplified by Northern Trust Company, whose main line of business is corporate money market accounts. Over a four-year period, Northern Trust successfully combined automated voice response with intelligent call routing. The automated voice response system came first. It allowed customers to do a variety of routine tasks, such as checking balances and transferring funds. Voice technology was later enhanced by a sophisticated call-routing system, which connects an account code with the customer database. The agent handling the account can pull up on a screen one year's data from a mainframe computer. The third part of the technology mix is a document imaging system from IBM. This permits agents to display their mainframe screen next to images of relevant documents scanned in the cash management department. With these systems, Northern handles 70,000 customer calls with just 22 service representatives. While business volume of this unit grew by 32 percent, no new staffers were added to the payroll.

However, the news is not all good. Technology by itself cannot improve productivity in many instances. For example, many firms have provided sales personnel with laptops so they can wire in call reports. However, this does nothing to increase sales calls. A salesperson must spend the same amount of time in writing his or her report, regardless of whether it is done on a laptop or a typewriter. If the job of a salesperson is to call on clients, laptops by themselves do not advance productivity. Why not simplify reporting or eliminate it altogether? A firm can enhance productivity only by fitting technology to a task in "smarter" ways. For example, Fannie Mae, America's biggest buyer of home mortgages, was unable to keep up with the growing volume of business despite its imposing array of mainframe computers. To overcome this problem, in 1990 the firm replaced the centralized computer system with decentralized work teams operating "user friendly" personal computers and software.

In 1992, the increase in refinancings nearly doubled the volume of new loans. But Fannie Mae added only 100 employees to its workforce of about 3,000. Fannie Mae found the key to better performance was an intelligent use of technology and well-planned changes in organizational structure that changed the ways of doing work.

Another example is that of Aetna Life & Casualty Co. In 1992 Aetna ran 22 offices, with a staff of 3,000. It took 15 days to send a basic policy to a new customer. Aetna overhauled its operation, cutting its office centers down to four, and reducing its staff to 700. Yet the firm was now able to route policies to customers in five days. How? A single rep, hooked up to a server, could call up all the data needed to process customers' applications and transmit policies over a computer network to the Hartford headquarters. There they are printed and mailed out within 24 hours. Productivity gains were accomplished not merely by installing PCs, but by reorganizing work. Before, 60 different employees handled an application. Now, a single individual does all processing of an application. Aetna estimates that the new system of processing policies will save the company $40 million a year.

These are not isolated examples. We picked these simply to illustrate several points:

- Technology by itself is often incapable of increasing output in service jobs that are nonroutine.
- In knowledge work, technology must be married to managerial innovation—rearranging how tasks are done.
- Managers can no longer ask how to get machines to imitate employee tasks. Rather, they must ask what tasks need not be done. Firms must change the configurations of work flow charts. Only then will technology be used more intelligently and productively.

How New Is New?

An innovation denotes something new. But how new must a product or process be in order to be classified as an innovation?

Since practically all innovative ideas are rearrangements of known elements, the amount of newness is a matter of degree. It is the difference between the innovation and what had previously existed. This can range from new products virtually indistinguishable from old to novelties which have no existing counterpart. Booz, Allen & Hamilton, a consulting firm specializing in new products, calls radical departures "new-to-the-world" products.

Thomas Robertson, a business school professor at Michigan State University, visualizes newness as existing on a continuum, with small, imperceptible degrees of newness at one end and the maximum amount of newness at the other. Robertson labelled these extremes as continuous and discontinuous innovations. These labels are based on usage patterns. Products toward the lower part of Robertson's continuum are presumed used in the same manner as products they replaced. Contrarily, innovations that are highly novel cause discontinuity. People must learn how to do things in different ways.

This grading scheme is abashedly general in nature. There is no way of placing something new at a precise point on a scale. "New" is a qualitative concept, not a quantitative one. Without an objective way of measuring innovative behavior, there is no sure way of predicting its outcome.

In the late 1970s Merrill Lynch introduced its Cash Management Account (CMA). This product simply combined in one account a number of well-known investment vehicles, such as money market, check-writing, credit cards, and stock and bond trading. This seemingly banal arrangement of investment options revolutionized Wall Street. Today, CMA accounts make up more than half of Merrill's $475 billion in assets.

Banks, insurance companies, brokerages, and mutual funds widely copied the "do-it-all" idea, and along with Merrill, keep multiplying the options offered to customers. Recent additions are CMA's with no annual fee, bill-paying and automatic savings, private insurance of $500,000 per brokerage account, check coding and summary statements for each coded category, and various types of mutual funds. At the time Cash Management made its appearance, not even its most ardent supporters could have foretold how this idea would change the face of an industry.

Despite our inability to measure precisely an innovation's newness or to predict its consequences, sociologists have outlined a number of useful generalizations for planning new products. Most of these sociological principles deal with technology, goods, and social behavior. However, they are in varying degrees applicable to financial service firms. These guidelines were derived from studies linking innovation characteristics with usage.

The most important characteristics to be considered in planning new financial services are:

Newness. The more radically a financial service departs from its predecessors, the more time it takes for potential customers to adopt the innovation. Unfamiliarity breeds caution. In dealing with the unfamiliar, a firm should be prepared to spend more on public relations and sales promotion. Heavier expenditures are required to instruct customers in new concepts and new ways of doing things.

Complexity. Complexity is often associated with newness. Complex services have slower acceptance rates. Users have more to learn and comprehend. Automatic-teller machines, introduced in the late 1960s, took a long time to catch on because people didn't understand how to use them. Fourteen years after their introduction, only one out of every three eligible card holders used the machines. Even today, older bank customers have a much lower usage incidence than young people who have more experience with computers.

When a service depends on technology, machines must be made user-friendly. Home banking began in 1983, and was once the rage at many of the nation's leading banks. The system has yet to take hold and fulfill its full potential, especially among segments of the population who are not familiar with computers.

Divisibility. A service that can be used in small quantities reduces risk and encourages trial. Many investors try new mutual funds on a small scale before investing more money. When high-priced products cannot be broken down into small units, as illustrated by a home banking system, acceptance lags.

Differential advantage. The greater advantage of the new service over competing ones spurs faster adoption of the innovation. An important advantage of financial services is better performance, particularly for services that compete on higher returns. Mutual funds and brokerages fall into that category. Another advantage is low prices that firms can charge clients for the same service. Credit card issues, for example, compete on price and interest charges on outstanding balances.

Commitment. If all other things are equal, expenditures of money and effort affect how quickly a service achieves market penetration. In turn, a faster introductory period lessens a firm's negative or low earnings. But risk must be taken into account. The value of a short product introduction must therefore be traded off against potential costs of failure. These tradeoffs are particularly vital when new products are radically new and introductory costs are high. Spreading out the introduction in time reduces risk, because the firm can always withdraw from the market if sales lag. But it loses the competitive advantage of first-in-the-market.

New to Whom?

Since decision making takes place within a company, innovation can be viewed from a microeconomic perspective. A product is new only to the firm that develops it. A company's new product may be markedly similar to other services already offered in the marketplace. Every firm has three, broadly based product options.

1. *Same services.* A company keeps its products unchanged. This is the most common situation within companies, where managers must deal with the current services a firm offers.

2. *Revised services.* Most innovations are modifications of existing services, modifications undertaken to meet competitive pressures. They involve small, incremental changes, but may alter the nature of the service over time.

3. *New services.* These are services that the company has not offered previously. The new service may be similar to others already on the market or it may be quite unique. Services without facsimiles, or those which require new technologies, usually fall outside the scope of operational planning and management. Results are difficult to anticipate.

These alternatives—same, modified, and new services—are usually carried out at the same time because firms usually turn out product lines consisting of multiple offerings. A firm must remain flexible, keeping open all options, so as to fit strategy to circumstances.

Pioneer or Follower?

The company that is first in the market with a new service is usually credited as its pioneer. This definition admits of only one leader; the rest are followers.

The advantages of being first-in-the-market were extensively studied by Robinson and Fornell in 1985 using the PIMS database, a project of the Strategic Planning Institute. This database contains records of more than 2,000 businesses. The Robinson-Fornell study, published in the *Journal of Marketing Research*,[1] found that out of 371 mature consumer industries studied, pioneers held a 29 percent market share. This compared with a 17 percent share for early followers and only 12 percent for late entrants.

Why? The "pioneer" benefits from a time advantage. The longer it takes competitors to copy the innovation, the more time the pioneer gains to entrench his or her position in the marketplace.

A head start allows the pioneer to gain customers as well as experience. Since the pioneer has a greater market share than followers, it also has a greater cost advantage. This relative advantage grows with the passage of time, provided the leader can sustain its larger market share.

---

1   William T. Robinson and Claes Fornell, "Sources of Market Pioneer Advantage in Consumer Goods," *Journal of Marketing Research* (August 1985), pp. 305-317.

As an industry reaches maturity, the number of potential customers available to competitors continues to shrink. At some point a firm gains business only by taking customers away from a rival. But most services are continuous, and getting buyers to switch providers presents great difficulties. The obstacles are especially great when confronting a market-share leader. The dominant firm always enjoys a cost advantage, and a good reputation for quality and expertise. Only some catastrophic event or lapse in management would dislodge a market leader. An example is Solomon Brothers being charged with illegal trading in government bonds.

Nothing illustrates clearer the staying power of a leader than the case of Merrill Lynch. New customers flocking to the brokerage firm for cash management accounts have greatly slowed down after about ten years. A large number of competitive firms have entered the market with similar offerings. Yet Merrill in 1993 still retained a two-thirds share of a growing cash management market.

Should financial service firms then always strive to be first-in-the-market with new services? The price of leadership is often higher risk, and many firms cannot afford to gamble on risky ventures.

When automatic teller machines were first introduced, very few banks ever made money on them. The machines suffered from mechanical problems, and were difficult for most people to use. ATMs were "out-of-order" more than they were "in-service." Only the large banks could afford a long period of "debugging." Since the public had to be educated on how to use the new-fangled machines, banks that installed them had to spend heavily on public relations and promotion.

Home banking is now the in-thinking of technology gurus. The first bank in New York to embrace the idea, Chemical Bank, spent more than $20 million to bring its home-banking system, Pronto, on-line in 1983. Not to be left behind, Chase Manhattan and Manufacturers Hanover Trust followed closely behind. On the basis of discounted cash flow, home banking did not pay for itself at any of these New York institutions.

The introduction of "new-to-the-world" services is not for small operators, especially when big promotional budgets must accompany high capital outlays. In that case, to paraphrase Shakespeare's Polonius, advising his son Laertes, neither a pioneer nor a close follower be. The best alternative is to be opportunistic.

Information Systems: In-House or Out-of-House?

Financial institutions have traditionally operated integrated information systems, with development, maintenance, and data processing done in-house. Competitive cost pressures have spurred firms increasingly to go outside the corporation for those information-related services. The largest operations that are outsourced are electronic data processing of transactional databases, ATM processing, credit card programs, and marketing database maintenance.

The preference for internal operations has been shifting over the years. According to Ernst & Young, banks in 1987 divided their technological expenditures 50-50 between internal operations and outside vendors. By 1992 banks' internal staffs received only 46 percent of a $17 billion spent on technology. Outside agencies obtained a 54 percent share. Outside service bureaus are currently processing more banking data than banks themselves. What underlying factors generated these changes?

The decision to outsource depends on several business considerations, not information handling. The main considerations are: cost savings, balance sheet improvement, lower investment risks, and selective functions.

Cost Savings

Lower costs prove to be the main reason for buying outside technical services. Ernst & Young studied relative costs of outsourcing with do-it-yourself decisions of banks. Costs were expressed as percentages of total assets. The study found outside data processing firms charging banks between 23 and 36 basis points on assets, with larger banks paying more than small ones. Service bureaus must invest larger sums to service larger banks. But cost savings are comparatively greater for smaller banks; they have the most to gain from outsourcing. Table 4–1 demonstrates the cost savings for banks of various sizes.

As the table shows, cost savings fall as a bank's asset size increases. Since large banks have sufficient volume to achieve scale economies, outsourcing offers little in the way of savings. But a cost reduction of 21 basis points for small banks is highly significant, translating into a 15 percent before-tax profit. By combining many accounts, an outside vendor can offer small firms the advantages of a large data processing center with sophisticated systems.

Balance Sheet Improvement

Investments in information technology are represented as liabilities on a firm's balance sheet. Outsourcing transforms fixed costs into variable costs. Firms need not incur equipment costs and related overhead. Consequently, buying technical services on the outside offers immediate additional earnings which can be invested in revenue-generating projects.

Critics charge that firms adopting the outsourcing route mortgage their futures for short-term gains. They give up control of vital operations, and cannot readily adopt new technologies. The early gains, opponents claim, tend to evaporate over the length of an average 10-year outsourcing contract.

Table 4-1. Relative Costs of Data Processing

Bank Assets (in $bils.)	Data Processing Costs (In Basis Points)		
	Outside	In-House	Cost Savings
$5–$10	23	44	21
$10–$20	24	38	14
$20 and more	26	36	10

Source: Brian Whitehead and Brendon O'Sullivan, "When to Say Yes or No to Outsourcing," *ABA Banking Journal* (June 1991), p. 65.

Yet few financial institutions have the potential to match efficient data processing operations. Whitehead and O'Sullivan, partners at Ernst & Young, estimate that less than 1 percent of our nation's banks have the capacity to run top quality information processing systems.

Lower Investment Risks

In the early stages of any emerging technology, there are few widely-accepted standards. Firms that rush in to buy expensive systems must consider the proposition that the value of their purchases may depreciate quickly. Costs of new technologies usually decline rapidly as equipment sales rise and unit production costs fall. Emerging technologies also experience waves of new product introductions and changing standards. There is no way to predict which versions will achieve general acceptance. In these circumstances, first adopters run high risks of buying systems that may soon become obsolete. Using short payback periods to justify technology purchases may limit risks. But short paybacks don't help much when capital investment is large and resulting benefits accrue over a long time period.

Investments in imaging present this type of situation. The technology promises dramatic savings by streamlining operations. Some vendors estimate their imaging systems can reduce staffs about 30 percent, reduce document storage space about 50 percent, and increase productivity from 20–40 percent. But the new imaging technology is costly and a fully-operating system requires a long lead-time.

In these circumstances, outsourcing offers an alternative to large uncertain investments. Outsourcing is seldom an all-or-nothing proposition. Financial companies can implement systems piecemeal by using outside agencies, or they can hire outside specialists to advise and manage particular functions. Banc One Corporation, which does a huge volume of retail banking, employed EDS in 1991 to co-develop Strategic Banking Systems, an upgraded system of client/server applications.

The exact arrangement depends upon contractual terms agreed upon with the outside agency. Service bureaus such as IBM, Systematics, and EDS provide facilities management, during which clients retain their own systems and technical personnel. Today roughly 18% of banks' mainframe data centers are run by service bureaus.

New software coming to market often operate on equipment that financial firms own. A FileNet imaging program, based on Microsoft Windows, runs on PCs. DST Stystem's software works on IBM's AS/400 minicomputer with PS/2 workstations. Metafile Information Systems sells software which banks can use to develop their own applications on PC networks.

Several other software houses developed similar systems. Broadway & Seymour, for example, brought out a system in 1991 that gave banks the option of using small computers to create check images on bank statements. IBM offers outsourcing in stages: first, check-capture imaging and second, back-office procedures. Even a technologically-elite bank like J.P. Morgan outsourced desktop trading with BT North America, Inc. The system permitted dealers to input trades from PCs.

Spreading a customer information system throughout the organization is a prime consideration. Getting a complete system on-line takes about five years, and integrating an imaging system at the same time may well require assistance from an outside vendor.

Selective Functions

Many peripheral activities do not justify in-house operations, especially when they involve specialized functions. In those instances, outsourcing provides expertise which is too costly to bring in-house. Credit card, student loan, and marketing database management are such examples. AT&T farms out its credit card operations. The Sears Discover card is now a part of Dean Witter, Discover, Inc.

In the event outsourcing is used for any job, negotiating the terms of a contract is of utmost importance. The client must specify the exact tasks and provide for possible contingencies. These should cover such things as:

- service levels a vendor must deliver;
- continuous innovations, such as changes in levels and costs of service (Small modifications should not have a material effect.);
- obligations on the part of the vendor to keep technology updated;
- rights to inspect on-site performance, regardless of where processing takes place;
- negotiating rights to enlarge or reduce the volume of work under various circumstances;
- conformance to changes in government laws, rules, and regulations;
- a method for handling and charging for errors caused by either client or agent;
- backup systems for interruptions of service;
- terms for generic or product-specific services only, if the firm wants a voice in future software; and
- a system for resolving disputes.

Business or Technology Management?

Some outsourcing decisions are really part of a much broader management decision: Who is responsible for assessing the impact of technology investments? At most financial firms, responsibility for planning the use of technology rests with technicians. This locus of responsibility leads to problems. One problem relates to evaluating the impact on business. Since a computer is often shared by many groups and departments, the technology group finds it difficult to measure results directly. Business units are charged for amounts of time and other costs, some direct and some imputed. But are the costs worth the benefits?

Investment plans are usually justified by showing the effect technology has on output. Does it speed up processing time, increase the number of computational functions, and reduce labor? Critics charge that such analyses overlook the impact on a firm's bottom line.

A second problem concerns itself with those responsible for processing—internal data processing people as opposed to an outside service bureau. Though many technicians claim they ask outside firms to bid on jobs and then compare their bids with internal costs, suppliers often do not believe that competition is conducted in an objective, arms-length manner.

Jonathan Palmer, head of Barnett Technologies, a subsidiary of Barnett Banks, says that "if you want to survive, you had better act as if you're in competition with outsiders—because in effect you are."[2]

But do insiders really compete with outsiders? Since internal operations involve joint costs with allocated overhead, technical departments have large leeway in cost comparisons. M. Arthus Gillis, president of Computer Based Solutions, Inc., admits that financial organizations pay lip service to the competitive concept. But "in practice," he says, "forget it." He claims that information management merely pretends to match or beat competitive bids. Like all bureaucracies, technical departments resist losing processing work to outsiders.

Paul A. Strassman, author of *The Business Value of Computers*,[3] insists that technology decisions should be made by business managers, not by technical managers. His extensive studies of the subject found no relationship between corporate spending on technology and ultimate business profitability. He views technical personnel as incapable of assessing business effects of technology expenditures. To integrate technology planning with business decisions, Strassman believes that budget decisions should be in the hands of nontechnical managers.

2   Reported in Karen Gullo "New Way to Tell If Technology Is Worth the Cost," *American Banker* (February 15, 1991), p. 1.

3   Quoted in Nell Margolis, "Bank IS fights Outsourcing Challenges," *Computerworld* (June 1, 1992), p. 12.

Continental Bank in 1991 was the first money center bank to outsource most of its information processing. That decision, made by senior management, came only after a business crisis and a radical restructuring that ended retail banking in favor of servicing business customers. But Continental's experience is an exception which cannot be generalized to other financial organizations.

Some banks have spun-off portions of technical operations, as First Fidelity Bancorp did in 1990. Barnett Banks set up a wholly-owned subsidiary, Barnett Technologies, Inc., to provide information services to the parent company. This move decreased dependence on centralized data centers. Some banks have taken small steps to integrate business units with technological units. For example, Banc One assigned authority for technology planning to a committee composed of the head of the technology unit, the chief financial officer, and heads of holding company banks. But this move does not give business units authority to make important decisions on budgets and investments. BankAmerica has gone the furthest, assigning technical people to business units. But the budget still remains with technologists, while business managers have veto power over technology plans that affect their units.

In general, however, financial firms have been reluctant to strip control over systems from technical units. One reason is they are apprehensive of having business managers make technical decisions. Are they sufficiently knowledgeable about information technology? Conversely, technical managers have not made good business decisions. In all probability financial institutions will handle problems by trial and error, hoping that they hit upon a workable solution.

Summary

An innovation can refer to a product or a process. Product innovations are revenue-generating; they create transactions directly. Process innovations improve internal operations by reducing costs or enhancing productivity.

In the financial services industry, new technologies reduce costs when they are intelligently coupled with tasks, especially non-routine jobs. New technological tasks can be performed in-house or outsourced.

Acceptance rates for new financial products depend upon several factors. Longer adoption times are associated with an innovation's degree of newness, complexity, divisibility, comparative advantage, and required commitment. There are advantages to pioneering new services as well as following the leader. Each firm must decide for itself which course of action to pursue.

5

Making Innovation Work

Chapter dealt with innovation concepts and strategies. This chapter emphasizes implementation—the ways of carrying out new ideas. It also covers the seven generic stages of new product development, as set forth by Booz, Allen & Hamilton. The main points covered are:

- The prime elements of a new product strategy
- Considerations of risk, uncertainty, and potential rewards
- Sources of ideas for new financial services
- Formal and informal methods for developing new products and processes
- Idea evaluation and business analysis
- The ingredients of a marketing plan for a new venture
- Market tests or sales tests—when to use them and when to avoid them
- Carrying out the commercialization stage of a new financial service

An On-Going Activity

Products age and wear out. As aging occurs, growth in sales and profits erodes. The aging factor in business is often referred to as "the product life cycle." For example, new technologies make current processes obsolete, eating away existing cost advantages. These trends are ongoing events that are always with us. Consequently, a business needs a constant flow of new products to offset the aging of its older products. The road to success thus becomes a three-pronged investment in products, distribution, and managerial skills—Schumpeter's triad on which innovation rests.

As an on-going activity, new product development almost never involves a single, discrete decision. Rather, it calls for continued planning, for a series of decisions that can be changed at any time. The consulting firm of Booz, Allen & Hamilton has conceptualized new product planning as consisting of seven steps: new product strategy; idea generation; screening; business analysis; development; testing; and commercialization.

The Booz, Allen & Hamilton model is based on products composed of goods, but it can equally apply to services. The new product planning model is visualized in Figure 5–1.

Dividing the new product process into defined stages has value for expository purposes, such as breaking the process down

Figure 5-1. Stages of New Product Development

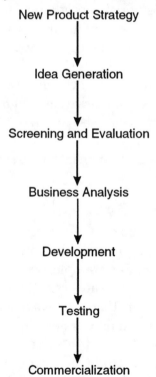

New Product Strategy

↓

Idea Generation

↓

Screening and Evaluation

↓

Business Analysis

↓

Development

↓

Testing

↓

Commercialization

into components that can be evaluated separately. In reality, however, these stages do not occur in a rigid, sequential manner. Product testing is often carried out in conjunction with development. A detailed business analysis may sometimes wait until testing results become available. In varying circumstances, some steps may be omitted altogether, such as screening and market testing.

Tasks at different stages are highly differentiated, requiring different skills. Idea generation is a creative process. As planning goes down the line toward commercialization, prosaic, repetitive tasks take over, tasks such as defining distribution channels, meeting schedules, and covering the market with promotional messages and sales calls. To illustrate the proposition with two characters from Thackeray's *Vanity Fair*, idea generation needs a Becky Sharp, a person who lives by her wits. Commercialization needs a Dobbins-type manager, who plods on regardless of obstacles placed in his way.

It might be argued that creativity applies to all stages. Ad agencies promote creativity as a vital element in commercialization. But as most "new" products are modifications or extensions of old products, current business relationships are not discarded. Radically new techniques in rendering a service are seldom the prime ingredients for success. Most are back-office operations. Customers are neither aware of them, nor familiar with them. New financial services are commercialized using pretty much the same formulas. This is not to say the old way is necessarily the right way. But the burden of proof always falls on the manager who favors a new approach.

Tasks are different at each stage, and management methods must vary to fit the job at hand. For example, feedback techniques are of little value in generating ideas, but are absolutely necessary in tracking performance when the product is placed on the market. Product design might have no place in markets where financial services are highly standardized. To be flexible, new product management must integrate and coordinate various functions.

New Product Strategy

Strictly speaking, new product planning is operational. It deals with transforming and commercializing a new product concept. It entails devising a blueprint in order to formulate the service and succeed in the marketplace.

While product development is mainly operational, it must nevertheless conform to product policy as enunciated by corporate headquarters. For example, Merrill Lynch sets longterm profit goals as 15 percent after-tax return on equity. A proposed project that does not meet this "hurdle rate" would have difficulty in receiving approval. Similarly, an ongoing project whose yield is below the 15 percent return would be in danger of termination. In the 1980s, Merrill Lynch established Interfunding, a $1 billion small-company loan portfolio. In 1990 its prospects fell below Merrill's "hurdle rate." At that point the firm decided to wind down the fund. Since obligations persist for several years, termination was scheduled for 1996.

All new product proposals must address the issue of risk. Managers can calculate risk only when they can assign a known probability of success to an event. But this cannot be done with a new product that has no history. When the new product resembles an existing one, past experience can offer valuable clues. Nevertheless, an estimate of this kind rests on analogy. It substitutes subjective assessments for objectively-derived probabilities. Projections of profit and loss therefore contain various degrees of uncertainty. When a new project has no precedents, there is *only* uncertainty.

Products new to the market have highly unpredictable outcomes. A case in point is videotext, an interactive technology which made its appearance in the early 1980s. Its promoters trumpeted this system as the wave of the future. They pictured consumers eagerly waiting for a chance to make bank deposits and pay bills electronically from the comfort of their homes. But the mass conversion of people's homes into electronic cottages never took place. Videotext may yet come into popular usage. But when?

Another ill-fated project was Citibank's "Reward America" program. The bank offered shoppers incentives to use "smart cards" at checkout counters. The card had a PIN number (personal identification number) for each participating customer. Shoppers who signed up for the program received monthly summaries of their purchases along with certificates for earned rebates. Supermarkets and other retailers were offered payments for handling those certificate redemptions. Citicorp planned to get reimbursed by selling shoppers' names and purchases to advertisers. The system was supposed to eliminate paper coupons, material proofs-of-purchase, while allowing self-service marketers to build customer databases with monitored purchase data.

Citicorp introduced the plan in 1990 with great fanfare, after testing for six months at 26 stores. The purported goal was to build an eventual database of 25 million consumers—a critical mass to attract manufacturers and sellers of packaged goods. After a full year of operations and expenditures running into the millions of dollars, Citicorp witnessed only a constant flow of red ink and no end in sight. In December of 1990, the project was unceremoniously terminated.

Why did "Reward America" die? Postmortems were many, but most of all explanations boiled down to value offered for price demanded. Tracking purchases does not increase the total volume of consumer expenditures, and so there was no reason for retailers to support the program enthusiastically. And Citicorp failed to apply lessons from its own marketing experience—the price of a product must be commensurate with its value. Manufacturers of low-priced goods in supermarkets were not willing to pay high prices for shopper names or use high-cost media to promote sales to those prospects.

Product planners must always balance rewards with risks. When markets are volatile, risk tolerance becomes skittish and varies considerably, even among companies in the same line of business.

To illustrate, consider three companies: PaineWebber, Salomon, and J.P. Morgan. All three did proprietary trading. All three had good and bad years. As new products in capital markets multiplied, so did risks. PaineWebber, whose returns were never outstanding, viewed the growth of complex derivatives as too much of a gamble. In 1990 the firm decided to shut down its $2 billion proprietary trading operation. Lee Fensterstock, executive vice-president, was reported as saying, "I just don't see how you can run a company and have this sort of volatility. I don't think the losses are controllable."

Salomon and Morgan could avoid losses no more than Paine-Webber. In the first quarter of 1993, Salomon reported a loss of $250 million from trading, a substantial hit even for a firm of Salomon's size. J.P. Morgan likewise suffered hefty losses from unpredictable price swings. Though providing no specifics, the firm's 1992 Annual Report notes that trading revenue in "debt instruments" dropped $467 million from the previous year. The decline came mainly from mortgage-backed derivatives. But neither Salomon nor Morgan were prepared to withdraw from proprietary trading. Morgan's Annual Report affirms that "rather than seeking to avoid risk," the firm "identifies and assumes risk in connection with our diverse business activities." Consequently, the company formed a "Corporate Risk Management" function which operated independently from all business groups. This risk management unit can define, monitor, and set limits to perceived risks, but it cannot control such key variables as price swings, interest rates, and market liquidity.

Risk-reward considerations encourage small, incremental changes. Product modifications, which are mainly services within a product line, clear rather quickly through the product development pipeline. New products destined for well-established markets relate to existing activities. Whether a new service fits into a product line or creates a brand new line, product development tends to move in a "horizontal" or "concentric" direction. These services relate to existing activities, and therefore, allow multiple uses of a firm's assets. As a result, the firm benefits from economies of scope.

Idea Generation

In the beginning is the idea. Before you can have a new service you must have its concept. In product development, the thought precedes the deed.

New ideas can come from almost any place in a corporation. Because most new financial services are related to existing services, operating managers are the prime movers in product development. They must continuously evaluate the performance of their own products as well as that of competitive ones. Since operating managers are in charge of the new or improved services, they assume roles of product advocates. Their proposals, however, emphasize incremental changes. They seek to improve what exists, and to make it more salable. Objectives of "creeping incrementalism" are various: greater market share, higher quality of service, reduced costs, and lower prices. They compete by implementing those goals.

Firms that service institutional clients may find them invaluable sources of new product ideas. Sales personnel, who are in constant contact with customers, often form the vital communication link. They receive information on practically every call they make. Their call reports are virtual "gold mines" of useful data, since they contain the prime ingredient of innovation—a potential for commercial value. Client ideas come in three distinct forms: new product ideas, problems, and generalities.

A new product idea arranges components in a novel or unconventional manner. These ideas can be conceptualized in different ways and developed into concrete services. If they contain both novelty and potential value, they stand ready to be developed and marketed.

Clients present many ideas as problems—either as complaints or as queries. These spotlight some deficiency that currently exists. A solution might transform the problem into a viable new product idea.

Many ideas arrive incomplete and grandly vague. Product planners might transform such generalities into ideas for new services. But these are indefinite, and thus less likely than problems to emerge as genuine new product ideas.

Informality characterizes product planning in small firms. In contrast, large, diversified companies usually centralize the process. Some firms split the function into search and development, with different personnel assigned to each task. Other firms employ the same people for more than one job. Regardless of how responsibilities are split up, the group in charge of search acts as a collection point to which all new product ideas flow.

A search group does more than hope for new ideas to come from others. An enterprising search unit generates new product ideas by its own efforts. It has many methods at its command, such as: individual analysis, brainstorming, focus groups, and surveys.

The most effective methods employ creative people who understand the business. Business planning departments, however, emphasize research, analysis, and number-crunching. These tasks ascribe the highest importance to logic, while idea generation often calls for a leap of faith. Even if a firm makes strenuous efforts to recruit creatives, there is no way to prejudge a person's creative contributions. Saddled with unenterprising, Dobbins-type employees, search units fall back on what they know best, formal research techniques.

Brainstorming

Brainstorming is one of the oldest research techniques, dating back to the 1930s, when first used by ad agencies. Copywriters who ran out of ideas would hold "rap sessions." The technique was formalized during the 1950s, and applied to various businesses.

Brainstorming calls for employee group sessions consisting of five to ten participants. These people are recruited from different parts of the company, ostensibly to draw on diverse points of view. However, the best practice recommends that groups contain people at roughly similar levels of the corporate hierarchy. A vice-president and a file clerk should not be put together at the same meeting. Rank commands deference. The clerk will say little, while the officer will rashly expound on everything. This runs counter to what brainstorming is supposed to accomplish: a contribution from all who participate in the session.

The key figure in this scenario is the group moderator. This person must keep the session interesting, keep ideas flowing, and make all participants feel relaxed and at ease.

The group leader must rigidly adhere to "deferral of judgment," thereby not allowing one member of the group to criticize another's opinion, no matter how far out the idea. People should be able to freely interject their ideas without inhibitions. If they fear they might be ridiculed, they clam up. The aim of brainstorming is to elicit as many ideas as possible, quickly and cheaply. Evaluation comes later.

Critics have berated brainstorming on many counts. The technique, they say, produces simple "top-of-the-mind" solutions to business problems. Such results, detractors argue, represent managed incompetence; they replace thoughtfulness with shallowness.

Although brainstorming yields an extremely low percentage of usable ideas, and formal research provides few innovative ones, brainstorming might trigger creative thinking at a low cost. If brainstorming opens mental vistas and fires the imagination of those responsible for generating new ideas, then it has served its purpose well. If it works, use it. If not, discard it.

Focus Groups

Focus group actions are highly similar to brainstorming sessions. The greatest difference is that focus groups are composed of consumers rather than employees.

Focus groups were developed by market research companies servicing firms producing goods for mass markets. Financial firms have employed those techniques to generate new product ideas for consumer markets. These consumer-based sessions are particularly popular with ad agencies to develop advertising and direct mail promotions. In many instances, ad agencies outrageously misuse these "research findings."

Ad agencies frequently cite "findings" of these sessions to justify their creative proposals. Buyers make their decisions based on this or that variable. Such assertions take qualitative data from small nonprobability samples and generalize them to a finite population.

The data also reflect answers of a group which is influenced by the moderator and fellow participants. The session recordings do not represent behavior or attitudes of people thinking and acting on their own in normal situations. When people are placed in a group and asked to expound on subjects they know little about, they tend to act like "experts." If these consumers have better ideas about products than professional mangers, the firm should hire them and fire its managers. Like their brainstorming cousins, focus groups do not produce new product ideas. They can only trigger ideas which corporate personnel might choose to explore.

Surveys

Marketing research surveys have been applied mainly to goods and mass-produced financial services. These surveys come in great varieties, and there are no common standards by which they are classified. However, they can be visualized as falling into three broad groups: motivational, attitudinal, and behavioral.

Motivation research seeks to find out why people act the way they do. The methods are essentially Freudian, influenced strongly by abnormal psychology. The "real reason" why people do things is assumed to lie below the level of consciousness. Motivation researchers believe they can probe consumer minds *en masse* by employing watered-down versions of clinical techniques, such as depth interviews, word association, story-telling, and role playing. The techniques are subjective, and surveys have frequently yielded results at odds with each other. Focus group interviews, counterparts of group therapy sessions, remain the last vestiges of motivation research.

When used to develop new product ideas, attitudinal and behavioral surveys can yield insights into consumers' purchase patterns. Both types of surveys deal with consumers' thoughts and actions in the present. They cannot forecast future behavior. The analyst derives such predictions through inference. Accuracy depends on the assumptions that are made and variation in the behavior projected. Above all, research has never formulated a new product. These come from the imagination of company personnel, who use research as input to devise creative output.

Inference

Most new product ideas in financial services arise from inference. An inferential act proceeds from facts or premises to propositions believed to follow logically. The premises are largely descriptive in nature, and usually classified as "secondary" research. The difference between "primary" and "secondary" revolves around the purpose for which data is collected. Often, that difference hews a fine line. "Primary" research is defined as an original study undertaken to solve a problem at hand. "Secondary" information thus had to be primary at some time.

In any event, both types of research can be internal or external. The most common form of internal data is the company's database of existing customers. By analyzing behavior patterns, managers can make useful inferences about future potential actions.

The most common providers of such outside information are government, trade publishers, private research companies, and trade associations.

"Secondary" information from external sources offer company research departments many advantages:

- The information is readily available. Can existing information help with a current problem?
- Existing data saves an enormous amount of time and money. There is no sense duplicating what has already been done.
- In many cases, existing information is of better quality than data a firm can obtain by its own efforts.

The advantages of combining creativity and inferential reasoning were dramatically illustrated by Fidelity's New Millenium Fund, which began operations toward the end of 1992. Writing about the fund in *Forbes*[1] February 1, 1993 issue, Mary Beth Grover amusingly entitled her article, "The Ouija Fund." She prefaces her story as follows:

"Some people pick stocks on financial criteria and some on volcanic eruptions. Neal Miller at Fidelity's New Millenium Fund has had good luck with volcanoes."

This bit of journalistic license creates attention, but exaggerates the stock-picking methods. According to its prospectus, the fund's objectives are capital appreciation by "identifying future beneficiaries of social and economic changes." How?

The Millenium brochure announces with a flare that the fund employs "change analysis," which it terms a nontraditional investment approach that continuously explores social and legislative factors. In reality, the technique is not much different from those of other financial firms. What firm does not continuously monitor the social and economic context of business? Like other funds, Millenium's managers scan thousands of media and research documents.

The fund also finds support from Fidelity's extensive research department, which includes personal visits to more than 6,000 companies a year. Perhaps what differentiates this fund from other growth funds is its search for little-recognized opportunities and Miller's inferential musings. Mr. Miller enjoys a solid reputation on Wall Street as being highly creative in his investment approach.

Asset-backed securities are common examples of inferentially-created new products. Almost anything can be "securitized." Firms have packaged loans and receivables and have traded them like securities. The largest securitized market consists of home mortgages. But now financial institutions are creating a wide variety of asset-backed instruments, ranging from loans on boats and aircraft

1   Mary Beth Grover, "The Ouija Fund," *Forbes* (February 1, 1993), p. 110.

to computer leases. Salomon in 1992 marketed the first issue ever of railcar leases. Merrill Lynch developed a securitization issue of small-business loans.

Andrew D. Stone, director at Daiwa Securities America, puts no limits on securitization. "The imagination is our only constraint—and time," he claims.[2] Securitization transforms illiquid assets to liquid form. These products, born of imagination, has opened large markets for what had been illiquid debt.

Idea Evaluation

Evaluating new business ideas is done continuously, from their inception to their introduction into the marketplace. Along the way, previous analysis and past decisions get modified in the light of more recent information.

Formal screening and business analysis are early forms of the evaluation process. They concern themselves with sorting out ideas and choosing those that look attractive. Once chosen, the ideas go into development. From that point to commercialization is where companies spend most of their money for new products. That being so, it behooves a firm to evaluate new ideas before it commits large funds.

Screening

Idea evaluation usually unfolds in a series of steps, the first of which is screening. Although firms go about this task in many ways, all procedures have certain features in common. First, they are quick, simple, and inexpensive. Second, they are elimination techniques; they aim to reject ideas that fail to meet company objectives or those which have high probabilities of failure.

Screening must address company-specific concerns. Though over simplied, these fall into four categories: corporate objective; feasibility; resource utilization; and probable outcome. Table 5–1 illustrates these considerations in the form of questions.

A beginning type of screening is the checklist, such as a "yes-no" answer to the questions of Table 5–1. Of course, firms may attach

---

2   Quoted in "You Can Securitize Virtually Everything," *Business Week*, July 20, 1992, p. 78.

Table 5-1. Main Considerations in Screening

I. *Corporate Objectives*

Can the product attain an acceptable market position?

How will the service affect existing product lines?

What is the rate of overall market growth?

II. *Feasibility*

What technological requirements must be met?

Does the service involve any legal problems?

What additional manpower would be required?

III. *Resource Utilization*

How much investment outlays will be necessary?

Does the service fit with existing facilities?

Will we have to develop new distribution features?

IV. *Outcome*

Will the product yield adequate sales and profits?

Will the product meet ROI goals?

What is the profit-risk ratio?

---

different degrees of importance to each answer. Even the same factor, such as market growth, may have various definitions. Firms will judge screening criteria ideosyncratically; a management's style tailors standards.

A more elaborate screening method is a product profile rating. The basic form is the ordinal rating scale, which ranks ideas on a number of key factors. Table 5–1 has 12 characteristics. If each one were to be ranked on some sort of scale, such as good, bad, or indifferent, we would have a rating profile. These scales are used to compare various proposals, so as to forward only the most promising to the business analysis phase.

An ordinal scale tells whether one rating is better than another. But it cannot tell how much better. This makes answers clear-cut only at the extremes. When patterns are not distinct or when they take on irregular shapes, sorting the best ideas from a large lot becomes troublesome.

For this reason, screening favors quantitative methods, the most popular of which is the summated rating. As with ranked data, ideas are rated on various criteria, but in terms of numerical values. Scoring done by several people is averaged. Each criterion is given a weight in accordance with its presumed importance. The system multiplies weights and scores and sums their products to obtain an overall rating. Table 5–2 illustrates a summated ratings scorecard, using 10 criteria and scoring each on a five point scale.

Although summated ratings provide a quantitative means of comparing ideas, they suffer from a number of flaws. These are as follows:

- Assigning numbers to categories like good and poor does not change the nature of an ordinal measurement.
- The numerical values remain arbitrary. Is "good" worth twice as much as "poor"?
- Can managers rate ideas as finely and precisely as scaling implies?
- When assigning weights, do managers know the contribution of each criterion to marketplace performance?

Table 5-2. Illustration of Summated Rating

Criteria	Weight	Highest (5)	Good (4)	Average (3)	Poor (2)	Lowest (1)	Total
1	.20		x				.80
2	.15			x			.45
3	.15	x					.75
4	.10		x				.40
5	.08		x				.32
6	.08		x				.32
7	.07					x	.07
8	.06	x					.30
9	.06			x			.18
10	.05	x					.25
Total	1.00						3.84

- Scores may be related to weights. Evaluators may judge ideas with high weights more stringently than those with low weights.
- All evaluators may not score in a consistent manner, a common human failing.
- Do cut-off points accurately mark a dividing line between success and failure? Firms with a great many new services have more experience with which to judge. But under the best of circumstances, cut-offs are subjective.

Concept Tests

Many firms selling services to consumers pass over managerial screening in favor of sales analysis or opinion research. These so-called concept tests concern themselves with whether or not to perpetuate the new idea.

One method proceeds along an indirect route. First, analysts identify existing services that are similar to the new idea. Next, they examine sales trends, assuming that the proposed service will act similarly to products currently on the market.

Another method takes the direct route. It presents the concept directly to potential buyers and solicits their reactions by a survey. A firm can sponsor its own study or use a standard survey offered by several marketing research houses. The test is usually confined to short verbal descriptions of the new offering. Sometimes, firms test several variations of a service.

Most concept tests contain some measure of buying intentions, a key result in a go or no-go decision. Prospects are asked to indicate their buying intentions after being presented with the concept of the new service. The following is a typical example of a buying-intention question:

"Which of these phrases best describes how likely you are to buy the service?"
Definitely will buy . . .
Probably will buy . . .

Might or might not buy . . .
Probably will not buy . . .
Definitely will not buy . . .

There is almost universal agreement that such conjectural questions cannot predict buying behavior. Neither the Michigan Research Center nor the Conference Board have been able to predict consumer purchases from their national surveys that query people about buying intentions.

Because these surveys overestimate actual demand, many managers deflate intentions-to-buy data by some factor. Some deflators are subjectively derived, while others are empirically based, developed from data of past sales.

However, even empirical deflators have serious flaws. The adjustments do not apply uniformly to all answers. A question checked "definitely will buy" has a higher probability of an actual sale than a designation "probably will buy." However, these probabilities are also product specific, and few firms have enough data to build deflators that can predict sales with any degree of confidence.

At best, concept tests are crude devices for separating extremes—for sorting out very good ideas from very bad ones. Core ideas that rate highest or lowest seldom present problems. But many array themselves somewhere in the middle, and make discrimination impossible. Concept tests should be used to screen out clear-cut choices, and no more. They cannot be used for "fine-tuning."

Business Analysis

Business analysis is a continuation of idea evaluation, but in greater detail. It concentrates on economic results, such as supply and demand factors.

The supply side deals with monetary outlays. Some expenditures are long-term. They entail standard capital budgeting with return on investment as the determining forecast. This calculation must account for the present value of money.

Other outlays are short term, such as wages, salaries, and expenses. Unlike capital spending, costs and expenses are in part dependent upon demand factors. These expenditures, for example, vary with volume. In turn, volume is associated with the amount budgeted for distribution and with the marketing mix used. These associations are embodied in *pro forma* P&L projections.

Forecasts of demand for a new service are less predictable than those of costs. A firm can control costs, but not the demand for its offerings. Thus, estimates of market potential and actual sales always encounter difficulties. The most tenuous forecasts are those for services new to the market; they contain more uncertainty.

Many services that have no counterpart on the market perform the same functions as those already in existence. In that event, sales depend on the rate of substitution. The new service might also have an "income effect"—enlarging the total market by attracting customers who previously shunned the past offerings. In estimating demand, both substitution and income effects should be considered.

A special case of substitution occurs when the new product takes business away from other company products. Here, the effects on the overall organization versus the competitive services involved must be separated. Shifts by current customers add no new business. Only business that was previously a competitor's adds to a company's total sales. Consequently, business analysis must take into account intra-company as well as inter-company effects. It is the net gain or loss that matters.

In some instances, however, a firm may find virtue in pursuing a new product even if it produces no net gain in business, as when failure to offer a new product means a loss of customers to competitors.

To illustrate: As interest rates dropped in the early 1990s, money began flowing from certificates of deposit to securities. To keep savings from going to mutual funds and brokerage houses, banks developed a host of new products. By 1993 some 75 percent of banks with more than $750 million in deposits offered attractive alternatives to low-paying CDs.

Today, most banks sell products of the large mutual fund managers, such as Fidelity, Oppenheimer, and Vanguard. Some large banks, like Chase Manhattan and First Interstate, have their own proprietary funds. These banks typically partner with a financial service company to circumvent laws that prohibit them from selling securities. A partnering arrangement usually has the financial house do the underwriting and record-keeping, but in some instances, banks license their own personnel.

Banks expect these new products to cannibalize their CDs, providing them with no net gains. Nevertheless, the no-gain strategy is desirable when compared to a bad alternative of losing customers to mutual funds and brokers.

A bank's offer of different investment vehicles can go beyond the purely defensive objective of holding onto customers. These offers can help a bank compete more effectively with brokers and fund managers for the small investors' savings. People are more apt to regard a bank as a fiduciary agent than they do a brokerage or financial firm. In addition, banks use salaried employees, and so have lower investing costs than most financial firms, which typically pay commissions of 35–40 percent to their brokers. Banks currently account for about 30 percent of all mutual fund sales, half of which cover proprietary funds.

Recently, banks have introduced a number of innovative products directly targeting small investors. These new financial products are "derivatives" that allow gains from capital appreciation, but guarantee the investment value of principal. One such fund is the Citicorp Stock Index Insured Account. This vehicle pays twice the average 5-year percent increase of the S&P 500. If the Index drops, fund holders are guaranteed their original investments. Republic New York Corporation, Bankers Trust, and Shawmut introduced similar index-linked CDs.

To counter bank competition for consumer dollars, brokerage houses have begun to imitate the bank's innovations. Merrill Lynch's Market Index Target-Term Securities resemble bank products, but are traded securities rather than CDs.

Development

Development involves transforming the product concept into an exact service that is offered in the marketplace. The development stage manifests two main aspects: technical and marketing.

The technical portion usually deals with designing computer software for proper performance of the service. The collaboration of operating and technical personnel is of utmost importance, for several departments may contribute to the arrangement of product specifications.

While the majority of new services call for applications of existing technology, the design is vital. It determines the exact features of the service. It spells out how the service will be performed. As such, it is a determinant of cost.

As development proceeds towards commercialization, the emphasis shifts from technical to marketing concerns. The new emphasis deals with issues such as distribution, selling, pricing, promotion, and merchandising. All these aspects are included in the marketing plan, which is drawn up in the latter stages of development.

A marketing plan for a new service is essentially the same as that for an existing service. However, the marketing plan for the new product is an extension of the business analysis; it adds the specifics to make product planning operational.

Briefly, the marketing plan contains four main elements associated with sales generation: situational analysis, marketing objectives, strategy and programs, and operating budgets. Table 5–3 outlines the subject matter managers might include under each heading.

Testing

Testing comprises the final stage of new product planning. This is a company's last chance to evaluate a financial product before pushing it into channels of distribution. Many kinds of test methods exist, such as opinion surveys, use tests, and market experiments.

Table 5-3. Brief Outline of a Marketing Plan

I. *Situational Analysis*

    A. *Projected Sales*

        Sales trends (units, dollars) for the total market and substitutable services under that category.

        Sales trends by region, customer characteristics, and distribution channels.

    B. *Competitive Data*

        Main competitors and their marketing strategies, shares of market, promotional effort, pricing and offer terms, and patterns of distribution.

    C. *Problems and Opportunities*

        These are inferred from an analysis of A and B.

II. *Marketing Objectives*

    A. *Financial*

        Sales estimates over time in both dollars and units, market share, and contributions to profit and overhead.

    B. *Nonfinancial*

        These are subfunctions, which might include sales force goals such as customer calls; advertising goals such as lead generation and media reach; distribution goals such as recruiting agents and brokers.

III. *Strategy and Action Programs*

        Exact details by which marketing strategy is implemented and its objectives achieved. Must contain a schedule of operations, and the intended results for each discrete operation.

IV. *Operating Budget*

        This is nothing more than an operating plan put in financial terms, such as projected costs of media and promotion. Must include a plan of monitoring, so that intended results can be compared with actual results.

However, the sales test, or test marketing, is the most reliable. It gained wide popularity in the packaged goods field, where it is referred to as test marketing. A firm actually offers the new product in one or more markets in order to measure sales.

Though honed in supermarkets and drug stores, test marketing offers greater advantages to the financial service industry than it does to packaged goods manufacturers. Already possessing built-in test markets in the form of databases, financial service companies can monitor sales directly at a relatively low cost. Such firms also have more flexibility in designing samples of testing units, and can exercise greater control of market operations.

Some test markets may be combined with "use" tests. A branch bank can try out a new ATM machine at one or several locations. Other examples of combined sales-use tests are vending machines, "smart cards," and direct trading on exchanges.

The purpose of a test market is two-fold: to predict future sales volume and to improve marketing operations. The first objective—sales forecasting—is by far the most important role of market testing. The sales test is preferred to other methods because actual market transactions turn out as the best forecasting method of eventual sales.

A second objective of market tests is to correct any observable marketing problems when introducing the product into normal distribution channels. These problems should confine themselves only to marketing, and not to inherent product flaws. The test market is not the proper place to begin experimenting with alternatives in rendering a service.

Nevertheless, not every new product should be market tested. The "don't-test" financial services may be classified as follows:

- Low risk products. Modifications and line extensions require little or no investment in support of distribution facilities. When the value of time and money expended on the test exceeds the risk value of plunging into wide distribution, a firm should forego the test market ritual.
- Limited life-span products. Fast-changing markets make testing impractical. Rapid changes render sales projections invalid.

- Products with high capital costs. Market tests are not justified when investment runs high, regardless of operating volume. A product that requires extensive computer programming is a case in point. If large outlays have already been made, a test market cannot lower risk.
- Products with first-in-the-market advantages. A test market means a firm virtually goes public with its new product. When a firm perceives advantages by being first in the market, testing gives competitors more time to imitate the innovation. In this situation, a firm must weigh the risks of not doing a market test against the gains of a first-in advantage. Since financial services can often be imitated quickly, test marketing often lessens the advantage of being first.

Commercialization

Commercialization is the result of a comprehensive process of new product planning, not just a single aspect of it. The new financial service has supposedly gone through all steps of the developmental process, and is now ready to meet the acid test in the marketplace. If the test market has correctly simulated the actual marketing operation, the outcome should approximate the forecast.

Some financial products are tested concurrently with their introduction to the market. This is a version of the "roll-out" plan. For example, a firm may begin with market testing in certain geographic areas or among specific market segments.

If early results seem favorable, the firm can then "roll out" or expand its markets until it covers the geographic areas or marketing segments visualized in the overall marketing plan. This procedure reduces risk because it does not introduce the product in all areas simultaneously. This approach enables a firm to correct shortcomings in its offering more expediently than pouring out all marketing effort at once. The strategy is one of postponing decisions to the last possible moment in time.

But this piecemeal approach also has disadvantages as compared to the all-out approach. It takes more time to penetrate the whole market. It may also be costlier, because piecemeal operations do not take advantage of volume expenditures.

An all-at-once or a piece-by-piece marketing effort depends on managers' confidence in success. When managers feel highly confident that a new product will succeed as forecast, they should "go for it." When forecasts are not quite as assuring as managers would like them to be, they should hedge their bets and proceed cautiously with the new product introduction.

Summary

Although the Booz, Allen & Hamilton model deals with physical products, it is applicable to new financial services. Firms use both formal and informal methods for generating ideas for new financial services. Among the formal methods are brainstorming, focus group research, and surveys. In almost all instances, inferential reasoning must be combined with formal and analytical methods.

Ideas must be evaluated before being put into development. The main methods of idea evaluation are screening, concept tests, and business analysis. While these assessments link risk to potential rewards, risk is often shrouded in uncertainty rather than in success-failure probabilities.

Marketing plans are usually put together toward the last part of new product development. These are frequently tested by some form of sales area test. However, not all plans for new financial services should be tested.

Commercialization can be carried out in one of two ways. "Roll-out" plans involve a piece-by-piece approach. A contrasting method is the "all-out" approach. The method employed depends on several factors, such as company resources and perceived risks.

Part III

Marketing Strategies

6
Segmenting and Bonding Markets

Approaches to defining markets follow two main routes. The most traveled one is segmentation. This marketing strategy divides customers and prospects according to their buying or usage propensities. It then creates products to meet these diverse group needs. In recent years, however, financial services have trended away from segmentation as dissimilar financial products competed more and more for the same groups of customers. Companies found it more profitable to combine segments in order to achieve broader market reach.

Accordingly, this chapter addresses such issues as:

- The basic ways of segmenting markets, and the strengths and weaknesses of each method
- Segmenting markets with supply-side considerations
- Why the much heralded "segments-of-one" have crippling limitations
- How multiple products blur distinctions among market segments
- Methods of countersegmentation, and when to use them

Segmentation Theory

The concept of market segmentation entered the business literature in the 1950s, and is still a popular subject in professional journals and trade publications.

The segmentation concept first drew its inspiration from the writings of John Chamberlain and Joan Robinson, two economists who led an intellectual revolt against neoclassical economics. These economists rejected the notion of competition governed by "an invisible hand." Rather, they saw business competing on unequal terms in market landscapes pitted with "uneven playing fields." Sellers did not offer identical products, and buyers did not demand identical goods and services.

As a business strategy, segmentation is market-oriented. It views markets as diverse buyer groups, each having different needs and wants. Each distinct segment represents a homogeneous demand that differs from the demands of all other groups. As a consequence, purchase behavior displays minimum variation within market segments and maximum variation between buyer groups. This idea is illustrated in Figure 6–1.

In Figure 6–1 each segment is represented by a circle, designated by a letter. Each circle contains certain numbers of buyers, depicted as dots. Ideally, the distance between any units in a circle is smaller than the distance between units in different circles. Ide-

Figure 6-1. Representation of Ideal Market Segments

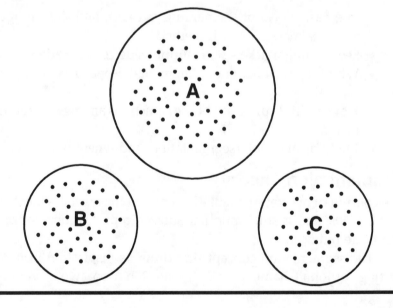

ally, the idea is to cut up markets so as to minimize buyer differences within segments and maximize differences between market segments.

Segmentation theory states that firms should offer unique products to specific segments in order to take advantage of market divisions. This approach customizes products. The presumed advantages are:

- A firm is in a better position to spot market opportunities.
- A firm can make better product adjustments to suit customers.
- By considering reactions of various segments, budgets are more attuned to market response.
- A company can improve its selling appeals. By directing offers only to interested audiences, sellers would never waste money communicating to nonbuyers.
- A logical corollary of this idealized proposition is that companies would confine their activities to what they do best. Consequently, firms would engage in businesses that offer them the highest probability of a competitive advantage.

Despite its volumous literature, the segmentation concept had limited application before the 1980s. At that time most firms communicated to the public through general media, such as newspapers and television. These media reached out to everyone—young and old, rich and poor, white collar workers and laborers. There was no way of "targeting" market segments with special offers. General media transmit "to-whom-it-may-concern" messages. Not until later, when computer technology made large databases economically feasible, did financial companies have a means of identifying marketing segments and directing their offers to the desired buyer groups.

Quest for a Differential Response

Analysts can segment markets in many ways. There are few defined rules regarding segmentation. The lack of conformity comes about because segmentation is industry and company specific. There are two general approaches in the financial service markets: a supply-side emphasis and a demand-side emphasis.

When priority tilts to the supply side, a firm tries to fit buyers to products, rather than the traditional method of fitting products to customers. There are several methods by which marketing activity can accomplish this. One way is to target the most productive part of the market, such as advertising in selective media. Direct mail, for example, entails spending more per contact. But if mailouts are directed to better prospects, they can provide higher returns per dollar.

Another way of improving returns is by selective transaction policies, perhaps best exemplified by Advanta. Card issuers in 1991 wrote off about 25 percent of all revenue they collected. The amount of writeoffs totalled approximately $8.4 billion. Meanwhile, Advanta's receivables grew far above industry rates, with defaults far below industry averages. Avanta accomplished this by extensive credit screening and fitting customers to card terms. Like most credit card issuers, Advanta culls applicant names through major credit bureaus, grading them on two criteria—income and timely bill payments. It then runs those names through some two dozen other proprietary databases, scoring prospective customers on the following: total outstanding debt, balances due on other credit cards, and interest rates on obligations. Advanta then fits applicants into groups with different interest rates and credit lines, seeking to reduce the number of deadbeats. Then Avanta can offer qualifying applicants terms that are superior to competitive offerings.

Similar selective policies are practiced widely in mortgage financing, insurance, and securities trading. Banks alter the terms of real estate loans in accordance with the financial conditions of borrowers. These institutions take into account such factors as current income, consistency of earnings, net worth, and asset quality.

Brokerage houses and mutual funds set up levels of service, called service linings, for customers who meet specific criteria, usually a certain level of transactional volume. Vanguard, for example, established a group of funds in 1992 that cut expenses to a mere 0.15 percent of net assets, an extremely low ratio.

These funds, however, are not for everyone. They are only for investors who begin their portfolios with a minimum outlay of $50,000. Fidelity Spartan and Dreyfus Basic Funds, similar to those of Vanguard, require a lower minimum investment of only $20,000. Nevertheless, these high-yielding funds are unable to reduce costs as much as Vanguard, and though relatively low, expense ratios amount to about 0.45 percent.

Supply-side considerations such as operating costs are particularly important in financial services because they affect performance. A Morningstar 1994 study clearly shows that annual expenses make a big difference in the total returns of mutual funds. According to Morningstar, the average diversified stock fund returned 108 percent before expenses from 1989 to 1994. After expenses, returns fell to 95 percent, well below the 97 percent registered by S&P's 500 stock index. By targeting only large investors into their family of funds, these firms can substantially reduce account servicing expenses and share higher profits with their customers.

A growing number of mutual funds emphasized the link between supply-side factors and performance by refusing to accept money from new shareholders. Most of these funds invested in small-cap, thinly-traded stocks. Thomas Marsico, manager of the Janus Twenty Fund, made the following statement regarding refusal to sell shares to new customers: "We think we can get better performance that way."[1] Jon Fossel, chairman of Oppenheimer Management Fund, voiced the same opinion. "There are some funds where the public's appetite for a fund can outstrip the ability to manage the money well." In these circumstances, internal factors to accomplish investment objectives drive market policies.

When emphasis is on the demand side, financial firms try to match products to general market needs, and business tactics often resemble those of mass marketers. Large banks such as Citicorp and

---

[1]   As reported in "Janus Twenty Is Latest Fund to Bar the Door, *The Wall Street Journal,* January 4, 1993, p. C1.

Nationsbank have conducted direct mail campaigns in which 30 to 40 million credit card applications have been sent out.

The sheer size of these marketing programs virtually bars a highly selective approach. Though mailing areas are prescreened, such mass mailings contain large percentages of nonprospects. Greater selectivity may yield higher profit margins to the Avantas. But it generality yields larger numbers of customers, which more than offset high margins. Mass marketing thus invariably results in more profits to the Citibanks of the world.

The two approaches—those from the demand side and those from the supply side—often are carried on simultaneously. One does not preclude the other. But no matter which route is taken, segmentation strategies must be designed to exploit differential responses to reach their goals by virtue of exploiting differential responses.

Differential responses are the heart of all segmentation strategies. There must be a clear difference in the way customers respond to product offers. If all customers were to respond in the same way, selectivity among segments makes no sense. A firm might as well offer the same service to everyone on the same terms, for to do otherwise only limits opportunities.

Ways of Segmenting Markets

Three basic methods describe the most frequent ways in which financial services companies segment markets:

- behavior
- geography
- demography

These methods often are combined in a single program. For purposes of exposition, though, we'll consider each of these ways separately.

Behavior

Behavior implies actions, and there is no better way to segment markets than on the basis of actual customer response. That is the only rationale for these market division tactics. Action indicates exactly what a person does.

Customer or prospect databases are essential to successful marketing programs based on consumer behavior. Customer databases provide clear information about differential responses. These databases record and track sales of customers according to the volume of their transactions, separating heavy traders from occasional traders, big spenders from penurious ones, large accounts from small accounts, and timely bill-payers from deadbeats. By analyzing activities, firms can separate customers into the good, the bad, and the ugly.

Many financial products involve a relatively small percentage of customers contributing a large proportion of a company's revenue. This often is referred to as the 80-20 principle. A small number of customers—perhaps 20 percent—brings in a disproportionate amount of revenue—perhaps as much as 80 percent. Egalitarianism has no place in business, so why not concentrate on the more productive customer segments?

To compete for the upper 20 percent, financial services have taken a page out of the airline industry's "frequent flyer" programs. Credit card issuers affiliate with airlines, auto rental agencies, hotels, and restaurants to run "frequent traveler programs."

For example, Chase Manhattan cardholders earn bonus dollars for purchases, which they can then use to obtain free airline tickets, and steeply-reduced rates at ITT Sheraton hotels and Hertz. To encourage more use of its cards, Chase also offers lower interest rates to qualifying customers who maintain larger balances. American Express launched a "membership miles" program in 1991 which credited members with one mile for each dollar charged on the card. Once the cumulative annual charge volume exceeds $5,000, the cardholder may trade in credits for various airline travel arrangements or packaged vacations. Spartan Brokerage, a special division of Fidelity Investments that services "active" traders, gives clients a 10 percent credit in any month that brokerage commissions exceed $350.

These types of best-customer programs were employed long before the segmentation concept was formalized. Brokerages adopted the practice of dividing their house lists into active and dormant accounts. While customer transaction files show frequency and volume, these data leave out many relevant variables that affect decisions. The main ones are as follows:

- Transactions, critics charge, reveal only past behavior. Best customers today will not necessarily remain best customers tomorrow.

  This proposition is true up to a point. There is clear evidence that past behavior is one of the best predictors of future behavior, especially in the short run. Current high-volume accounts will tend to do better than low-volume accounts a week or a month from now. To cope with changes in time, many financial service firms built predictive systems into their databases.

- Customer files contain only partial information. For example, a customer doing little business with one firm may transact a large volume of business with a competitive firm. Today's small customer might be tomorrow's big customer. But a firm can only know transactions carried in its own files, and not total financial services used by any individual.

- Over time, a customer database erodes. Customers drop out or become inactive for many reasons. Relying solely on current customers assures an eventual decline. The erosion of old customers must be offset by the acquisition of new customers if the firm is to grow and prosper. Therefore, companies make use of outside databases and various media to replenish losses of customers.

Demographics

The principle reason for treating customers differently is because they offer differing potential sales. You want to spend more on marketing to other customers. But transaction records alone contain insufficient information for making fine distinctions about buying potentials. For example, transactions do not tell what types of consumers are most likely to respond to an offer and the probable value of that response.

One of the most common ways of linking differential response to customer type is by the use of demographics. Banks design special services for customers of a certain age group such as those 50 and over. Benefits of these programs vary widely from bank to bank, and can include such goodies as interest on checking and lower minimum balances, free personalized checks, special rate CDs, discounts on shopping, eating out, travel and recreation, financial newsletters, pharmacy services, common carrier accidental death insurance, and even medical insurance claim filing assistance.

What do banks get out of these programs? Hopefully, more business by cross-selling services, such as: credit cards, trust services, CDs, safe deposit box rentals, automatic deposits of social security and pension checks, brokerage and travel-related services. The Plus 50 clubs that have sprung up all over the country are vehicles for expanding a potpourri of financial services to a broad, upper-age segment.

The same is true of younger age groups, though product offerings undoubtedly differ. Sears found success in mailing Discover card solicitations to newlyweds. Younger families have greater needs for car and college loans, life insurance, and retirement funds.

Wealthy customers have long been a "target" of many financial service firms. One yardstick is household income, because it reflects "disposable" or "discretionary" funds. A valuable indicator of "disposable" income is luxury car purchases. R.L. Polk, which collects auto registration records, is a valuable source of such statistics. Donnelly's DQI database holds information of more than 89 million households which combine telephone listings and car registrations.

Personal assets also indicate wealth, though asset distribution cannot readily be tied to individual households. There are generally two sources for information about income and asset ownership: private research firms and government agencies.

Private sources include a host of information services. Among them are list compilers and other list vendors who make names available to direct marketers. Metromail is one of the largest list compilers, culling 85 million names from phone books, tax rolls, and other sources. American Express uses cardholder names to run promotions. These usually offer a discount if the AmEx card is used at the merchant's place of business. Other card issuers engage in similar ventures with merchants, receiving a percentage of the sale. TRW, a credit checking agency, combines a number of databases with its own to estimate household income and assets based on credit utilization. Carol Wright, Metromail, and large list houses marry their mailing lists to census information for purposes of selecting affluent households.

Most demographic information derives from government agencies. The basic source is the Census Bureau, which sells tape files. Its CD-ROM, an acronym for "compact-disk read-only-memory," runs on personal computers.

A major limitation of the decennial census is loss of accuracy with the passage of time. While Census Bureau's *Current Population Reports* provide updated demographics, these pertain to large areas. Relatively large errors occur when population statistics are projected to small geographic units. Though many list compilers claim they update census information, users should always find out the methods they use to do so. For example, data for small geographical areas are often extrapolated from larger area surveys. Such updates usually assume that change occurs uniformly. In other instances, changes in small area statistics cannot be monitored economically. New buildings create radical changes in block statistics, and there is no way of projecting the composition of new residents without conducting a survey or census of the area.

A number of private research firms offer enhanced census data. Donnelly Marketing Information Services, for example, adds auto ownership and mobility data to its updates and 5-year projections. Its financial database called 'Wealthwise' uses some 75 product profiles to divide consumers into 26 financial-related clusters.

Many firms overlay both customer files and prospect lists with these enhanced census data. The results of such list matching tell a great deal about neighborhoods in which households are located. But the overlay does not tell about income or other financial assets of any individual household. When such matched data are used, firms adopt the old aphorism about birds of a feather—neighbors act in much the same way with respect to financial services. Yet even the most affluent communities have various proportions on not-so-wealthy residents. Besides, being rich does not guarantee that a person will act in a predetermined way. In fact, numerous studies have shown only weak associations between socio-economic data and buying behavior. Weak statistical relationships indicate faulty predictions.

Geography

Geography is one of the oldest methods of dividing markets and establishing sales territories. Banks evaluate geographic areas when opening, establishing, or closing branches. Many brokerages and financial firms operate local offices to take advantage of propinquity to customers. Insurance agents operate on the basis of geographical territories.

Financial databases today regard the individual as the basic information unit (BIU). An individual is the smallest unit for which records are kept. From an operational perspective, however, segments of one person are obviously impractical. It is not economical to create a unique product for every individual. Usually, individuals are grouped by geography. Financial firms must know how to communicate with customers, such as when sending summary statements, transaction confirmations, tax information, and bills and credits.

BIU data can only be aggregated, never disaggregated. A bank can combine all customers within a particular zip code, and then add up zip code data to get the total for a county. But if the bank has only county figures, it cannot derive counts for zip code areas.

Likewise, banking statistics cannot be obtained for counties if BIUs pertain to states.

BIU selection depends on a firm's operations and on information usage. A large credit card issuer which sends out millions of mailing pieces might want to sort its mailouts in accordance with postal carrier routes. A local bank, however, may deem zip code areas sufficient. Visa and Mastercard want zip codes for servicing accounts, but want areas of dominant influence (ADI's) for running general advertising campaigns on television. An ADI is an Arbitron designation that defines television coverage areas, with counties as their BIUs. On the other hand, a mutual fund advertising in a specialized financial journal might require only total circulation counts. However, if the journal has a paid circulation, ABC breakouts may be more relevant.

Geodemographic Databases

Firms that have adopted demography as a diagnostic tool often unite it with geography. The U.S. Census underprops practically all geodemographic databases. It accumulates mountains of data about persons and households for a large variety of geographic designations—regions, states, counties, metropolitan areas, zip codes, census tracts, and blocks.

A number of research houses have "enhanced" the census database by combining several demographic variables within geographic boundaries. The most popular census-based systems are ACORN, ClusterPlus, and Prizm. All three use statistical multivariate techniques to divide the population into "lifestyle" clusters. These are basically "social classes" following the conventional socio-economic definition of income, education, and occupation.

ACORN, produced by CACI Market Analysis of Fairfax, Virginia, divides the country into 44 clusters, each with distinct demographic characteristics. For example, its "Old Money" segment contains large proportions of families with high incomes, college educations, and expensive homes. ClusterPlus is a product of Donnelley Marketing Services, a division of the A.C. Nielsen Company.

The database incorporates more than 1,600 variables to derive 47 unique "lifestyle groups." This information can be projected onto any geographic or geometric area in the nation.

Similarly, Claritas Corporation's Prizm database contains more than 500,000 separate localities grouped into 52 unique segments. People in each geographic segment should have the same characteristics, yet differ importantly from residents in other segments. These clusters are described by colorful but expressive nicknames, such as "Money and Brains," "Blue Collar Nursery," "Bohemian Mix," and "Blue Blood Estates." Prizm bears a close likeness to its sisters, ClusterPlus and ACORN. For example, PRIZM's "Blue Blood Estates" is markedly similar to ACORN's "Old Money" segment. However, even similar clusters are not exactly equivalent; each system has different numbers of clusters.

All three geodemographic systems are linked to various syndicated marketing surveys, the most important being those of Simmons Market Research Bureau and Mediamark, Inc. These are essentially magazine readership surveys which contain product purchase information.

Demographic Mapping

A feature of the 1990 Census is TIGER, which stands for Topologically Integrated Geographic Encoding and Referencing. Eight years in the making, TIGER maps the entire United States. This computerized file contains every street, highway, bridge, river, political boundary, and physical entity. When combined with Census data, the TIGER file promises enormous benefits for firms using small area analysis in planning their business.

The Census Bureau began selling the TIGER software in 1991 for $84,000. Small businesses can buy partial tapes that cover any particular area desired. Every state has an affiliate Census Bureau office, usually located at a school, where TIGER tapes are made available.

Despite wide distribution of data-user services, most businesses use private research houses, mainly because they want the value-added features. Some of these features include client-proprie-tary information, and some include enhancements appended by the vendor.

One such private mapping company is Minnesota-based Data-map, Inc. The software generates demographic data in both tabular and graphic form. The areas covered are of two types. One type consists of "standardized geographic units," such as zip codes or postal carrier routes. A second type encompasses radii around a site. When clients provide tapes or disks with data relevant to their business, computer-generated maps are customized. Table 6-1 illus-trates an example of demographic mapping in tabular form, while Figure 6-2 illustrates a map of postal carrier routes delineated by household income.

Mapping demographics has many uses. The more important among them are:

- *Site selection* - Demographics of local areas are particularly important in assessing a site's potential and in assessing the nature of facilities required for a each site. Many areas may not support a bank with a full-service office. Residential neighborhoods with modest income distributions may not warrant a trust department or a foreign currency exchange section.
- *Customer profiles* - Profiles help firms wishing to match cus-tomers' transactions with socioeconomic data. Analyses of this nature furnish clues as to sources of business.
- *Market potential* - Demographics are related to purchases of financial services. Many firms reasonably infer the value of markets by comparing demographic profiles of their cus-tomers with those of markets.
- *Operational efficiency* - Small area analysis reduces costs in relation to revenue. Firms marketing products through di-rect mail, such as credit cards, find postal carrier routes offer more selectivity than zip codes. Because postal carrier routes

Figure 6-2. Presentation Map of TIGER Streets
Overlaid with Postal Carrier Routes
Shaded by Demographic Income Variable

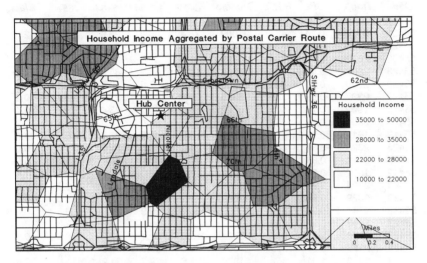

Source: DATAMAP, Inc. © 1989.

are smaller than zip codes, mailers can often eliminate areas with low potential returns.

- *Sales territories* - When designing them, firms must account for how customers and prospects are clustered. Sales people can make less calls when destinations are widely dispersed, more calls when travel distances are short.
- *Regulatory compliance* - Legal requirements often relate to geographic areas. For example, the Community Reinvestment Act mandates that banks make loans in areas from which they obtain deposits. Computer Mapping clearly shows this relationship between loans and deposits.

Evaluating the A Priori Approach

The division of markets based on geodemography is aptly called *a priori* segmentation. A firm using this model first selects socio-eco-

Table 6-1. DATAMAP™ Sample Tabular Report

Zip Code	Carrier Route	Dist. from Site	1987 # of H.H.'s	Avg. H.H. Income	PCT. Persons In Age Group				Pct. Black	Pct. Hisp.
					0–17	18–34	35–64	65+		
55423	2340	0.00	168	21009	18.4	36.8	28.9	15.9	2.3	0.8
55423	2324	0.14	487	21009	18.4	36.8	28.9	15.9	2.3	0.8
55423	2338	0.29	528	15790	12.7	37.5	31.4	18.4	0.4	0.9
55423	2332	0.42	324	15790	12.7	37.5	31.4	18.4	0.4	0.9
55423	2308	0.47	186	24566	17.9	30.2	35.5	16.4	1.4	0.8
55423	2330	0.49	353	45260	20.1	27.8	40.7	11.5	0.9	0.3
55423	2337	0.69	388	25378	24.6	28.8	37.9	8.7	0.2	0.3
55419	1902	0.73	471	16722	16.7	41.0	23.4	18.9	4.4	0.4
55423	2331	0.78	354	23550	25.0	28.0	35.2	11.8	0.2	0.0
55419	1917	0.79	471	16722	16.7	41.0	23.4	18.9	4.4	0.4
55423	2325	0.81	404	27279	21.5	28.0	39.5	11.0	0.0	0.5
55423	2314	0.88	389	45260	20.1	27.8	40.7	11.5	0.9	0.3
55419	1912	0.89	341	28299	17.2	25.0	42.2	15.6	1.6	0.6
55423	2304	0.91	323	25811	15.1	27.0	41.4	16.5	0.0	0.3
55423	2329	0.94	300	22639	18.9	26.7	39.1	15.3	0.0	0.3
55423	2341	0.94	378	25862	24.0	29.9	36.4	9.6	0.0	1.4
55423	2318	0.95	472	17277	14.0	41.4	32.3	12.3	0.7	0.4
55423	2326	0.97	346	22723	19.8	32.1	37.5	10.6	0.1	0.2
55423	2317	0.97	339	27004	23.6	29.3	37.5	9.7	0.6	0.7
55419	1910	1.01	367	31870	26.6	29.7	31.9	11.8	2.6	0.2
55419	1916	1.05	402	20164	17.5	40.3	26.0	16.1	4.9	0.6
55419	1920	1.06	528	21783	15.4	29.7	31.4	23.5	1.4	0.8
55419	1921	1.07	105	21783	15.4	29.7	31.4	23.5	1.4	0.8
55423	2319	1.18	369	28581	18.5	28.8	44.8	7.9	0.0	0.5
55423	2323	1.18	341	20144	19.5	28.3	36.8	15.5	0.3	1.7
55423	2321	1.23	408	19126	17.8	45.2	29.6	7.4	1.5	0.9
55419	1919	1.24	384	31870	26.6	29.7	31.9	11.8	2.6	0.2
55423	2310	1.26	378	19663	12.8	33.2	37.6	16.4	0.2	0.0
55419	1906	1.27	382	30020	18.3	29.2	36.0	16.5	0.2	0.2
55423	2303	1.29	331	17277	14.0	41.4	32.3	12.3	0.7	0.4
55417	1703	1.32	353	24037	17.7	29.8	33.4	19.2	5.8	0.7
55423	2309	1.33	349	27004	23.6	29.3	37.5	9.7	0.6	0.7
55419	1918	1.33	425	21801	19.3	33.4	25.8	21.5	0.9	0.0
55419	1907	1.34	332	28029	24.7	28.9	35.2	11.2	0.4	0.0
55423	2312	1.35	375	24420	25.1	33.9	33.3	7.7	1.3	0.0
55423	2339	1.36	359	28108	22.0	25.1	43.2	9.6	0.0	0.0
55419	1913	1.37	455	25512	21.5	33.9	26.4	18.3	3.8	0.4
55423	2336	1.37	332	23409	19.3	23.2	42.6	14.9	0.2	0.1
55417	1706	1.40	368	26937	17.0	25.8	33.5	23.7	0.0	0.7
55423	2315	1.44	450	22928	24.8	33.9	33.5	7.9	0.3	1.0
55423	2311	1.45	403	25156	22.5	29.4	40.5	7.6	0.0	0.2
55419	1915	1.46	300	26316	13.3	23.9	22.6	40.2	0.6	0.6
55410	1010	1.50	372	26359	20.8	37.6	34.5	7.0	1.4	0.9

15890 = TOTAL HOUSEHOLD COUNT
SOURCE: DATAMAP, INC.

Pct. Owner Occ.	Pct. Moved 5 yrs	Pct. Sing	Pct. Mar	Avg. House Value	Avg. Rent	Pct. Blue Collar	Pct. with Child	Median # yrs School	City/ County
40.0	41.7	30.7	52.1	61814	287	16.0	24.1	12.7	Richfiel
40.0	41.7	30.7	52.1	61814	287	16.0	24.1	12.7	Richfiel
32.5	50.9	35.9	47.6	60326	222	25.6	15.9	12.7	Richfiel
32.5	50.9	35.9	47.6	60326	222	25.6	15.9	12.7	Richfiel
83.9	42.3	35.9	54.4	60985	262	20.3	39.8	13.1	Richfiel
91.3	10.9	28.3	63.4	59204	322	18.7	35.5	12.9	Richfiel
86.6	32.3	27.0	65.9	63809	307	22.1	50.0	12.8	Richfiel
23.9	62.1	29.6	44.5	63787	285	20.7	23.2	12.7	Diamond
96.6	39.1	17.9	71.2	64754	381	20.2	33.0	12.9	Richfiel
23.9	62.1	29.6	44.5	63787	285	20.7	23.2	12.7	Diamond
96.7	17.1	22.8	71.9	62607	375	29.3	26.0	12.7	Richfiel
91.3	10.9	28.3	63.4	59204	322	18.7	35.5	12.9	Richfiel
96.3	19.9	21.9	64.2	69970	354	21.9	27.0	13.0	Diamond
84.3	25.3	31.5	55.8	63270	296	23.9	21.3	12.6	Richfiel
85.0	26.5	23.6	67.6	61588	293	20.3	31.6	12.8	Richfiel
95.0	38.3	18.8	69.9	65400	373	12.0	34.0	14.6	Richfiel
51.0	43.3	31.1	47.5	58603	223	21.9	15.1	12.7	Richfiel
76.8	40.7	27.2	61.7	58867	255	24.0	32.8	12.8	Richfiel
96.3	16.4	25.8	63.6	61675	364	22.9	40.9	13.0	Richfiel
95.6	30.2	17.2	75.3	70692	342	5.6	36.5	14.8	Diamond
48.1	49.2	32.2	52.6	66376	280	23.4	21.4	12.8	Diamond
82.2	31.0	22.7	56.6	62319	285	12.7	18.6	12.8	Diamond
82.2	31.0	22.7	56.6	62319	285	12.7	18.6	12.8	Diamond
94.7	31.4	27.6	66.2	62762	377	16.5	34.5	12.7	Richfiel
79.0	33.8	25.9	53.2	57315	276	25.0	24.2	12.7	Richfiel
31.4	63.6	40.2	44.5	67293	287	20.6	23.5	13.0	Richfiel
95.6	30.2	17.2	75.3	70692	342	5.6	36.5	14.8	Diamond
54.1	16.6	26.4	56.4	57391	241	23.3	15.4	12.9	Richfiel
92.1	20.4	26.4	66.5	60266	346	22.0	20.7	12.8	Diamond
51.0	43.3	31.1	47.5	58603	223	21.9	15.1	12.7	Richfiel
87.6	26.2	20.7	60.6	58821	302	26.7	20.7	12.7	Nokomis
96.3	16.4	25.8	63.6	61675	364	22.9	40.9	13.0	Richfiel
62.1	58.2	26.4	55.9	73388	256	9.4	26.7	14.3	Diamond
95.9	39.6	33.1	57.8	65043	409	16.5	39.5	13.0	Diamond
93.5	21.7	28.6	59.6	58024	310	23.4	43.9	12.8	Richfiel
99.5	34.0	20.2	70.1	61409	0	15.3	36.0	12.8	Richfiel
81.9	44.4	27.7	58.3	66842	268	12.9	27.0	14.3	Diamond
75.3	25.4	21.0	69.9	71284	307	13.4	28.1	12.8	Richfiel
90.0	30.7	17.4	61.3	64561	321	9.3	24.4	13.5	Nokomis
85.2	37.8	20.6	57.7	58183	322	26.0	44.0	12.9	Richfiel
98.0	33.0	27.3	60.7	58798	0	26.9	35.5	12.7	Richfiel
93.9	34.2	25.1	42.2	67323	356	13.9	30.1	12.7	Diamond
79.8	48.3	33.8	49.5	60053	359	19.2	36.0	12.8	Edina Ar

nomic criteria, and then goes about choosing areas in which to operate. The rationale for this approach is an apparent connection between services and socio-economic factors. Common sense tells us that this is true for many products. Trading in stocks and bonds is related to income, as is insurance, new car loans, mortgage-backed loans, and many other financial services. After all, a person must have money to buy a money-related service.

How would an *a priori* approach work? Suppose a financial house describes its customers in terms of income and occupation. It further chooses its BIU as a census tract, a supposedly homogeneous area containing roughly 1,500 homes.

First, the firm specifies that one-third of the families residing in a tract must earn more than $75,000 annually and at least half the wage earners must hold professional or managerial jobs. The next step is to scan designated areas and select tracts that qualify on those criteria.

This approach yields soft probabilities, not hard sureties. Besides, the definition of a prospect contains vast ambiguities. Is the firm saying a good prospect is one who qualifies on both income *and* occupation? Contrarily, does the definition specify "prospects" as people who have a high income *or* who work at managerial-professional jobs?

This either-or segment encompasses larger numbers than when people must qualify on both counts. The income *and* occupation criteria implies a joint-probability, and such statistics cannot be derived from census data. Summary tapes record each demographic individually, and do not cross-tabulate them. In any event, the size of a joint-probability segment can only be estimated by analysis of similar data. When projected to small area divisions, such estimates contain large degrees of error.

The either/or proposition also presents difficulties. Two criteria yield three possible combinations:

1. Professionals/managers with high income.

2. Professionals/managers who do not qualify on high income.

3. High-income families who do not meet the occupational standard.

Since we do not know the size of any group, we would do double-counting if we look at statistics of single demographics. We would also come up with vastly different profiles for our BIUs. For example, administrative centers like Washington, D.C. and university towns have large percentages of professionals and managers, but lower proportions of high incomes.

In contrast, high-income professionals and managers form a large percentage of many towns in the Connecticut county of Fairfield, notably Darien, Greenwich, New Canaan, Westport, and Wilton. A segment based on "either-or" demographic qualifications may thus lack homogeneity.

Lastly, every *a priori* system must show a meaningful connection between demographics and behavior. If that link is lacking, the result is a sociological study. A differential response is only assumed, not authenticated. Most of the geodemographic databases project product information from surveys such as those of Simmons Market Research Bureau and Mediamark, Inc. These magazine readership surveys incorporate product information as "add-ons." The studies use "global" questions, such as: "Do you own stocks or bonds?" "Do you have a credit card?" "Do you own a mutual fund?" From a practical point of view, such questions can hardly yield enough details to segment markets with any degree of effectiveness.

Segments of One

During the past several years a number of books, articles, and speeches have fervently prophesied a new age of personalized products. *The Wall Street Journal* recently lent its prestige to that prophesy by publishing an article whose title mimicked what the Boston Consulting Group calls "segments-of-one marketing."[2] *The*

---

2   Kathleen Deveny, "Segments of One," *The Wall Street Journal* (March 22, 1991), p. B4.

Journal article noted that the focus of the 1990s is "you" as the "target" consumer.

This idea had been widely popularized by Stan Rapp and Tom Collins, principals of a direct marketing agency. In their book, *The Great American Turnaround,*[3] the authors claim that business has dramatically shifted in a steady progression from "mass" to "niche" to "individual." At an AMA Sales Promotion Conference in 1990 Rapp was more explicit about this shift. "The death of mass marketing is official," he animatedly proclaimed. During the 1991 annual meeting of the American Association of Advertising Agencies, Florence Skelly, social researcher and president of Telematics, averred that the mass market "will never return." Nevertheless, the reported demise of mass markets, like that of Mark Twain, has been grossly exaggerated.

Segments-of-one as an object of business strategy derives from the expansion of computer technology and software, such as the new "relational" databases. This state-of-the art method cross-indexes separate files, like those holding names of investors in funds X,Y, and Z. For example, if you want to find out how many new investors were added to the fund, or the sources of sales, old-type databases commonly mandated running the entire customer file and sorting transactions into different categories. The cross-reference system provides the same information, but more economically. We need only run three smaller files—those of Funds X,Y, and Z to ascertain changes in these funds, and where the additions came from. The computation can also relate ownership of other funds with investors in X,Y, and Z.

Some financial firms personalize products. J.P. Morgan provides a personal banker to clients worth a minimum of $1 million. U.S. Trust recently lowered qualifications for personal banking from $1 million to $250,000, though customized service at banks commonly starts with $300,000 (exclusive of home values). Barry Kaye Associates renders financial planning for estates worth more

---

3   Stan Rapp and Tom Collins, *Great American Turnaround*, Englewood Cliffs, NJ: Prentice-Hall, 1990.

than $3 million. But special services for a handful of wealthy clients do not constitute individual segmentation. Financial houses practiced such selectivity long before databases and segmentation concepts came into vogue.

The rich and the famous are the exceptions, not the rule. Many financial services cannot be produced economically as single entities. Unless the service sells for an inordinately high price, it cannot be individualized. Pension funds will fit services to large clients, but that is also not viewed as segmentation. It differs little from practices of security underwriters bidding for the business of individual companies in a larger, almost homogeneous market of corporate securities.

Most financial firms in consumer markets provide minor variations of standard prototypes. For example, many asset allocation funds and variable annuities permit investors to choose different proportions of investment types, such as stocks, bonds, and cash. To help investors design their portfolios, mutual fund companies like Dreyfus, Fidelity, T. Rowe Price, and Stein Roe give customers worksheets that suggest an asset allocation. Customers can choose how their money is to be apportioned in standard funds run by professional managers. But many of these asset allocation funds do not allocate assets to suit individual predilections. Rather, they practice what is known as "tactical asset allocation." They change the percentages in stocks, bonds, and cash, depending upon which types they deem attractive at the moment. Many commentators see these tactics as a form of "disguised market timing." At any time, customers may find their portfolio mixes departing radically from the asset allocation suggested in their initial worksheets.

Customers today have many more choices. Wider choices came about not because providers of financial services customized their outputs, but because computers enabled them to create more varieties of standardized services.

Mass, Class, or Hybrid Markets?

Many frequent-user programs are presented as if they were aimed at particular segments, or even at segments-of-one. The oft-quoted example is that of special discounts or premiums to "best customers." Credit card issuers, for example, reward big spenders with attractive bonuses and rebates.

Do bonus programs exemplify segmentation? Yes and no. Yes, because they cull out customers who respond differently from the rest and give them special treatment. No, because the same rewards and bonuses are available to *all* consumers. The freebies are analogous to the S&H Green Stamps of the 1960s, stamps which individuals laboriously pasted into books and presented at redemption centers. Today, computers do this tedious work, keeping track of a person's purchases and recording cumulative values.

Another version of bonuses involves giving rebates and discounts. Holders of the Discover card earn yearly cashbacks on annual purchases. Other credit card companies pack billing envelopes with price-off coupons. Mastercard periodically promotes retail discounts at cooperating stores. A "MasterValues" program in late 1990 was supported by more than $10 million in a special holiday advertising campaign. Brokerage firms reduce commissions for securities trades involving a larger number of shares, or for do-it-yourself investors who trade directly on-line from a personal computer. Likewise, mutual funds offer lower fees for larger investments.

All such programs are forms of price competition. Lower charges and givebacks based on purchases have been practiced from time immemorial. They represent volume discounting, cumulative for credit card companies, noncumulative for securities trading. Since the product and terms of the transaction remain the same for everyone, it violates segmentation theory.

Segmentation is a seller's program, not a buyer's. For example, a department store advertising a sale in general media such as a local newspapers tries to communicate with everyone. The store engages in "undifferentiated" marketing. Shoppers invariably respond differently. Some ignore the ads, some buy a little, and some buy a lot. The fact that consumers respond differently to a generalized offer does not make segmentation. Similarly, financial firms that offer the same services to a market, no matter how varied, do not practice segmentation.

Multiple Product Usage

As a market matures, the number of products destined for that market grows almost geometrically. Products compete on horizontal and vertical levels. The horizontal type involves similar products. For example, bond funds compete with other bond funds. Capital appreciation funds vie with other funds having similar objectives.

Vertical competition involves completely different categories performing the same functions. For example, CDs, stock funds, bond issues, and annuities compete with each other for investment returns.

When multiple products compete with each other, market segments become blurred. Let us consider three competitive products: stocks, bonds, and money market funds. The same people might place money in all three investment vehicles, but in different proportions. In this example, what is the relevant segment? Though the three investment types are highly distinct, market segments are not, and certainly do not conform to the notion of investors existing in separate compartments. The segments are overlapping, without shape or form. Three competing investment types yield seven unique groups. These are persons investing in the following:

1. Stocks only

2. Bonds only

3. Money market funds only

4. Stocks and bonds

5. Stocks and money market funds

6. Bonds and money market funds

7. All three investment types

In this example, customers might be represented on an "investment proliferation map," depicted in Figure 6-3.

Nonexclusive investment practices result in fuzzy segments. Does a financial firm regard investors in money market funds as a separate category of investors as opposed to buyers of equity funds? Investors in both money markets and stock? All three? Under these conditions, firms competing in the same market may set their sights on the broadest possible group of potential customers.

The trend among financial service providers has been away from narrow segments to the direction of broader reach. Insurance firms, banks, brokerages, and mutual funds companies have gravitated toward "wrap" accounts. These envision selling several products to a customer in quest of a "share of the whole wallet." These products compete both horizontally and vertically.

Figure 6-3. Representation of Overlapping Segments

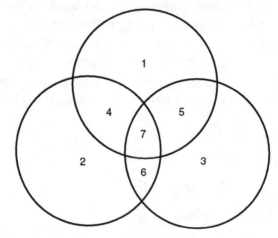

The horizontal competition is exemplified by line extensions, such as the proliferation of funds which often differ minutely from one another. For example, Fidelity Investments offers two types of money market funds, Cash Reserves and Fidelity Daily Investment Trust. Returns of both funds follow short-term interest trends, and only an expert would perceive the fine differences between them. Similarly, a number of "balanced" and "asset allocation" funds put out by the same firm have essentially the same objectives. A key question posed by line extensions: How much can similar products be increased without hurting profit margins and net revenue? In this instance, a market segmentation approach has little relevance. Traditional segmentation calls for "different strokes for different folks." Line extension strategies call for "different strokes for the same folks."

While firms pursuing horizontal competition seek a larger share within a set of similar products, vertical competition expands the set. CDs, mutual funds, and annuities vie with each other for a share of consumers' wallets. Economists sometimes refer to this strategy as "interlacing." Firms develop financial products that are but distantly related to their current lines. When they use available resources, they benefit from economies of scope. Brokerages and banks selling proprietary and outside mutual funds to current customers increase profit margins. Revenue gains are accompanied by lower incremental costs.

Interlacing is not merely for the sake of efficiency; it is for growth. As markets become saturated, a firm grows by entering new businesses. Line extensions basically aim at increasing revenue per customer. Interlacing produces different sorts of products, confronts new competitors, and extends its offers to new customers.

Outstanding examples are nonbanks that successfully penetrated the national credit card market, such as Sears, AT&T, GM, Ford, and H & R Block.

Sears took advantage of its huge customer base to develop the Discover card. Though Discover recently went public as part of

Dean Witter, Sears had developed a new business in which it still maintains an interest.

AT&T designed a card to attract additional long-distance calling volume, but at the same time grew a new business. Though Total Systems processes the Universal card, AT&T's contract gives the phone company an option to buy stock from the outside supplier.

Other examples of interlacing are numerous, such as banks and mutual funds setting up brokerage firms, banks increasing investment options for clients, nonbanks offering checking accounts, and various organizations co-sponsoring affinity cards with a card issuer.

Insofar as these programs enlarge a firm's markets by joining diverse financial service markets, interlacing is clearly a countersegmentation strategy. It may not change database operations. The basic units remain similar, but they are combined into enlarged segments, and product policy heads towards a larger customer group, and perhaps a "mass" market.

The trend in financial services today clearly runs towards countersegmentation. Greater profits accrue from selling more products to the same customers than from seeking new customers for a limited product mix. Offering prospects a greater variety of financial alternatives increases the likelihood of market expansion. At the same time, databases with multifunctional uses enable firms to benefit from economies of scope.

Breaking down larger markets into segments and joining smaller market units into bigger entities occur simultaneously. Most new products appear first as niches. As the number of their customers grow, other firms enter the business. For example, Charles E. Merrill, a founder of Merrill Lynch, did not think that mutual funds had much of a future. As late as 1976, twenty years after Merrill's death, the firm that bears his name ran but two small funds. As late as 1980 only about 5 percent of household equity assets were in mutual funds, but by 1992 household equity assets had grown to some 35 percent. Mutual funds provided 96 percent of total investments that went into stocks. Merrill Lynch, steering vast resources into the once neglected niche, developed 158 different funds, with more than $115 billion under management. At the same time, other firms bring out new financial products that form new niches by chipping away at the large market.

Segmentation and countersegmentation occur all the time. In allocating the firm's strategic resources, management must decide which strategy to pursue, and the intensity of that pursuit.

Summary

The conventional wisdom for defining markets is segmentation. While firms must consider supply-side issues, emphasis rests on demand.

There are three basic ways of segmenting financial markets: behavior, geography, and demography. Firms usually combine all three factors in defining meaningful marketing factors. There are no standard criteria for doing that. The exact combination of factors must be company and market specific.

Computers make it feasible to vary segment size from mass markets to units of one. Direct marketers have highlighted segments of one as the wave of the future. But this form of marketing can seldom be operationalized, and, when feasible, is rarely profitable.

Recently, the financial industry has witnessed giant inroads of countersegmentation. The impetus to this trend comes from product proliferation to achieve broader markets through diversification.

7

Marketing to the Customer Database

Marketing to a customer database implies revenue-generating activity. Customer files provide a ready means of communicating directly with buyers. Accordingly, direct marketing holds center stage.

The discussion that follows highlights how to exploit ties with buyers to build additional income. Specifically the chapter:

- Illustrates cross-selling techniques to maximize profits by using "marginal" principles
- Shows when multistage marketing programs justify high lead-to-sales ratios, and when they do not
- Discusses management trade-offs regarding sales, costs, and profit margins
- Explains the links between capital budgets, various product costs, and selling activity
- Spells out the reasons marketing must work together with other departments to achieve superior sales results

Functions of a Customer Information File

Customer information files are a vital link between financial services firms and the customers—commercial or retail. They serve many purposes. Among the most important are:

Accounting

These databases record transactions in order to process day-to-day accounting functions. Mainly, these databases represent passive systems. They record activity initiated by customers: banks keep track of deposits and withdrawals; brokerage houses credit and bill customers who buy and sell securities; credit card issuers record customer purchases and make payments to retailers.

Marketing

These databases reflect sellers' efforts to bring about customer action. Marketing retail services usually involves soliciting a response through use of media. Marketing to businesses often combines media solicitation with face-to-face selling. Marketing functions are also interconnected with accounting tasks. Sales involve billing and receipt of payments.

Customer Service

This category contains a bewildering array of activities, depending on the service. Customer service ranges from bank tellers handling deposits and withdrawals to account representatives assisting in solving clients' problems. These activities can also include the simple execution of transactions to giving advice on trusts, retirement funds, and taxes. Database uses for purposes of providing customer service obviously span a great variety of tasks.

This chapter emphasizes customer databases used for marketing purposes. However, marketing tasks are often closely associated with other corporate functions.

Customer-Based Marketing

Customer databases serve two major marketing functions. The most common is helping to generate revenues from existing customers. There are numerous methods of doing this, such as cross-selling newly-created or current products to existing customers. Marketing to current customers virtually mandates communicating with them directly. Since a company already knows how to contact its customers, direct mail and telephone are the most expeditious way of soliciting sales at the retail level. The method chosen for accomplishing this depends upon industry practice. Banks, insurance companies, and mutual funds make best use of the printed word.

Stock brokerages, which conduct most of their business by personal contact, do a substantial volume of prospecting by phone.

Business-to-business marketing places greater emphasis on sales calls, either by telephone or through personal visit. The two types of communication have become increasingly specialized in recent years. The telephone finds its greatest use in contacting small customers and qualifying leads. Personal visits favor large accounts and serious prospects.

Customer databases may also find employment as a planning tool to acquire new customers. When used in this way, the database becomes an object of quantitative or statistical analysis. The analysis aims to determine the likelihood of different customer groups acquiring particular financial services. These buying patterns of customers are then projected to a universe of noncustomers. Firms often carry out database analysis simultaneously with "cross-selling" activities. That is, they try to convert prospects into customers while still selling to current customers.

Direct Sales to Customers

Financial service companies have long practiced cross-selling. As part of these programs, a firm may offer multiple products of its own, or act as an agent for other companies. Banks and stock brokers sell their own company's mutual funds as well as the funds of others. Selling various financial services to a customer base provides many advantages:

- A firm can parlay its existing ties with buyers into additional income. Customers are far more likely to buy than are non-customers.
- Costs of selling to customers are much lower than costs of selling to prospective customers. To sell a retail product, a company can insert a promotional piece along with the monthly statement for little or no additional postage. While this sort of "piggy-backing" keeps incremental promotional

costs low, the probability of response is higher than with mailings destined to noncustomers.

- Costs of servicing a new business are low, especially when the firm uses existing assets. Many mutual funds offer the same product to different groups of customers. When a funds management company, for example, sells the same funds in a 401(k) plan to individual investors, incremental expenses decline and profit margins rise. By combining more assets into one portfolio, firms produce economies of scale.

The same low-cost, high-return benefits accrue to firms serving business customers. These financial houses usually maintain personal relations with clients, and reps can pitch new products during their regular calls.

Personal contacts in business play major roles in decisions to expand financial services or to enter new lines of business. A number of money center banks have gained regulatory approval from the Federal Reserve Board for corporate debt powers. Banks such as Bankers Trust of N.Y., Chase Manhattan, Chemical Banking Corp., Citicorp, and J.P. Morgan have moved into traditional underwriting and investment banking by extending their relationships with commercial customers.

Existing customer relationships permit these banks to enlarge their product mix. By doing so they open up opportunities for moving into more profitable fields. For example, sales of high-yield bond issues in 1992 exceeded $39 billion, and underwriting fees surpassed $800 million. Fees for such securities typically ran at 2.3 percent of a bond's value. This rate compares with 0.5 percent for an investment-grade bond. Given a choice, there is little doubt which type of bond a bank would prefer to underwrite. Enlargement of the product mix also shifts the banks' business risks away from money-lending to wholesaling financial services. Income sources shift from interest to fees when banks offer stocks, bonds, and cash management.

How "Cross-Selling" Works

To illustrate the principles involved in "cross-selling," consider the following example. A firm designs a program to market retirement funds to its one million customers who already own funds, but no IRA. In keeping with a widespread practice of ranking database names, all customers are separated into five equal groups of 200,000. This ranking is done by matching geodemographic data with internal information, and constructing a customer profile.

These groups are then assigned probabilities of responding to this special offer. To make the offer more attractive to customers, the firm eliminates all sales charges and service fees. Although transaction data are collected and maintained at the individual level, buying probabilities refer to the group. No predictive system can as yet fine-tune response for a particular person with any degree of accuracy.

By inserting the promotional material into quarterly statements, marketing costs to these one million customers are held to $.40 per unit, or $400,000. These costs include creative expenses, paper, printing, inserting, and sending out prospectuses to interested customers. Though group response rates differ, the firm assumes marketing costs are equal for each group.

The firm estimates the overall response rate for the IRA promotion at 5.8 percent, or 58,000 buyers. Further suppose the average investment of buyers amounts to $1,500, and first year net profits total $180,000 on new sales, exclusive of marketing costs. Sales to the 58,000 buyers would then bring in $580,000 of gross profits. Deducting marketing costs of $400,000 yields $180,000 net. The next table shows response rates and profits that are credited to each of the five segments of 200,000 each. All figures in Table 7–1 are hypothetical, but the example aptly demonstrates the principle of selling new services to customers.

Table 7–1 is based on costs of a single promotion yielding a one-year profit. It shows that:

- mailout to the top 60 percent of the list garners more profits than mailing to everyone. The top 60 percent produces net profits of $240,000.
- Mailing to everyone lowers profits by $60,000. The less responsive segments, those with buying probabilities of less than .06, simply lose money.

If a differential response exists among buyers—and the database adequately reflects this—a company has the capacity to expand profits. Let's look again at Table 7–1.

- The number of buyers—and sales volume—increases as mailings are expanded.
- But the growth of sales and profits proceeds at a decreasing rate. For example, the top segment produces $120,000 in net profits, the second best yields $80,000, and so forth.
- In theory, total profits reach their peak when marginal expenses equal incremental returns. At that point, every dollar of cost would bring in exactly a dollar of profits.

The five basic propositions for applying marginal theories in marketing to customer databases are summarized as follows:

1. Demand is not uniform. It varies among customers.

2. Databases can be constructed to forecast customer probabilities of acquiring additional services.

Table 7-1. *Hypothetical Example of IRA Offer to Customers*

Group	Probability of Buying	No. of Buyers	Net Profits	Cumulative Profits
1	.100	20,000	$120,000	$120,000
2	.080	16,000	80,000	200,000
3	.060	12,000	40,000	240,000
		Cutoff Point		
4	.030	6,000	(20,000)	220,000
5	.020	4,000	(40,000)	180,000
Total	.058	58,000		

3. When customers are grouped by these probabilities, a database is divided into hierarchical classes with different response rates.

4. A company communicates first with the best customers and works progressively down to less-likely buyers.

5. Offers cease where the incremental cost of marketing equals the incremental profits the effort generates.

These marginal ideas are visualized by the generalized response and profit curves shown in Figure 7–1. For illustrative purposes, the graphs are drawn to fit the data used as an example in Table 7–1.

The upper graph displays a sales response curve. Sales rise as mailings grow, but revenue increases at a decreasing rate. Mathematically, the sales function takes the shape of a second-degree polynomial: R (revenue) = ßϒ log M (mailings). The symbol ßϒ denotes the intercept on the graph, which is close to zero. It indicates few mailings are needed to begin making sales. Based on the average response in Table 7–1, every 17 solicitations bring in a sale.

A convex-shaped sales curve implies a differential response among customers. As offers go out to less-likely buyers, response rates get progressively lower. Maximum profits occur at point E. Given the assumptions and response probabilities made in the construction of Table 7–1, the firm reaches point E by mailing to 60 percent of the customer database. At that point, the last sale is a breakeven proposition. Its marketing cost equals marginal revenue, leaving no profits.

The graphs in Figure 7–1 are drawn as if the statistical data were continuous. They are not. In our example, response refers to the average of each quintal. This is why the true profit maximization point is seldom, or ever, achieved. We cannot accurately predict the probability of a single individual responding to an offer. But the group approach is a useful guide to decision making. In our exam-

Figure 7-1. Illustration of the Marginal Principle

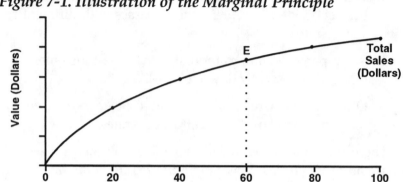

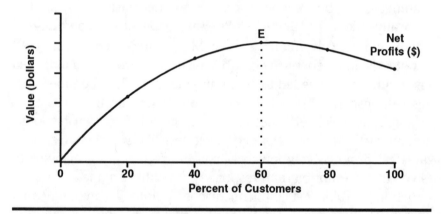

ple, mailings beyond the 60 percent mark would bring in more revenue, but no profit.

The crux of the matter is how to determine point E. The 60 percent is only an estimate or reference point. Actual response may exceed or fall below expectations. It may therefore prove expedient to send out offers sequentially, reducing the size of batch mailings as we approach point E.

Options and Tradeoffs

The sales response model depicted in Figure 7–1 implies a static business environment. Only a given response curve automatically determines a mailing cutoff point, and hence the extent of marketing efforts.

However, what would happen if profit margins varied? How would increases or decreases in profit margins affect a firm's marketing intensity?

An increase in profit margins shifts the area of maximum returns to higher levels on the sales response curve (see Figure 7–1). This would also increase the number of mailings because the higher margins lower the breakeven. In contrast, a decline in profit margins would have an opposite effect on how a firm uses its marketing resources.

For example, Table 7–1 shows that mailing to the fourth quintal would lose $20,000. But if the profit margin were to rise from $10 to $13.50 per sale, the company would find it worthwhile to market IRA funds to the less desirable fourth segment of the database. That effort would produce an additional $1,000 net profit for the year. Instead of sending out solicitations to 60 percent of its customers, it would pay to mail offers to 80 percent of the database.

Cost Reductions

Cost reductions or revenue enhancements increase profit margins, and there are many ways to accomplish this goal. Since resources are limited, the management of financial services firms often face various tradeoffs among options. Capital budgeting is a solution many firms have tried. This budgeting system involves large outlays, and various departments compete with each other for these limited funds. Capital budgets are used for two purposes—cost reduction and revenue enhancement.

Capital expenditures to reduce costs apply to both operations and marketing. Imaging technology, involving costly installations, promises banks significant savings from check processing. Similarly, ATMs appeal to banks because they promise to reduce labor costs. These electronic self-service systems are credited with eliminating about 80,000 positions in 1991–1992.

Technology also can be used to lower the cost of sales. A full-blown "marketing and sales productivity" system (MSP) promises benefits ranging from handling transactions more efficiently to reducing personal selling costs. An integrated MSP system supporting 500 sales people can cost more than $5 million. These sales-automation systems originated in manufacturing, and their adoption has been extremely slow in the financial service industry. A Harvard Business School-supported survey among 280 executives indicates an adoption rate of less than 7 percent, an extremely low incidence.

Increasing Revenue

Technology is sometimes used to increase revenue, like developing a computerized trading program. Revenue benefits from technology, however, are usually indirect. For example, several mutual fund companies developed software to assist in stock selection. They hoped that a higher return would attract more investors, or bring in more funds per investor. But who is to be credited for any revenue increases? Was the increase in sales caused by marketing efforts, more adroit trading, or automated stock selection systems? Since investments in technology and information work on sales indirectly, their revenue effects are difficult to demonstrate.

Essentially, marketing attempts to influence the sales response curve by changing customers' behavior. Efforts are "expensed" over the short term. Marketing seeks to increase profit margins by such non-technological solutions as:

- improving creativity in advertising presentations;
- selecting media more effectively;
- targeting would-be buyers more proficiently;
- "positioning" offers in ways more meaningful to buyers;

- creating value-added services to differentiate financial offerings; and
- achieving greater effectiveness and wider scope in distribution channels.

To sum up: both short-term and long-term budgeting increase profit margins in two ways: by cutting costs and by bringing in more revenue. The results apply to both technical and non-technological programs. This is visualized in the next diagram, Figure 7–2.

Tradeoffs and Complements

Marketing to database customers is primarily a revenue-generating activity. These expenses always involve tradeoffs of various kinds. Generous budgets created to enlarge a distribution network might leave insufficient outlays for upgrading data processing. A large capital expenditure for systems development and computer upgrading might mean belt tightening in the area of selling expenses. A large sales and advertising campaign might impede acquisition of hardware equipment. Marketers must justify budgets in terms of savings, revenue, and profitability.

Yet cost reduction and revenue generation often complement each other. By lowering operating costs and passing them on to their customers, discount brokerages generate revenue faster than full service brokers. Discounters today service more than three

Figure 7-2. Ways of Increasing Profit Margins

	Results	
Main Method	**Reducing Costs**	**Increasing Revenue**
Technical	Hardware Installation Software Development	Software Development Market Research
Operational	Restructuring "Reengineering" Cost Control	Ad effectiveness Sales effectiveness New product output Channel management

million investors, roughly 25 percent of all individual trading. In the mid-1980s only 15 percent of individual trading was through discount brokers.

Now firms find new sources or revenue by exploiting communications' technology. They can trade worldwide, 24 hours a day. Continuous improvements in computers and software have done more than lower processing costs. They have enabled financial firms to handle a vastly greater volume of transactions, and to bring out more new services and product enhancements.

Sometimes one cannot tell what task or what department in a company triggered a revenue increase. For example, Mastercard's Maestro, a software system, lets retailers deduct purchases directly from checking accounts. By the end of February, 1993, Mastercard had issued three million of such debit cards. Who was responsible for the increased revenue, the technicians who developed the Maestro program or the marketing people who sold it? Obviously, technicians do not sell. But marketers must have a salable product. Unless different groups work together, a firm cannot get the best results from varied efforts. Consequently, complements co-exist with tradeoffs, and rivalry with cooperation.

A Matter of Emphasis

While management consultants regard togetherness as a corporate virtue, collegiality does not mean equality in decision making. Different tasks are assigned different levels of importance within any organization. The exact importance given to any activity depends on the corporate culture and its nature of the financial services. Corporations are hierarchical organizations, and functions most associated with increases in income receive the highest priorities.

When competitive services display minor differences, emphasis rests on technologically-produced cost reduction. Mastercard and Visa, the two major credit card associations, see their core business as processing transactions for card issuers and making payments to retailers. Under these conditions, cost reductions lead to lower charges to clients.

Efficiency gives these organizations competitive advantages. Both organizations also try to make their cards unique. Mastercard International, for example, spruced up the card's orange and ocher logo and runs "image" advertising. However, results from these promotional efforts remain obscure. In 1992 Mastercard touted its cards on the air as "smart money." Did these advertisements convince television viewers that Visa or American Express cards are not as smart? Did Mastercard's advertising campaign increase customer usage of its credit cards? And by how much? The effect, if there is one, is difficult to prove.

Mastercard's share of market in 1992 grew by an unimpressive three tenths of a percent in terms of dollar volume. But that entire increase can be attributed to Mastercard's association with nonbanks, which Visa energetically opposed. General Motors, for example, had 4.5 million cards outstanding by the end of 1992, all of them Mastercards. The GE Rewards and H&R Block cards are exclusively Mastercard. AT&T has emerged as the largest Mastercard issuer, surpassing Citibank. Unlike Visa, Mastercard gave seats on its Board of Directors to companies outside the banking business, such as AT&T, GE, and Household International. Mastercard's warm reception of nonbank credit card issuers, not advertising, was responsible for its revenue increases.

Nor was Mastercard alone in its failure to demonstrate revenue accruals from advertising. American Express, with a much larger advertising budget, found prestige a hard sell and brand loyalty of little benefit in a fiercely competitive environment.

In 1992, it stopped an income decline by wooing retailers with better terms, not by "forcing" distribution with TV saturation campaigns. Advertising did not pressure retailers to accept American Express cards, because buyers did not demand that retailers do so. Ownership of all purpose credit cards averages about 3.7 cards per cardholder. Since holders of bank credit cards outnumber those holding travel and entertainment cards by about four to one, multiple card ownership is probably higher for American Express customers. If merchants don't accept one card, buyers can easily substitute another card that is accepted. Unlike a well-known defunct cigarette ad, customers would rather switch than fight.

When profitability depends on performance, companies compete on the basis of technology and information. Full service brokers can command higher commissions because they supply clients with marketing research and recommendations.

Of course, the recommended stocks must yield better-than--average results. Firms that do proprietary trading gear remuneration to individual trader performance. Mutual funds rely on fund managers, and also reward market analysts with key positions in the company. Banks, insurance companies, and financial firms that derive revenue from investment and trading place utmost value on technology, information acquisition, and market research. By demonstrating a consistent above-average performance, Fidelity Magellan became the largest mutual fund in the United States. Its top spot is well deserved, for when a mutual fund ceases to provide good returns, redemptions quickly exceed new investments.

Sometimes a firm must choose between performance and sales. This happened in 1992, when mountains of cash flowed out of CDs into equity funds which yielded higher returns.

A substantial number of mutual funds closed their doors to new investors when they thought that the burgeoning quantity of cash threatened performance. Most of these funds invested in small-company stocks. Funds that restricted new customers included such top performers as Janus Twenty, Fidelity's Low Priced Stock Fund, Oppenheimer Global Bio-Tech Fund, Babson Enterprise Fund, and Skyline Special Equities Fund. Managements that specialize in small company investments operate in thin markets and adhere to sharp limits on the number of companies their portfolios contain. In that way, they don't overweigh their portfolios to the extent where one company can push up the price.

The major problem facing marketing is uncertain returns. For example, cost-reduction programs set proposals in precise terms of dollar outlays and resulting cash flow. A proposal for a bank imaging system can fairly well estimate the investment in hardware and software. It can also reasonably calculate expected benefits from that investment, such as added processing capability, operating expenses, and projected savings. The entire operation is virtually self contained under internal control.

The results from revenue-generating activities, however, are more nebulous. Promotion and advertising are particularly unpredictable. Buying behavior is only weakly related to selling actions. Marketing influences sales in varying degrees, but it cannot dictate how markets behave. A marketing program cannot mandate that customers buy so much of this and so much of that. Consequently, past performance is not consistent with future results. A promotion that worked a few months ago may not work today. An ad that elicited a good response in the past may encounter apathy now. Finance executives are understandably reluctant to embrace a conventional wisdom that sees revenue-generating efforts in terms of John Wanamaker's often quoted aphorism: "I know that half my advertising works, but I don't know which half."

Multistage Selling

Many efforts to sell to existing database customers, as well as to noncustomers, are not one-shot solicitations. A large number of financial services employ marketing programs where solicitations are only preliminary endeavors, presale steps. Some of these programs are mandated by government regulation. A mutual fund advertising to new shareholders solicits only an expression of interest from would-be investors. An affirmative response triggers a second mailing, which includes a prospectus and an application. Lately, the SEC has proposed selling certain mutual funds directly without first having to mail out a prospectus.

Similarly, credit card solicitations are only a prelude to qualifying potential customers. Applications are usually checked for credit worthiness before accounts are opened for qualified customers. Firms selling financial services to businesses solicit inquiries, often following up requests for literature with telephone calls and personal visits. Insurance companies and brokerage houses also track leads with sales calls and further mailouts.

Because the initial response serves as a screening device, these marketing programs must be based on total costs. The largest part of selling costs may come later, particularly in marketing to business customers.

For example, suppose a mailing to 10,000 business firms brings in 800 inquiries. This amounts to an 8 percent response rate, and can be evaluated in terms of cost-per-inquiry. But suppose follow up calls by sales personnel result in 160 sales. That is, 20 percent of inquiries are converted to sales (160/800= .20). That means that the initial mailing resulted in a sales rate of only 1.6 percent (160/10,000=.016).

The important figure is derived from costs of the initial contact and subsequent calls. Evaluating this twin-phased cost can be described mathematically as follows:

$TC = (Cm/Rm)CR + Cs/S$, where

TC = Total cost of a sale

Cm = Costs of the initial contact

Rm = Response to the initial contact

CR = Conversion rate, or sales as a percentage of response

Cs = Costs of follow up selling

S = Number of sales

This equation reflects the common practice of assessing each part of a multi-stage program as though each phase were independent of the other. In many instances this may not be the case. For example, an ad may pique readers' curiosity and get a large number of inquiries from people who are not serious prospects. If all these leads were followed up with sales calls, either personally or by telephone, costs of the second stage may rise sharply. Contrarily, an ad may discourage poor prospects from responding, and the initial contact garners a low initial response, but the follow-up yields a high sales conversion rate. Cost distribution among the marketing stages determines which way is best—either getting the most leads you can or making lead generation selective. High lead-to-sales ratios may be justified when the service bears a high price, operates with high margins, or tends to have a high incidence of repeat usage. Financial services with opposite characteristics should have low lead-to-sales ratios.

Continuity Programs in Database Marketing

Financial services are rendered on a one-shot or continuous basis. Tax preparations and financial consulting can be one-time events; they stand alone. Although the company may contact the customer again, he or she may decline to use the same service provider. Past action is discrete, totally disconnected from anything done now or in the future. While satisfied customers may come back, future decisions have little relation to previous ones.

Most financial services, however, are a continuously used product. They perform over time. Some are open-ended, and customers determine the volume and timing of transactions. Checking accounts, mutual funds, brokerage, and credit cards represent this type of service. Other services are for fixed periods of time. Insurance policies, annuities, CDs, mortgages, and loans are fixed-term arrangements. The service contract covers a fixed period of time in which to meet obligations. A fixed-term service must be renewed in order to continue, such as insurance policies and certain forms of loans.

Regardless of time-related terms, all databases track transactions and update the financial status of customers. But performing the basic operational functions does not mean a company is doing database marketing. Operations and marketing are quite distinct from each other. Processing transactions is considered a "back-end" or back-office function. It is analogous to fulfillment in a goods-producing company, and is often linked with customer service.

"Back-end" departments are cost centers. They generate no revenue as they do not create transactions. They simply execute customers' orders, send out bills, accept payments, and adjust accounts. Customers observe only the results of these operations. They are seldom concerned with the mechanics of how their balance sheets or buy-and-sell stock confirmations are brought about. Many of these operations are technical in nature, and some are performed wholly by machines, such as ATMs at banks. Customers care only that ATMs work in certain ways, not how they work.

Other "back-end" operations are considered "trade secrets," such as computer-aided forecasting systems. Clients are appraised of the technical methods, and might even be instructed on how to use them. But they do not receive a course in how systems work internally. They do not run company computers, and probably have no desire to do so. Their only concern is that the machines don't make mistakes. In short, customers are largely divorced from "back-end" operations.

Many "back-end" activities enhance customer satisfaction, and they can affect customer loyalty and sales volume. But, revenue effects are indirect and difficult to measure, while expenses are more tangible evidence of company performance. Since the "back office" represents a cost center, the primary concern of those departments is cost-reduction at given levels of service.

Marketing programs are "front end " activities. The firm communicates with prospective customers, either through promotional media or face-to-face. The aim is revenue generation. When databases are used for that objective, programs are designed primarily to maintain or increase sales.

Many marketing practitioners describe these dealings with database customers as "relationship marketing." This form of marketing seeks to create long-lasting incentives for doing business.

Like most businesses, financial services thrive on repeat transactions. Acquiring a new customer frequently costs ten times as much as retaining an existing one. It therefore makes good business sense to develop long-term relationships with customers in order to build a bridge of trust and respect.

In *The Complete Database Marketer*,[1] Arthur M. Hughes argues that building relationships is akin to running a club: members "are your customers for life." Echoing the conventional wisdom, Hughes also maintains that by proper use of databases, firms can build relationships that will instill customer loyalty and insulate a firm's customers from competitive lures.

Benefits of relational marketing are often enunciated with fervor, as though they were "self-evident" truths. Yet this rhetoric gives rise to a number of unresolved issues.

- Can any program insulate customers from competition? This is sheer hyperbole.
- No one disputes the fact that customer loyalty produces benefits. But the key issue is: how does a company build customer loyalty?
- Are there universal principles for developing loyalty? Or are financial services so diverse that they require completely different methods? We reject universals in favor of an individualized, trial-and-error approach.
- What price customer loyalty? Building loyalty costs money, and returns must be commensurate with costs. If they are not, it is better to operate on a program-by-program basis, where each promotion must pay for itself.
- To calculate whether benefits are worth the costs, we must estimate the value of a customer.

In addition to such questions, relationship marketing is not a uniform activity. It embraces sets of very different, though related, goals. The prime tasks can be enumerated as follows:

- Raising customer retention rates
- Increasing transaction value per customer
- Selling customers a variety of different services

---

[1]   Arthur M. Hughes, *Complete Database Marketer: Tapping Your Customer Base to Maximize Sales and Increase Profits,* Chicago, IL: Probus Publishing Company, 1991.

  • Upgrading customer service to build loyalty

Customer Retention Rates

Many financial services represent fixed-period, positive option programs. Contracts, such as insurance and annuities, must be renewed
at fixed points in time. Marketing's role in these transactions is often
passive, serving in a routine order-taking capacity. Customers receive notices of termination and requests to renew contracts. Terms
may be the same or altered. When contracts involve small sums,
business is usually conducted by mail, and often carried out by
operating personnel who are not involved in the marketing effort.
Salespeople are very interested with renewals when sums are large,
as those of organizational clients. Here contracts are complex and
require extensive negotiations. Marketing personnel are similarly
involved in customer renewals when firms rely on agent distribution channels.

Regardless of customer size, type of service, or methods of
distribution, back-end operations are often a determining factor in
customer retention. These back-end functions relate to performance.
A homeowner who feels that an insurance adjuster shortchanged
him, on a damage claim will think twice about renewing a contract.
A shareholder may decide to sell out when a mutual fund performs
poorly. A bank depositor or an annuitant may chose not to renew
a CD when interest falls to unsatisfactory levels.

In some instances, financial firms employ a negative rather than
a positive option: if the customer does not say "No," renewal is
automatic. Credit cards and CDs are cases in point. But the customer
still has the final word on the matter. He or she can say, "No."

Customer Transaction Volume

When a financial service generates revenue for customers, such as
interest, dividends, or capital gains, good results encourage more
investments. A mutual fund with high returns will find customers
adding money to that fund or adding the fund to their portfolio if
they don't already own it.

A multiple product policy also tends to increase sales per customer. When interest rates dropped in the early 1990s, bank customers exited from CDs. Banks who could offer equity funds as alternatives were not hurt much. In fact, the most rapid growth of mutual funds in 1992 was through banks. During the first half of that year, banks sold $23 billion of mutual funds, either their own or those of others. This figure represented 14 percent of total stock and bond sales, and compares with $28 billion banks sold in all of 1991.

Cross-selling also is related to customer retention. Insurance companies found that the more policies a customer owns, the higher is the retention rate. A person who owns both car and home insurance from the same company is more apt to renew both policies. The same idea can be extended to other products. An annuity holder has a higher probability of renewing a life insurance policy with the same company. Depositors are more likely to renew credit cards from the bank in which they keep deposits

Selling Additional Services

Cross-selling raises several issues. Some services are substitutes for each other, such as "families of mutual funds." A switch from one fund to another merely shifts money within a company's coffers. But other types of cross-selling generate incremental sales because the financial products are unrelated to each other. For example, home insurance and car insurance are such services. When a car owner takes out a home insurance policy with the same company, it is as if the company acquired a new customer in a different line of business. While the customer already exists in the company database, the home insurance department can properly regard the sale as a new account, and the buyer as a new customer.

Many financial firms employ a concept described as "life-time value of a customer " in setting up marketing budgets. The customer is regarded as a long-term asset, and costs of acquiring that customer is handled as an investment. When cross-selling occurs, the buyer would probably be regarded in the same way as a new customer. The subject of "lifetime value" is discussed in greater detail in Chapter 9.

Customer Service

To many business gurus, customer service is the cement that binds customers to commercial organizations. But *how* a service is rendered depends upon *what* is being performed. Servicing a mortgage or a life insurance policy is quite different from servicing customers of mutual funds, brokerage houses, or credit card issuers. Some services emphasize back-end operations, while others stress front-end servicing. Chapter 10 discusses the subject of customer service in much greater detail.

Summary

Though customer databases are used for various purposes, this chapter emphasizes marketing. Selling to existing customers often involves cross-selling via direct marketing. This approach can build income by:

- enlarging the product mix,
- lowering selling costs,
- using existing assets to achieve economies in cost of sales, and
- reducing income volatility.

Cross-selling, in particular, is well suited to the application of "marginal" principals. A key factor is avoiding incremental marketing costs that do not yield commensurate returns.

Proper application of "marginal" concepts to marketing, however, must account for much more than sales and selling expenses. Unit pricing and nonselling costs are vital considerations. Capital budgets to reduce operating costs must be considered in conjunction with marketing expenses. Since "back-end" and "front-end" activities are interdependent, marketing must work together with other departments. Only an integrated corporate program can attain the yet unfulfilled promises of "marginal" theorists.

8

Acquiring New Customers

Because customer databases deteriorate over time, financial firms must constantly seek new customers. To solicit new buyers, companies offering financial services rely heavily on direct marketing.

Though mail and telephone are the mainstays of direct marketing, general media also have important roles in promotions to new customers. This chapter delves into direct marketing applications, such as:

- List "enhancements" in direct mail operations—when they work and when they don't
- Types of mailing lists and their uses
- Problems of name duplication when renting mailing lists
- Lead-qualifying techniques in marketing to business
- Effective uses of inbound and outbound telemarketing
- Generating leads in newspapers, publications, and television
- Problems of low response in direct marketing operations

While cultivating existing customers is a focal point of database usage, acquiring new customers is a necessary complement. At any given point, total revenue represented by a customer database equals business of retained customers plus business generated from new customers. This can be expressed by the simple equation:

$$\text{Revenue} = \left(\begin{array}{c} \text{Retained} \\ \text{Customers} \end{array} + \begin{array}{c} \text{New} \\ \text{Customers} \end{array} \right) \times \begin{array}{c} \text{Revenue Inflow} \\ \text{per Customer} \end{array}$$

This bookkeeping concept implies that by itself, cultivating present customers is not enough to sustain a company's growth and well-being. The acquisition of new customers is needed. The main reason is that the number of customers diminishes over time. Deteriorating databases must be sustained by infusions of new customers. While higher retention rates suggest a company can do well with fewer new customers, fresh batches of buyers are constantly in demand.

Financial service firms rely heavily on direct marketing to acquire new customers. What is direct marketing? It is paid-for communication in media that solicits a direct, measurable response. There are basically three kinds of response solicited: a sale, an inquiry, or a visit to the premises of the seller.

Many financial services require more than one contact. Mutual funds cannot be sold without a customer first reading a prospectus, though the SEC is presently exploring the relaxation of this rule. An insurance company or its agent must convey the terms of a policy before a sale takes place. Brokerage houses usually send applications that spell out key terms to new customers. In all these situations, a direct response solicitation is only a prelude to further contact. As such, the initial communication invites an expression of interest in the offer or a request for information. Direct sales without follow-ups normally involve financial products which are simple and familiar to almost everyone, such as CDs or credit cards.

Direct marketing that seeks to promote visits to a seller's premises is relatively infrequent. While customers commonly visit banks to conduct their business, retail banking does not rely on direct marketing to stimulate customer traffic. Rather, local banks and branch offices advertise in general media, such as newspapers, because their markets are not selective. Retail services are so widely used that true segments do not exist.

In consumer markets, financial services generally appeal to upscale segments of the population. That's where the money is. Firms therefore, eschew advertising in general media, such as television. Some financial segments border on mass markets, such as credit cardholders. People carrying plastic cards number more than 100 million, according to the Nilson Company. The largest bank card issuer, Citicorp boasts of servicing more than 30 million customers. Nevertheless, financial service companies concentrate on media that allow commercial messages to be directed to particular individuals rather than to general audiences. Advertising to general audiences incurs high proportions of "media waste," defined as readers or viewers who are disinterested in a commercial message or are not prospects for the service.

Direct mail and telephone are the two main pillars supporting the media structure of direct marketing. Mail and telephone, unlike general media, possess a quality which, for lack of a better word, we call "specificity." A mailing piece goes to a designated person at a specific address. A telephone call similarly is directed to a particular home. But specificity does not eliminate all media waste. A mailer cannot guarantee that a recipient will not consign the mailing piece to the trash unopened or unread. A telemarketer cannot be sure who will answer at the other end. But direct mail and telephone are considered to have lower incidents of "media waste" than general media.

About 85 percent of direct marketing expenditures find their way into these two media. As estimated by Robert J. Coen of McCann-Erickson, Inc., 1991 spending in direct mail totaled almost $24.5 billion. This figure averaged 19 percent of all U.S. ad expenditures in measured media (see Appendix 8).

Direct Mail

Direct mail is probably the most flexible of all media. In contrast to general media, mail is perfectly divisible. TV broadcasts deliver audiences on an all-or-nothing basis. Print media sells batches of circulation. Mailings are regulated by neither audiences nor circulation, by neither ratings nor a fixed number of copies. The marketer precisely controls the amount of transmitted messages, and so exercises better control over expenses. The firm can send out as many mailouts as it wishes, from several dozen to several million. There are no limitations or cutoff points.

Mailings can go out sequentially or all at once. A sequential mailing program reduces risk by having future mail contingent upon results of past batches. The marketer specifies the size and timing of each batch, and has the opportunity of making continuous modifications in the advertising program.

Another advantage of mail over general media is better selectivity. Firms can segment retail markets in almost any pattern they desire. They can direct mailings to geographic units with preselected demographics or lifestyles. These units can be as small as a Census block and postal route or as large as a county or Census region. Mail overcomes constraints of time and distance by funneling commercial messages to known prospects via the U.S. Postal Service.

Finally, direct mail imposes fewer restrictions in conveying an offer. The typical TV commercial lasts 30 seconds, and not much information can be presented in that time. Costs for longer commercials are prohibitive on all but the lowest-rated cable shows. Magazine and newspaper space can be expanded when offers require a lot of detail. But reader interest wanes as the text expands, and costs rise disproportionately in relation to response. In direct mail, costs of long letters and informative brochures rise more slowly than increments in data.

This communication feature of direct mail has a special significance to financial firms. Conventional wisdom among direct marketers holds that success depends more on the goodness of the offer than on anything else. This belief is particularly true of financial services, which are bought on a more rational basis than are most other articles of commerce. Financial services require "reason why" copy, which implies that promotional material contain a relatively large amount of text, and even statistical graphs and tables. Mailing pieces and brochures can present this material in black and white, and so save printing costs. Except for newspapers, color advertisements are either mandatory or expedient. The television medium runs entirely in color. Though magazines have lower rates for black and white, readers are more attracted by color. In direct mail the message stands alone, with no competition from other ads. Color adds nothing to a presentation of an offer for financial services. Black and white reduces printing costs while putting greater emphasis on content of the offer.

Consumer Lists

In order to mail, we need a list of names and addresses. Mailing to "occupant" violates a prime directive of direct mail: personalize the correspondence, or else response rates will fall.

To acquire customers not already on a company database, you must rely on external lists. There are two kinds: response and compiled.

Response lists are composed of people who transacted business by mail. Thus, a response list is someone else's house list. Owners have the right to approve or disapprove every rental order, and usually will not rent their lists to direct competitors.

Since responders have greater likelihoods of purchasing than those who don't buy through the mail, response lists cost more. However, some relationship should exist between lists and offers. Buyers of prescription drugs may not make appropriate "targets" for brokerage houses and mutual funds. But they may be valued by health insurers. Credit card issuers and insurance firms seem to make heavy use of catalog lists. But banks advertising home equity loans may bypass catalog list vendors.

Compiled lists are extensive compilations from such sources as telephone directories, voter rolls, and auto registrations. The major compilers are Donnelley Marketing, Metromail, and R.L Polk, which together account for about 90 percent of all compiled list rentals. The most authoritative source of list information is Standard Rate & Data Service, which publishes *Direct Mail Lists Rates and Data*.

Compilers offer numerous "enhancements" to their lists, such as demographic and lifestyle data. This feature permits financial service firms to select names that match desired profiles. The enormous size of compiled lists ensures that selective processes end up with "high quality" names in substantial quantities.

There are smaller compiled lists, such as those of new home buyers. Names on smaller lists usually have common characteristics, so do not offer enhancements. But these lists work well when they possess a dominant characteristic that a financial firm seeks.

Business Lists

Business lists combine both responder and compiled names. But enhancements, which are essentially segmentation techniques, are not important in business-to-business marketing. Business services are bought quite differently from the way consumers buy. Consequently, the type of list available to a business mailer is quite different from that of a firm marketing consumer services.

One big difference is in responder lists. A previous mail response by a business prospect may have little to do with the purchase probability of a company. Often, "buyer" lists are small, and difficult to obtain for specific services. For example, a company that just engaged a firm to manage retirement funds is not likely to be a "hot prospect" for another retirement management firm. A company that has just selected an underwriter for its bond issue is no longer a prospect for another underwriter. A buyer of computer processing has already made the selection, and is not apt to buy a parallel service. So-called "hot-line buyers" of goods have no counterparts in financial services.

Publication subscribers constitute another form of "responder" mailing lists. While subscribers responded to mail solicitations of publishers, they have not necessarily responded to an offer for a vendor's product. A subscriber list represents people interested in the editorial content of a given publication.

There are two broad categories of business publications: vertical and horizontal.

The vertical publication gears its editorial to all aspects of an industry. Subscribers to a horizontal publication work in various industries. *Iron Age* or *Advertising Age* are published for people in industry regardless of this position. The *Journal of Accountancy* gets mailed to accounting professionals irrespective of the industry in which they work. *Lab Management* caters to technicians and technologists working in various types of organizations, such as hospitals, medical centers, clinics, pharmaceutical firms, and independent laboratories.

Financial firms selling an industry-specific service would rent names from vertical magazine publishers. Most financial services appeal to a wide range of industries, and subscription lists come mainly from horizontal publications.

Many business publications screen subscribers, requiring them to meet certain criteria before they are added to the mailing list. Publications that do so offer names classified in a number of categories. The most common options are lists of job titles, job functions, and industrial sector such as Standard Industrial Classification (SIC).

A firm must exercise care when using subscription lists for direct mail. Areas of concern include:

- Qualifying data may be inaccurate. Many subscribers exaggerate their titles and decision-making authority, especially in controlled-circulation publications. Subscribers often lie about their jobs in order to get free copies. List brokers and other vendors don't disclose negatives, since it is in their interest to sell names. There is thus no way to ascertain the veracity of subscriber information without some kind of testing or research. However, returns of such research must justify their cost.
- A publisher may not update subscriber names frequently enough to keep classification data current for direct marketing purposes. For example, people's titles and job functions—and even the company they work for—undergo continuous change. The frequency of updating can often be checked from audit statements.

- Job title and job functions can vary dramatically from company to company. A vice president at a bank may be much farther down the ladder than a vice president of a brokerage house. This is also true for compiled lists.

Compiled lists are usually large, and often contain the same classifications appended to names as subscription lists: title, job function, company size, and SIC code. These names can be obtained at the lowest cost. Because information is derived from different sources with varying degrees of accuracy, it may be necessary to expend additional money on list testing.

Merge-Purge Techniques

Mailers do not want individuals to receive more than one copy of the same mailing piece. To prevent multiple mailings, firms employ a merge-purge technique.

An obvious advantage of eliminating duplication is cost reduction. Besides saving on mailing expenses, merge-purge distinguishes customers from prospects by matching outside lists with the customer database. For many reasons, mailers may not want to send solicitation pieces to their customers. Buyers who appear on other lists also may have higher buying probabilities, and a firm might make special efforts to promote its services to these "mail junkies."

The first step in merge-purge is defining the duplication unit. Is it an individual or the household? Some financial houses send out multiple mailings when individuals in the same home have separate accounts. Most firms, however, prefer the household as the relevant unit.

Duplication of business-to-business mailing lists poses completely different problems from those of consumers lists. Demographic matching is unusual in business-to-business marketing. A company's' direct mail may go to various addresses, some going to corporate headquarters, some to different units, and some to different post office boxes.

Business lists also contain many inaccuracies owing to changes in jobs, titles, and companies. Merge-purge techniques are used less frequently in business, and require more personal attention than the wholly computerized methods in consumer areas. For these reasons, merge-purge systems apply more widely to consumer markets, and this discussion will be confined to retail services.

A variety of software programs are available for merge-purge operations. Some programs use match codes, such as a zip code, digits from the address, and a fixed number of letters from a person's name and street. Some software uses every element of a mailing label to determine a match. Some programs run on phonetics rather than spelling, and some match names and addresses by complicated scoring formulas.

Regardless of methodology, errors are unavoidable. Kestnbaum & Company found wide quality differences among 25 merge-purge programs it studied. Problems ranged from shortcomings in computer programs to poor conditions of the lists. Compiled lists in particular show large variability because they are put together from wide varieties of sources.

For example, here are several hypothetical examples of possible name duplication. Can you tell which pairs are duplicates and which are not?

Example 1	John Brown 20 Russet Way Cranston, RI 02920	John Brown 20 Russet Way Cranston, RI 02920
Example 2	John Brown 20 Russet Way Cranston, RI 02920	Mary Brown 20 Russet Way Cranston, RI 02920
Example 3	Jane Little 10 Dingle Court Worchester, MA 01619	Jane Gross 10 Dingle Court Worchester, MA 01619

If individuals were the unit of comparison, practically all programs would pick Example 1 as a duplicate. Yet the names might be those of separate people, such as father and son.

Example 3 would rarely be tabbed as a match. Yet the two names may well belong to the same person. A female may keep her maiden name for business and her married name at home.

If the unit of analysis were a household, examples 1 and 2 might well be chosen as duplicates. Yet the two John Browns, father and son, might comprise separate households. Similarly, John and Mary in Example 2 might live together, being related by blood or marriage. Or they might comprise entirely separate households, though living at the same address in a multiple-dwelling unit.

Rates and Rentals

Name duplication gives rise to a number of problems concerning list rentals. Mailers using multiple lists find the same name appearing in different places. Outside lists also contain names already existing in a customer databases. Sending individuals identical or unnecessary mailings is wasteful.

Suppose one-fourth of a rented list duplicates names of a company's database. Buying the entire outside list raises cost per name by 33 percent. Costs of postage, paper, inserting, and other production costs go up by a like percentage; the mailing acquires no new customers by soliciting people who are already customers. Should a mailer pay for useless names?

A standard arrangement is the "85 percent net name agreement." This 85 percent rule obligates the lessee to pay a minimum of 85 percent for all names on the rented list, even if the usable portion falls below the 85 percent minimum.

Minimum payments, along with other rental terms, represent asking prices. But like many business practices, almost all terms are negotiable, especially when large quantities are involved. Firms renting a million or more names can easily get minimums down to as low as 70 percent. Some large mailers can even negotiate no minimums at all. This is called a net-net agreement—mailers pay only for the names they use. Deals depend on the size of an order and negotiators' skills.

Many list renters rely on list brokers to bring together available lists. Sometimes these firms take on consulting jobs for mailers, such as list searches and evaluations. But, list brokers primarily work for list sellers, usually at a 20 percent commission on sales. Brokers present potential customers data cards which show prices and key facts about each list, such as number of names, demographic information, schedules, test arrangements, and any restrictions on the use of the list.

Data cards, however, do not contain all information a list buyer should have. They rarely if ever tell when a list was "cleaned" last. A widely accepted standard proposes "cleaning" lists four times a year. But many lists are updated much less frequently. Mailers who buy outdated lists suffer from lower response rates and large percentages of undelivered mail.

Another controversial issue is the exact definition of a responder. Some sellers maintain names on a response list despite the fact that the accounts have been inactive for years. A mailer would hardly pay a premium for such names if that information were known. A sophisticated renter should ask about these issues, and even demand evidence of list owners' veracity.

Rental agreements generate other controversies, most of which are computer-related. For example:

- A merge-purge of two outside lists finds a number of duplicates. Which list gets the total number of names reduced? One way is a 50-50 split. But if the lists are of unequal size, the smaller list will always have a larger proportion of duplicates.
- If the lists are rented at different rates, mailers prefer to credit the costlier list with duplicates. The owner of that list will scream "unfair!"
- A company matches a house list against an outside list. The firm mails the "approved" piece to unduplicated names. However, it sends a special promotion to the duplicated names, on the assumption that they are "prime prospects."

Does the renter have to pay the list owner for those names? After all, they are part of the customer database. But the mailer would not have known about his or her customers' other activities had he or she not matched the outside list with the internal one.

- A house list is matched against an outside list which has personal information about clients. Can the renter add that information to duplicates? The matching process, in effect, permits a computer to transfer information from one source to another.

- After doing a merge-purge, a firm sends out a mailing to a list devoid of duplicates. The mailer requests a record of address corrections from the post office. Who owns that information? The mailer paid for corrected addresses, but has a right only to names that responded to the offer.

- A firm employs an outside source to look up and append phone numbers to a rented list. Who owns the phone numbers? Can the mailer follow up the mailing with phone calls without paying the list owner?

Many of these questions have no precise answers. But such issues should be anticipated when renting lists, and handled when negotiating list rental contracts. It is far better to reach some agreement on such eventualities before they become controversies, rather than after.

Telemarketing

The telephone is so pervasive that we readily accept it as part of our daily lives. Homes and businesses are joined in an extensive communication network that girdles the earth. Telephone expenditures of American businesses reach astronomical sums.

Telemarketing, the application of the telephone to marketing tasks, has two forms: outbound and inbound. Firms doing outbound telemarketing contact customers and prospects. Inbound calls occur at the initiation of customers, and firms relying on such calls usually have toll-free 800 numbers.

The tasks of both forms are quite distinct. The main ones in the financial service area are listed as follows:

Outbound Tasks	Inbound Tasks
Direct selling	Order taking
Lead followups	Inquiry handling
Sales support	Customer service
Account management	

Direct Telephone Selling Techniques

The unique advantage of selling by telephone is speed. Prospects are reached instantly. There is no time lag between transmission and response to a sales message.

One form of direct selling is the "cold canvass." This technique is sometimes used by insurance agents and brokerage firms, particularly to special offers and promotions. But the "cold canvass" is not common in selling financial services. "Cold" calling sometimes appears when business is low. For example, when sales of new securities lagged in 1990, stockbrokers found themselves making unsolicited calls to strangers. But these practices are often associated with "boiler room" operations, and do not prove productive.

Direct telephone selling is most effective when targeting people or organizations who are already doing business with the firm. Customers consider it quite proper for full-service brokerage houses to call them with advice and special offers. This is part of the service. But this kind of direct selling actually implies cross-selling, done with existing customers, and not with merely potential ones.

Lead Follow-Ups

In many instances, outgoing calls are follow-ups to incoming messages, often from media other than telephone. These follow-ups take various forms.

A prospect calls an 800 number in response to an advertisement placed in electronic or printed media. The firm follows up this inquiry or request for literature with a phone call, perhaps scheduling a face-to-face meeting with a company representative. Some insurance agents use this system, claiming that the telephone produces more sales than a follow-up by mail. Sometimes, the phone follow-up is used to stimulate sales with new customers. For example, Choice credit card, issued by Citicorp, calls new customers to explain benefits and special offers.

Financial services to business often rely on personal selling to generate new business. In these situations, the telephone plays a key role in tracking and qualifying leads. According to McGraw-Hill, the typical visit to a prospect costs more than $250. Unless an order involves a substantial sum, it will not cover selling expenses. In contrast, phone calls cost between $7.50 to $15, and a telemarketer can make as many as five contacts per hour. A salesperson might take a day or more to visit the same number of prospects. It pays to substitute the telephone for personal visits, whenever possible.

Telephone solicitations can be substituted for other media in various circumstances, but two kinds of substitution occur most frequently. One relates to sales potential. The idea is to divide potential accounts by their expected sales volumes. A 10(k) retirement plan with a large number of employees promises a strong stream of revenue. In those situations, a management team would normally be assigned to solicit that business. When the expected volume of business does not appear capable of supporting personal visits, telemarketing and mail follow-ups are used to make the sale.

A related use of telephone solicitation is lead qualification. When services are sold entirely by mail, you may have no need to qualify leads, just send out the mailing with an order or application form. When services are sold by personal contact, however, qualification by telephone provides an efficient marketing tool. It identifies promising prospects, permitting the higher-paid sales personnel to spend time calling on the best leads. The least promising leads might be contacted by phone.

"Telequalifying" is performed in several ways. Many lead-generating ads contain 800 numbers. When the prospect calls, qualification can be done by the operator answering the phone. A few simple questions during the phone conversation might be enough to evaluate callers. Some companies employ computerized lead-tracking systems, sometimes called "inquiry management systems." These complicated systems permeate an entire sales process, starting with lead generation and qualification, and reaching the eventual outcome: a sale or no sale. These programs can be developed internally or contracted from an outside vendor. An elaborate system is that of SPSS, which can be adjusted to each company's operation. This phone tracking system links phone numbers to various ads, and records the number dialed, date, and time of incoming calls. The SPSS program performs complicated statistical analyses which predict prospects' buying probabilities. It then tracks their actions to their final status: are they customers or non-customers?

All lead-tracking systems require input from the sales force. But sales personnel shy away from paperwork, and think their time is better spent selling. Why, they ask, should we do clerical work dreamt up by corporate bureaucrats? When salespeople are company employees, the firm can exercise control. But when selling is done by agents or employees working on commission, cooperation is difficult to achieve. In any circumstances, a lead-tracking system should be simple and require minimal paperwork.

Inbound Calls

Using inbound telephone lines to acquire customers works only in conjunction with other media. The 800 number has become the most common method of responding to advertisements in print and on television.

Most consumers prefer to use the telephone to answer an ad. They expend less effort in making a phone call than in writing a letter or filling out a coupon. Consequently, including an 800 number to a mailing piece increases response significantly—as much as

60 percent to 80 percent. This increment, however, does not occur uniformly for all financial products, and this raises the question as to whether the additional response justifies the costs of WATS lines. The Direct Marketing Association advises testing response before making costly commitments. Because response tests are widely practiced by direct marketers, the appendix at the end of this chapter discusses the subject in more detail.

Regardless of media, incoming phone calls are mostly leads. As a lead-generating device, television requires more phone lines than print. Individuals determine the pace of reading, which takes place over a period of time. Telephone calls come in driblets. But television viewing proceeds at a pace set by the broadcaster. Audiences see commercials at the same time. Incoming calls are bunched up. Telephone equipment must be sufficient to handle peak loads if callers are not to be put on "eternity holds."

Peak loads mean empty telephone stations in off-peak hours. Heavy calling intervals and possible overloads can be reduced by a more balanced television schedule. Financial services can avoid a deluge of phone calls by proper spacing of TV commercials. Most financial services telecast on specialized cable programs, such as CNBC's "Money Line." This type of narrowcasting appeals to small audiences, and does not set off eruptions of voluminous phone calls.

General Media

General media—primarily newspapers, magazines, and television—carry only a small portion of financial service ads. These media are primarily magazines, newspapers, and television. They are "general" because their editorial matter is not directed to specific individuals. A telecaster does not control who watches a show. Nor do print media know exactly who will read. While many publications go only to subscribers, media studies suggest that the largest part of magazine readership is made up of "pass-along readers." These people are neither subscribers nor single copy buyers.

Unlike direct mail or telephone advertisements, those in general media are encased in an editorial environment. Readership and viewership of ads are in varying degrees "involuntary." Television and magazine audiences are interested in editorial content, not in ads these media carry. People "shop" the pages of newspapers, but not for financial services. "Reader shopping" in newspapers is event-related, such as a special sale, a movie, or sporting event. In general media, advertising coverage is determined by media circulation patterns, and not by marketers' specifications. To have their ads reach potential customers, advertisers commonly match media readership/viewership to their markets.

Part of general media's importance to financial services is the friendly environment they provide for "image." This can be particularly important to such financial institutions, as banks, insurance companies and credit card associations. Image advertising provides a promotional umbrella while agents or association members do the direct selling. Image advertising may also be effective when a financial service is widely used and market segments are blurred or indistinct. Television and print campaigns for financial services are most noticeable for credit cards and insurance.

General media are efficient in performing a number of direct marketing functions. These media supplement other direct marketing efforts by extending media reach. They deliver audiences that are not reached efficiently by telephone or mail. A media mix also conveys different and more varied impressions than a single medium.

Print Media

The most important print media are newspapers and magazines. There are two types of papers: local and national. The overwhelming majority of newspapers fall into the local category. Magazines are also of two types: consumer publications and the business press.

Newspapers

Newspapers are basically local media. In 1991, advertising expenditures in newspapers amounted to $30.4 billion. Of that total, $26.7 billion, or 88 percent, was local. Banks are the largest advertisers of financial services in local newspapers. Like a supermarket, a local bank draws most of its customers from the surrounding area. Since almost every household is a potential customer, newspapers are the ideal media for bank advertising. Newspaper circulation blankets local markets with high penetration. Daily newspapers reach about two-thirds of all U.S. households, with 75 percent of all readers getting their papers by in-home delivery.

Lead generation plays practically no part in bank advertising, since most customers live in close proximity to the bank. Rather, banks prefer to have customers visit the site. Advertising therefore emphasizes special events, new financial products, and attractive rates for various services.

Circulation of large metropolitan dailies usually spreads beyond the range of local customers. To reduce ads going outside the normal trading zone, a local firm or branch can buy a less-than-full circulation run of a newspaper targeting particular geographic zones. By carefully selecting geographic editions, a firm can match a newspaper's circulation to the residential patterns of its customers.

Several newspapers extend their circulations nationally, though not evenly. The most prominent are *The Wall Street Journal*, *New York Times*, and *U.S.A. Today*. Because the editorial content of *The Wall Street Journal* specializes in financial news, this newspaper has wide appeal to financial service firms that operate on a national scale. Brokerage houses and mutual funds are especially heavy advertisers in *The Journal*, and most of their ads are lead-generating devices, carrying coupons, and toll-free 800 numbers.

Magazines

There are two types of magazines, consumer and business. This designation contains ambiguities, as many "consumer" magazines are edited for business people. For example, *Time* and *Newsweek* offer demographic editions that concentrate on professional and managerial audiences. Similarly, "consumer" publications like *Fortune* and *Business Week* are edited for business-oriented audiences, and are prime vehicles for financial service firms engaging in both general and direct response advertising.

Using consumer magazines to reach business audiences exemplifies "extreme horizontalness." A horizontal magazine is one that cuts across industries and is edited for general readers rather than for narrow specialists.

Some advertising meant for business readers verges on consumer advertising, so that often it is difficult to differentiate between the two. In any event, horizontal publications usually have more media waste—that is, readership which will have no interest in buying an advertised product. Media planners may have to contend with this type of unrelated advertising in order to achieve market coverage.

The business press carries the largest chunk of magazine advertising featuring financial services to business. There are essentially three major classifications of business publications: trade, vertical, and professional.

Trade publications are merchandising vehicles, and are seldom used by financial firms unless they have a product created specifically for distributors. Vertical magazines are similarly used by financial firms when a service relates to a particular industry. Vertical publications are edited for people in an industry. *American Banker* is an example of a vertical publication. Firms wishing to cover an industry can probably reach the majority of decision makers by advertising in one or two leading vertical publications.

Professional magazines go to individuals in particular occupations. These publications appeal to firms that wish to advertise to executives performing similar functions. Many of these magazines feature reader service cards, which increase requests for information and literature.

Television

As an advertising medium, television is fragmented, and it will probably continue to be. Its main segments are network, spot, and cable.

In order to acquire customers through direct marketing, financial services use cable almost exclusively. Direct marketing, which requires longer commercials, regards neither network nor spot television as economically viable.

Cable television is an old system, initially developed to help remote areas pick up signals. But satellite broadcasting and computer technology have changed the shape of cable broadcasting. This change is still in progress. Satellites have expanded channel capacity, and, combined with computers, offer the possibility of two-way communication.

Unlike broadcast television, cable appeals to specialized audiences and uses innovative programming. One development in cable is the use of teletext, originally created by the British Broadcasting System. This process codes text material digitally, telecasts it, and decodes the messages by a set translator. Text can appear as moving type across a television screen. Some financial programs and newscasts carry these as ticker-tape stock prices.

Most financial services use cable to generate leads. Advertising intended to produce leads should adhere to these guidelines:

- We should measure returns from media expenditures in terms of cost-per-sale, not cost-per-inquiry. The lead is only a means of getting a sale.
- The program must be related to the content of the commercial. A commercial for a financial service should appear in a program geared to audiences interested in financial matters. We should not want our phones flooded with callers who have only a peripheral interest or are calling out of curiosity.
- The commercial should focus on the object of the lead, and not on the characteristics of the service. This permits the use of shorter commercials and thereby lowers cost. A lead-getting commercial can be shorter than a typical sales-getting commercial, since it does not have to spend much time "selling" a prospect or creating a transaction.

- A lead-generating commercial should give an accurate impression of the service being promoted. When creatives succumb to temptations to expand inquiries by puffery, we get high inquiry rates but low customer sign-ups. If maximizing inquiries is not the objective of an ad, it should not shout superlatives that won't be reflected in the follow-up literature, or the marketplace realities.
- Close monitoring of response is a must. Testing can yield unreliable estimates of response. In addition, scheduling patterns and frequency of telecasting also affect response, and results cannot be known before commercials are actually aired.

Direct Response

As long as direct marketing is the cornerstone of customer development, response is the name of the game. Net income accruing from new customers must exceed acquisition costs. When media are used, costs-per-response is compared with the expected income-per-response. When personal selling becomes a part of the acquisition process, order-getting costs must be factored into the calculation.

Low rate of response is the greatest problem in direct marketing. Exact figures do not exist, but the industry sets the norm at 2 percent. This rate, however, is not uniform. It varies substantially in accordance with the nature of the financial product, the contents of an offer, the markets to which the offer is directed, and the media used in conveying an offer.

If the average response rate is 2 percent, it will be lower for new customers. Most direct marketing of financial services probably yields a lower-than-average rate. For example, newspaper ads generally produce less than one new customer for every 100 copies of circulation. Depending on the type of financial product, 100 mailing pieces might produce two new customers. These calculations are admittedly rough, and even speculative. But even highly accurate estimates would not significantly alter conclusions of low response rates.

The entire communication process in marketing can be likened to a giant funnel, which demands a large amount of input but yields a small output. Large efforts result in small effects. It is more correct to say that 98 percent did not respond to an ad than to say that 2 percent did. Those who responded are exceptions; those who did not respond represent the mainstream. This characteristic of direct marketing has important implications:

- Because responders are oddities, we cannot precisely predict the behavior of these individuals. How can we pick out the one individual who will act from a group of 50 or 100?
- When response occurs at such low levels, it becomes highly variable. It takes very little to swing results from success to failure or vice versa. When the norm is 1 percent, an increase of only 1 percent doubles marketing productivity. In such circumstances, advanced testing of offers may be necessary to meet reasonable goals.
- Conversely, the only basis of business action is the audience. If we send out 100,000 pieces of mail, we are likely to obtain a certain number of new customers.
- A larger mass increases the probability of overall results approximating "normal" expectancies. This mathematical proposition of safety in numbers lies at the heart of "the central limit theorem." But a strategy of lowering error by large numbers exacts a high price. Building a substantial body of customers by mass promotions requires large outlays of money.
- Even then, large scale promotions do not eliminate risk. The theory of large numbers assumes the existence of a stable, consistent universe. It takes no account of market aberrations, unexpected events, and economic irregularities. It assumes that norms will maintain a certain constancy. But

anomalies are always with us, and they become particularly damaging to large commitments.

The twin problems of low response and high volatility long have been major concerns to direct marketers. For the most part, they have concentrated on "proactive" methods to increase marketing productivity. This approach focuses on the "success ratio." It requires practitioners to improve methods for getting people to respond to their solicitations, such as opening a new account, transferring an IRA or credit card, or buying an insurance policy.

Thus, marketers work at refining prospect selection methods. They start with the best prospects and work down progressively to the worst customers. To improve response, they compare the "pull" of new ads and mailing pieces against a "control"—a commercial message that already has generated an acceptable response level. To achieve more creative promotions, they test each new campaign against some established norm.

These "proactive" actions are laudable, and frequently result in successful entries into new markets. Yet all our sophisticated measurements and meticulous analyses have given no evidence that direct marketing has succeeded in raising the average "success ratio."

This dismal conclusion has given rise to what Lester Wunderman, chairman of Wunderman Worldwide, calls the "failure ratio" approach. His line of reasoning is as follows: when promotional messages are unanswered by 98 or 99 percent of an audience, communication is misdirected. If we cannot improve response we should concentrate on reducing "communication waste." We should use the "failure ratio" approach. How? By not sending out promotional material to poor prospects.

If a company sends out 100,000 pieces of mail and obtains 1,000 sales, the response rate is 1 percent. If that company can eliminate 50,000 mailings to the least probable buyers, the response rate will rise. The degree of increase depends on the efficiency of identifying nonbuyers. In many instances it is easier and more profitable not to market to marginal buyers than to influence prospects to take action.

The proactive approach is probably best achieved when markets are small, and key buying groups are clearly distinguishable. For example, J.P. Morgan seeks individual accounts of $500,000 and up. Morgan would gain nothing by programs to eliminate nonprospects because it does no mass promotions in the first place.

Many financial houses are satisfied with more modest balances than J.P. Morgan. Many mutual funds solicit IRA accounts as low as $500. When markets are large but nonprospects are numerous, the "failure ratio" approach might be the way to go. Nevertheless, companies often can benefit by pursuing proaction at the same time.

Summary

Customer databases cannot be kept intact indefinitely. Financial firms must solicit new accounts constantly, and direct marketing is the main method of doing so.

Direct mail to acquire new customers relies on external lists. List "enhancements" are frequently used in solicitations to consumers. They are not important in business-to-business marketing.

Mailers operating in retail services employ "merge-purge" techniques to eliminate list duplication. However, name duplication poses many problems in list rentals. These should be addressed when negotiating list-rental contracts.

Usage of general media are mostly confined to editorially selective vehicles. Solicitations in these media are usually lead-generating advertisements. Firms marketing financial services to businesses can substantially reduce follow-up costs by "telequalifying" leads.

Regardless of media used, low response rates induce high variability in marketing outcomes. Conventional wisdom advocates proactive moves to bolster the "success ratio." A contrary opinion has recently emerged which recommends a "failure ratio" approach.

Appendix 8a

Table A8-1. Estimated U.S. Advertising Expenditures (in millions of dollars)

Media	1985	1991	% Increase
Newspapers	25,170	30,409	21
Magazines*	5,341	6,739	26
Television	21,022	27,402	30
3 Networks	8,060	8,933	11
Spot	11,718	14,675	25
Cable	724	1,941	68
Syndication	520	1,853	256
Radio	6,490	8,476	31
Yellow Pages	5,800	9,182	58
Direct Mail	15,500	24,460	58
Business Publications	2,375	2,882	21
Outdoor	945	1,077	14
Miscellaneous	12,107	15,773	30
Total	94,750	126,400	33

*Combines consumer and farm publications.

Source: Based on "Estimated Annual U.S. Advertising Expenditures," Prepared for *Advertising Age* by Robert J. Coen, McCann-Erickson, Inc. Printed with permission.

Appendix 8b

Testing Response

Testing response has always been an important part of planning in direct marketing. It still is. The aim of testing is to determine in advance the best way, or a satisfactory way, of generating response, given a set of alternatives. The rationale of testing is the well-founded principle that firms should reduce risks as low as possible in undertaking business decisions.

Response tests cover two main elements of a marketing program—message and media. Message effects include both form and content, or copy and offer. Copy refers to the presentation of the offer, and often cannot be separated from specific terms of the tender or proposition. Tests of message response hold out several options:

- Test different offers embodied in a highly similar presentation
- Test different presentations of essentially the same offer
- Test combinations of copy and offer

When media effects become the objective, tests concern themselves with the devices that carry the message, such as mailing lists, telephone numbers, magazines, television shows, and newspapers.

Whether marketing researchers test messages or media, estimates are of two kinds: relative and absolute. A relative estimate compares one score in terms of another. For example, which ad pulled best, A or B? A common practice is to compare results with a "control." A "control" ad is one that ran previously and yielded a highly satisfactory result.

An absolute estimate provides a probable number of returns from a promotional action. Firms project this number to some known universe, such as mailing or telephone lists, publications, and television schedules. A relative estimate tells which action is best. But even the best may not result in a payout. An absolute estimate is therefore necessary for a business decision.

The types of response tests can be visualized in Figure 8b–1.

Basic Designs

Tests of response fall into a class of research designs called "experimental." The basic idea is to manipulate one or more variables while holding all other things constant. Any effect can thus be ascribed to the variable tested.

The greatest advantage of response testing is its focus on action. These tests ignore "soft data," such as awareness of the message, recall of details in an offer, attitudes toward the company of the service. Tests evaluate response under actual market conditions. Researchers measure behavior in terms of inquiries, sales, and customer traffic.

The "experiments" are commonly of two broad types—single tests and comparative ones. By its vary nature, the single test implies an absolute measurement. The comparative test evaluates two or more alternatives, so that decision makers can choose the best option available.

Figure 8b-1. Types of Response Tests

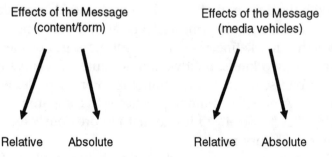

The Single Test

The single test measures one variable, one time. For example, a financial firm develops a mailing piece and wants to know if it will pay off. A test of this sort can be represented symbolically as follows:

$$X \qquad\qquad O$$

The symbol X denotes the item tested. The symbol O signifies the response.

The procedure calls for drawing a sample of the mailing list under consideration. If the sample is large enough, the firm can make a reasonable estimate of response, and then decide whether to go ahead with the program on a larger scale.

This model is low-cost and easy to execute. A key assumption is that the value of O before the test is zero. No prior knowledge of the product, or experience, or preferences had been built up. This makes the single test best suitable to new financial services, and perhaps to radically new offers. However, extraneous variables are but weakly controlled, and predictions can be adversely affected by timing of the test.

Comparative Tests

One the most elementary basis, the comparative test evaluates two variables. A test of this type can be represented as

Sample 1:	X(1)	O(1)
Sample 2:	X(2)	O(2)

If the message is tested, the two samples must represent the same universe and be statistically identical. For example, a test of two offers may be tested with two matched samples from a mailing list. Since both presentation and medium are constant, any difference in response is assumed to result from differences in the offers.

A popular form of message testing in print media is the A/B split. In this design, alternate messages go into every other copy, producing two identical or matched samples. Since each sample is exposed to the same audience, response is imputed to the ads. Many magazines, however, do not offer A/B splits, and newspapers seldom do.

A media test keeps the offers constant, but varies media vehicles. For example, the same ad may be placed in two different magazines. Response differences are then credited to the pulling power of the magazines, because offers and presentations are the same. No matter what the test, ads must be keyed so that returns can be traced to their sources.

A comparison of two alternatives has certain weaknesses. First, timing can affect the outcome of the test, especially if there are seasonal variations. Second, neither alternative may yield a satisfactory response. To overcome these shortcomings, many tests add a "control." For example, a "control" ad is one that has a proven record of satisfactory response when run in a given medium. When a "control" is used the design is diagramed as follows:

Sample 1:	X(1)	O(1)
Sample 2:	X(2)	O(2)
Control Sample 3:	X(3)	O(3)

Because the control is a known entity, all messages can be evaluated in relation to the "winning" format. Extraneous variables are assumed to affect all groups alike, thus canceling out their impact. The firm would then go along with the alternative that yields the highest return.

Conceptually, the comparison test can be extended to any number of alternatives. However, a large number adds costs and administrative problems.

The comparison test may also be inappropriate for intermedia comparisons, because there is no way to hold copy constant. How do you make a television commercial of the same quality as a printed advertisement? What is the print equivalent to a television commercial, a full-page, four-color ad or a black-and-white ad?

Response-Testing Issues

Response testing gives an appearance of science. The experimental method was adopted from the scientific laboratory. Many of the sampling and analytical techniques were developed in agricultural testing by R.A. Fisher, who was knighted for his contributions. But testing response in the marketplace bears little similarity to testing in a laboratory, where the environment is highly controlled and variation in results are generally low.

One problem with response testing is sampling error. Because response rates are low, reliable estimates require large samples. Table 8b-2 shows sampling errors at the 95 percent level of confidence. The absolute error tells the amount of chance variation that would occur 19 out of 20 times, if the identical measurement took place an infinite number of times. The relative error is simply the absolute error expressed as a percentage of the estimate. Both types of errors assume that the only variation is that of chance, and that nonsampling errors do not exist. Though response tests usually focus on behavior—a certain number of people took action or did not—nonsampling error does exist and often may be substantial. It cannot be ascertained, but there is no reason to assume that what cannot be measured does not exist.

Table 8b-2. Sampling Errors at the 95% Confidence Level

Sample Size	Response Level (%)				
	1.0	2.0	3.0	4.0	5.0
	Absolute Error				
1,000	.61	.87	1.06	1.21	1.35
3,000	.36	.50	.61	.70	.78
5,000	.27	.39	.47	.54	.60
7,000	.23	.33	.40	.46	.51
10,000	.19	.27	.33	.38	.42
	Relative Error				
1,000	61	44	35	30	27
3,000	36	25	20	18	16
5,000	27	20	16	14	12
7,000	23	17	13	12	10
10,000	19	14	11	10	8

Both absolute and relative error decline as sample size increases. Because response is generally low—perhaps only 1 percent for many customer acquisition programs—sample size must be substantial for results to be meaningful. For example, a response rate of 2 percent based on a sample of 1,000 contains a sampling error of 0.875. That is 44 percent of the estimate. To reduce that relative error by half, to 22 percent, we need a sample of about 4,000, which would just about quadruple our costs.

For comparative tests, samples must be larger. When expected results are only one or two percentage points, any observable differences can only be marginal. But the relative error of this difference is roughly 50 percent larger than shown in the table of relative errors. This is because errors of the two samples must be taken into account simultaneously. Consequently, costs shoot up exponentially.

Sampling seems to be a major culprit in what has come to be known as a "regression toward the mean." It seems common for full-scale results to yield much lower response rates than indicated by testing.

The sampling argument runs as follows: Suppose a firm tests three versions of an offer. By "matching," all three samples should be equally responsive. But these samples contain sampling error, or error caused by pure chance. Thus, some results may be upwardly biased, and some may contain a downward bias. We don't know what the true figure is. We have only probabilities. On the basis of this test, the firm chooses the offer with the highest return. But when the list is used in its entirety, high and low biases average out, and the highest returns observed on the test are never duplicated in reality.

This explanation was evaluated empirically by Raab Associates using information which encompassed 475 mailings of 12.7 million names over an 11 year span. According to Raab's analysis, the "regression toward the mean" theory explains only a small part of why tests do better than full-scale operations. Other factors that make results variable relate to inconsistencies in the marketplace.

All other things are simply not the same at all times. Consequently, test conditions may differ substantially from market conditions when a company executed the overall plan.

Raab Associates recommends the use of larger samples—about five times larger than those used currently. But if test results differ from actual results because of elements other than those of pure chance, larger samples will not solve the problem. Nonsampling error will still be present, and higher costs associated with larger samples will not make results more predictable. Perhaps the only way is to add a "risk factor" to the calculations. If a test shows a sampling error of 1 percent, increase it to 2 percent. But that sort of adjustment can be made only on the basis of experience.

9

Geodemographic Databases

Whether databases are internal or external, most large computer files are "geodemographic." They contain both geographic and demographic information. These databases are used primarily for marketing purposes. This chapter deals with such uses as:

- Organizations offering geodemographic databases
- Computer mapping
- Illustrations of types of maps
- Targeting in direct response and general media
- Relationship marketing
- Applications of lifetime-value-of-customer concept
- Structure of Geodemographic Database

Configuring Demographics

As explained in Chapter 6, a geodemographic database provides socio-economic data about individuals and households in various geographical areas. Computer technology permits these geographical configurations to be of any size and shape. These areas can be as large as Census regions or as small as city blocks. The possibilities of analyzing and displaying information by mapping are almost endless. Demographic information featured on a map is called "attribute data."

Such information, frequently stored in a database or tabular format, remains independent of the map itself. But attribute data are easily linked to area maps. An example is a map which marks out density patterns of retail customers for almost any type of financial service—local banks and branch offices, insurance firms and agents, mutual funds and credit card issuers. Each firm must fit areas and demographics to its own particular operations.

There are two broad classes of geodemographic databases: internal and external. An internal database is usually comprised of a company's customers. Some company files may contain prospects, such as people who responded to lead-generating advertisements but were not converted to customers. An external database always contains population characteristics for various geographic areas. They may also contain names and address of residents.

Internal Databases

All customer databases of financial firms are basically transactional. They track customer activity on a periodic basis, such as bank deposits and withdrawals, mortgage and loan payments, credit card charges, securities trading, IRA contributions, and account balances.

How do these transactional databases become geodemographic? Since customer records contain names and addresses, these files are already coded geographically—by city, state, and zip code. Firms that send out large quantities of mail might further organize their files according to postal carrier routes.

Demographic data enter customer databases in one of two ways:

1. The firm solicits personal information on application forms, especially when extending credit or assuming contingent liabilities. For example, a mortgage application makes queries about marital status, occupation, personal assets and liabilities, and net worth. Firms also check applicants credit ratings with outside agencies.

2. Demographic data from external databases are overlaid on customer files. This method provides information about the neighborhoods in which customers reside.

External Databases

A large number of organizations offer geodemographic data. These firms can be divided into four broad categories.

1. *List compilers,* such as Metromail and Carol Wright. These sell lists to direct marketers and conduct coop promotions.

2. *Demographic research houses,* such as CACI Market Analysis, Donnelly Marketing Services, and Claritas. These firms offer "enhanced" databases. These enhancements include socio-economic clusters of small areas, media statistics, and data taken from sources other than Census.

3. *Computer mapping services,* such as Datamap, Inc. and Strategic Mapping, Inc. Some of these services do actual mapping for clients while others sell mapping software.

4. *Bureau of the Census,* a division of the U.S. Department of Commerce. The Census Bureau provides government data on disk or tape, along with mapping programs, to allow companies to perform their own analyses. The Census also conducts special analysis on request of individual clients. Its regional centers offer consultation and support services to business customers.

Firms in each of the above categories may provide more than one type of service. For example, demographic research houses perform mapping for customers, while list houses provide demographic analyses for individual clients.

Uses of Geodemographic Data

The key to all data usage is implementation. Information must be actionable. Geodemographic data are most useful when population characteristics are of critical importance and operations call for area selectivity. From this perspective, the major applications of geodemographic databases fall into the following four general categories:

1. Assessing market and sales potentials

2. Direct marketing applications

3. Directing distribution channels

4. Managing site locations

Market and Sales Potentials

Demographic data, particularly household income, are often used to assess business opportunities, such as the potentials of a market. The term "market potential" has several distinct meanings. It can mean maximum sales a market can absorb. In that sense, the definition implies a sales ceiling of all competitive products. A "potential" often denotes actual sales, and therefore estimates are synonymous with industry sales forecasts. A third definition refers to either the maximum or actual sales forecast of a particular company.

Regardless of definition, estimates based on geodemographics must establish a link between attribute data and sales. For example, a credit card issuer might surrogate household income for buying on credit. A joint study by the Census Bureau and Conference Board evinced a relationship between total income and discretionary spending. A car insurance company might employ the auto ownership incidence of an area as the relevant attribute. A mutual fund offering CD alternatives to yield-hungry investors might use a combination of age and income. Conservative investing, partly a function of age, has preservation of principal as its goal.

There are two major ways of calculating sales potentials, top-down and bottom-up.

The chain-ratio is probably the most popular top-down technique. It starts with a total which is subsequently decomposed. A branch bank, for example, might start with total bank deposits in the area it serves. It then estimates the household income of each market segment, if income is the prime attribute. The last step divides total deposits according to the percent of households at given income levels in each branch's territory. Thus, the bank imputes a share of total deposits to each submarket.

The bottom-up approach is known by names such as "aggregative" or "market build-up" methods. The bottom-up approach starts by using attribute data to estimate the sales potential of each submarket. The individual estimates are then added up to derive a total for the entire area in which a company plans to operate.

These two forecasting approaches form the bases for other marketing operations, such as locating retail sites, managing distribution channels and sales territories, and targeting customers and prospects.

Site Analysis

Assessing local business sites often involves combining demographic attributes with other types of information. For example, a bank might merge customer addresses with loans and deposits, population attributes, and competitive locations. Figure 9–1 is a computer-designed map by Strategic Mapping, Inc., illustrating how information is combined to evaluate business potentials of branch offices and ATMs.

The map shows one- and two-mile rings encircling the site. As distance increases, the proportion of customers decrease. We can see three shopping centers near the two-mile periphery. If population at those boundaries is outside the site's trading area, the bank might install ATMs at the shopping centers. Or ATMs might be installed at shopping areas in the southwest corner of the map.

There are several ways of depicting distances from a site. Figures 9–2 and 9–3, mapped by Strategic Mapping Inc., illustrate two different versions of a site ringed by a two-mile radius. Figure 9–2 shows selected zip code areas within or touching the two-mile buffer zone. Figure 9–3 displays those zip code areas whose centroids lie inside the two-mile radius of the site. The optimum method for aggregating the data for either map is to area-weight the data for each zip code included. Thus, the analysis considers only the data included in the actual trade area.

Figure 9-1. Trade Area for Potential Site

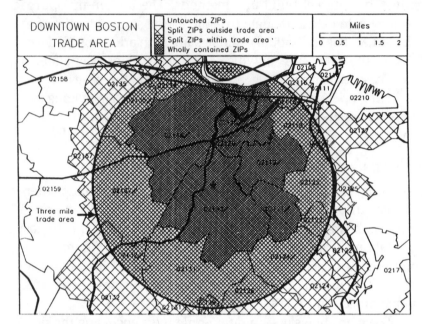

Source: *The Desktop Mapping Guidebook,* Strategic Mapping, Inc., Santa Clara, CA,1991, p. 25.

Managing Distribution

Financial services may be distributed in many ways—by a company's own personnel, by outside distributors and agents, or by a combination of both. No matter which method a firm chooses, managing a distribution channel shares many features in common.

When sales potentials rest on geodemographic data, sales areas are probably unequal in size. They are also likely to vary in terms of growth rates and sales goals. But a spatial allocation of resources remains optimal when a given budget produces the same marginal returns in each geographic area.

However, there is no general agreement on how to do that. For example, a firm can allocate more funds to weak markets with high potentials. Yet returns there may be low because of strong

Figure 9-2. Zip Code Boundaries Touching Two-Mile Radius

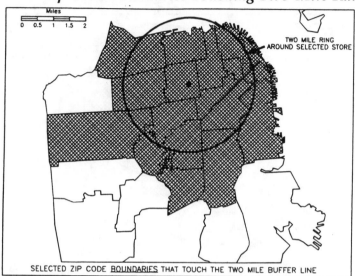

Source: *The Desktop Mapping Guidebook,* Strategic Mapping, Inc., Santa Clara, CA,1991, p. 25.

competition and cost disadvantages. On the other hand, incremental expenditures in areas with high market share may yield below average returns. By and large, the allocation process features trial and error, sometimes called "sequential commitment." The company edges toward a more satisfactory position in small steps, modifying its actions as it goes along.

Targeting

Targeting refers to directing promotional messages to specific segments rather than to everyone. Many financial products are specialized, and targeting implies the matching of media and copy with market segments. "Copy" is an advertising term that embraces both the form and content of an ad. Direct mail, the most common direct marketing media, necessitates sorting geographic or geodemographic segments by zip codes or postal carrier routes. Firms often overlay their in-house transactional files with geode-

Figure 9-3. Zip Codes with Centroids inside Two-Mile Radius

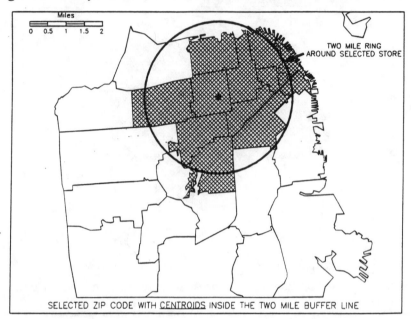

SELECTED ZIP CODE WITH CENTROIDS INSIDE THE TWO MILE BUFFER LINE

Source: The Desktop Mapping Guidebook, Strategic Mapping, Inc., Santa Clara, CA,1991, p. 25.

mographic databases in order to develop customer profiles. That is, the process identifies postal areas that contain a high proportion of households in the target group. These household profiles then form the basis for mailings to potentially-responsive segments.

When financial firms use mass media, "targeting" is more difficult. The more mass the medium, the more general the audience. Advertisements cannot be directed to target audiences with as much precision as promotional mail. In that event, advertising incurs larger "audience waste." More commercial messages go to people who have no interest in using the product.

Advertising for financial services that appear in mass media are of two kinds. One type is general advertising, which promotes a company's "image." This type does not sell products directly, but supports sales efforts. A second kind of mass media "targeting" is direct response advertising. Ads carry coupons and toll-free 800 numbers that solicit a direct response.

Practically, TV direct response "targeting" occurs only on cable narrow-casts. But even here a financial firm faces many obstacles in matching audiences to "consumer targets." One reason is that stations transmit signals to large areas, usually two or more metropolitan regions. A marketer therefore pays for the messages broadcast to a wide geographic area. Financial services that enjoy extensive distribution channels and advertise widely-used products incur minimum media waste. Each company must decide for itself how much waste to accept. There are no precise rules.

Ad space in national carriers usually is bought on the basis of audience. There are two major readership-measuring services: Simmons Media Research Bureau (SMRB) and Mediamark, Inc. (MRI). Both are notorious for putting out statistics of dubious accuracy. The following table compares print audiences used most often in advertising financial services, as reported by SMRB and MRI.

As Table 9-1 shows, audiences as reported by the two services differed from 19,000 readers for *The Wall Street Journal* to more than two million readers for *Money*. In terms of percentages, readership

Table 9-1. Adult Audience of Select Magazines

Publication	Audience (mils.)		Difference	
	SMRB	MRI	Number	Percent*
Barron's	1.27	1.03	167,000	23%
Business Week	6.83	6.31	520,000	8%
Forbes	3.44	3.67	230,000	7%
Fortune	3.85	4.01	160,000	4%
Kiplinger Per. Fin.	2.02	2.75	748,000	36%
Money	6.24	8.31	2,070,000	33%
Wall Street Journal	4.65	4.46	19,000	4%

* Percent differences were calculated by dividing the higher audience estimate by the lower one.

Source: Adweek, *Marketer's Media Guide* (Spring-Summer 1992).

differences ranged from 4–36 percent. Three out of the seven publications recorded differences of better than 20 percent.

The lack of uniformity in audience measurements gives clear evidence that media efficiency depends on the set of figures used—and there is no way of determining which set is correct. While direct marketers use cost per response as the criterion for media selection, past experience is the vital element. Even then, results of any ad can differ radically from past results. Under these circumstances, financial firms would do well to:

- Test ads before running them in full editions of costly publications. But predictions from copy testing are far from prefect.
- Buy space based on circulation, not audience. Publications guarantee their rate bases, and the Audit Bureau of Circulations (ABC) audits paid copies.
- Assess copy distribution. Publishers have exact figures of mailings, and will make counts available for select zip codes. This approach assumes that such analyses are worth the cost in terms of improved response.

Relationship Marketing

Previous chapters discussed how databases allow financial firms to maintain closer relationships with buyers. In many instances, customer databases enhanced with demographic information provide marketing departments with better tools for anticipating demand. As a result, the use of such customer databases has given rise to "relationship marketing."

Advocates of "relationship marketing" present it as an idea that will open a whole new world of marketing. Undoubtedly, there is merit to promoting customer loyalty. Continuity is the backbone of a thriving business. Many firms would not survive without their customers' repeat business.

But is this idea really a new one? Emphatically, no. The new and old paradigms agree on fundamental ideas; they differ only in their emphasis on certain practices.

For example, both relationship and conventional marketing are customer-oriented. They both accept the idea that buyer satisfaction translates into buyer loyalty. Both philosophies preach that companies can ward off competitors by responding to buyer's needs. But how?

Conventional marketing seeks to differentiate offerings either by changing product attributes or by influencing consumers' choice with advertising. These views are intellectually at odds with a "customer-is-king" theorem. Do consumers really need small, meaningless changes? And how can marketers insist they give consumers what they need when they spend huge sums to "educate" consumers as to what they should need?

The new school sees product loyalty driven by relationships. Advocates of relational marketing would use demographic data in customer files to bind buyers to a company's products. For example, a fund management company might promote growth funds to younger people and to families saving for their children's college education. As customers mature, company mailouts might stress more conservation investments.

Nevertheless, relationship marketing contains a fatal flaw. Modern business is impersonal. Friendly and close relationships built up naturally over years of personal contact can hardly be created by marketing. Does anyone really regard Citicorp in the same way as a neighbor or friend with whom to share a glass of beer after work? A missed payment on a credit card bill would automatically trigger a dunning letter from the bank's computer. Queries about account balances are answered by robots after punching in the proper numbers on a telephone.

Companies should strive to give customers good service, and build favorable images with informational newsletters and promotional pieces. But managements should not delude themselves that direct marketing can protect them from competitive inroads. The best defense is an offense; the best competitive weapon is a better offering.

The concept of lifetime customer value is an extension of relational marketing. If customers are long-term sources of income, then marketing must take that into account. Profits from continued transactions usually exceed earnings from the original sale. For this reason, financial firms are often willing to lose money on an initial sale in order to acquire a new customer. The firm makes money on subsequent sales from the customers acquired. This "loss-leader" concept raises the vital question: how much is a customer worth?

The theory of a customer's "lifetime value" (LTV) is a recent attempt to answer that question. Though the idea relates to almost any database operation, it applies primarily to continuity programs. Insurance companies, credit card issuers, banks, mutual funds, brokerages, and a number of other financial services operate on the basis of repeat, continuous business relationships with customers. This business concept regards customers as long-term assets, in effect, construing customer acquisition as investment.

Firms that embrace this life-value view of a customer "buy into the market." They allow for initial sales that do not cover their costs, counting on future revenue flows to offset short-term losses. A number of insurance companies have modeled the long-term net worth of policy holders in order to calculate how much they can spend on making a sale.

There are several ways of doing such calculations. The most common method involves a two-step procedure. The first phase is to analyze the historical record, especially customer retention rates, revenues, operating costs, and net earnings. The next step extrapolates these statistics into the future, predicting what would happen in a set of tomorrows.

To illustrate: Suppose a financial house drew a sample from its database of 10,000 new clients at some period, and tracked their behavior for five years. The study can be done retroactively, such as picking a sample among customers acquired five years ago. Say analysts find a 50 percent annual rate of attrition, or about 5.6 percent dropouts a month, an average revenue of $550 per cus-

Table 9-2. Net Earnings from 10,000 New Customers

Year	Av. No. of Customers*	Average Revenues	Net Income**
	(#)	($000)	($000)
0	10,000	—	—
1	7,080	3,894	175
2	3,540	1,947	88
3	1,770	974	44
4	885	486	22
5	440	242	11
		Total Income	340

*Customers as of June 30, at a 50 percent annual attrition rate.

**Assuming a combined tax rate of Federal, State, and local governments of 40 percent, with no tax loss carryforwards.

tomer, and after-tax income on that revenue of 4.5 percent. A *pro forma* financial statement might be as shown in Table 9–2.

Net income figures are annualized. To simplify the exposition, there is no depreciation. Net income and net cash inflow are the same.

If the investment in customer acquisition is assumed to have a five-year life, how much can the company afford to lay out in advance? A common practice in handling problems of this sort employs a present value concept. This idea sees the future value of an investment that generates cash at compound interest. To evaluate this future sum, we must discount expected earnings by the time-value of money and compare the results with the initial outlay.

To do this calculation, we must place a value on the cost of capital. The accepted method is to determine what sources of capital exist, their after-tax costs, and the weighted average of their costs. For example, if capital consisted of 50 percent debt and 50 percent equity and the after-tax costs were respectively 8 percent and 12 percent, then the weighted average cost of capital would be 10 percent. This number is then used for discounting future expected cash flows.

Table 9-3. Present Value Estimates

Year	Net Income	Discount Factor @ 10%	Present Value
	($000)		($000)
1	175	.909	159
2	88	.826	73
3	44	.751	33
4	22	.683	15
5	11	.621	7
Total	340		287

For illustrative purposes, suppose the firm valued its capital costs at 10 percent. Present value estimates would then look like those in Table 9-3.

As long as the present value exceeds the initial investment, the firm's capital cost requirements are met. That is, the firm is earning more than its cost of capital.

Given the present value in Table 9-3, the company can spend up to $287,000 to acquire 10,000 new company clients. This expenditure amounts to $28.70 per customer. Customer acquisition costs must include advertising, promotion, and selling expenses. It must also account for any third-party charges, such as sales commissions to agents and brokers, payments to video and commercial production houses, and any outside marketing and creative consultants. Future charges associated with these channel members, such as royalties, must be included in calculations of net earnings.

Capital budgeting has a number of pitfalls. These are well enunciated in any Finance 101 course at a decent business school. Briefly, the major shortcomings are:

- The calculation might not include inflation's effect on both the projected cash flows and the cost of capital.
- Several methods exist for figuring the cost of each component of capital, yielding different results. For instance, the cost of issuing new equity might be estimated on the basis

of the capital asset pricing model, the divided growth model, or the bond cost plus premium approach.
- The calculation involves forecasts which perceive the future as substantially the same as the past. This assumption departs from reality as time passes. Indeed, the assumptions underlying the projections of net cash inflows over the life of an investment may turn out wrong for reasons we cannot presently know.

The application of capital investment theory to database marketing brings with it additional suppositions, some of which are dubious. The idea that a company can spend $287,000 and still make a profit may be accurate. But it also may be misleading when used as a business strategy. Profit maximization is achieved at the margin. It is possible that the best solution might be to spend just $100,000!

The rendition of most services has two parts, a "front end" and a "back end." The front end concerns itself with selling face-to-face to a customer. The back end is essentially "back office" operations conducted out of customers' sight. The life-value-of-a-customer calculation virtually credits front-end operations with the whole profit over the life of an investment. And there lies the rub.

For many financial services, customer behavior is significantly molded by back-end operations. When a mutual fund reports above average returns, shareholder attrition declines and revenue per customer jumps up. When basic metal and real estate industries wallowed in the doldrums in 1990, mutual funds specializing in these areas saw customers closing their accounts or reducing their investments. When these depressed industries turned around in late 1992 and 1993, customers opened accounts and increased their commitments.

Similarly, real estate investment trusts took on a new popularity and demand for REITs swelled on Wall Street. Bank loan officers find shrinking demand when business conditions turn sour and new loan applications when customers are more optimistic about their prospects.

If customer acquisition is treated as a long-term outlay, benefits accruing from back-end operations should be accorded the same treatment as front-end operations. This is particularly true when sales are heavily influenced by monetary returns to customers. Both front-end and back-end operations should be included into the present value calculation. If this is not done, the omission results in an inefficient allocation of resources.

The life-value concept is most effective when markets are highly stable and product changes are few and far between. Some "standard" insurance policies, annuities, and closed-end bonds may be of this nature. These services are characterized by long-term periods of continuous operations.

But insurance companies, like many other financial service firms, cannot separate marketing from other financial operations. Insurance companies invest money they receive from policy holders and annuitants. That investment has nothing to do with customer acquisition, but cash flow is obviously linked to revenue accruing from customers. Since insurance firms invest in long-term fixed securities, such as corporate bonds and real estate obligations, what happens when these investments sour? As the "lifetime" stream of income goes awry, so do estimates of returns from investments in new customers.

Many financial products are interest rate sensitive. What would have happened to a bank that in 1990 used lifetime value to budget marketing costs for selling CDs? Calculations of CD renewals would have been as unsubstantial as dreams. Even staid long-term bonds were not immune to Federal Reserve interest policy. Firms which had early cancellation clauses in their contracts quickly terminated the lifetime of their bonds by refinancing their debts at lower interest rates. The present value of investors who bought those bonds never materialized. Customer acquisition costs were sunken costs, and therefore had no effect on refinancing outcomes.

Some authors recommend estimating customers' lifetime value for new products and cross-selling. However, returns depend on whether such sales represent additional revenue or funds transfers. For example, when banks began selling mutual funds to stop CD money from flying out the door, the new investment for setting up funds was incremental. So were outlays for convincing customers to transfer their money from CDs to mutual funds. But revenue was not additional. Money flowing into funds came mostly from nonrenewed CDs. Whether funds are additional or switched opens a new can of worms for life-value-of-customer concepts.

If money is switched from CDs to funds, then is the life-value of a customer terminated and does a new life cycle begin with mutual funds? If so, returns on customer acquisition of CDs may be negative. When returns on marketing CDs were so volatile, can those on mutual fund selling be less? What if interest rates reverse and we have inflation? How should we regard investors shifting funds again, but this time to CDs? Should all people transferring funds be regarded as old customers? In that event, should programs for new financial products be considered investments or current expenses? There are no ready answers to such questions.

When back-end and front-end operations are perceived as parts of an integrated system, management is presented with more meaningful alternatives. It confronts all tradeoffs and priorities. It no longer assumes unchanging attrition rates. Forecasts are no longer projected into a changing future.

It often makes no sense to budget for customer acquisition on the basis of outcomes in some hypothetical tomorrow. Why not plan the product or service first, then set marketing budgets? In reality, marketing and product development comprise a continuous process? The core of any business is not selling, but making products that users want. In this approach, success will not depend on a correct forecast of repeat business, but will depend on doing the right thing in the right way at the right time. Only by handling back-end and front-end operations as an interconnected whole can a firm muddle through changing times.

Summary

Large databases are basically geodemographic. It does not matter whether they are internal or external. When customer files add personal information about individuals, a transactional database is transformed into a geodemographic database.

All geodemographic databases have marketing as their primary purpose. Some database functions are concerned mainly with geographical considerations, such as site selection, distribution channels, and sending out mailings. Other marketing functions are concerned with promotion, such as targeting customers and prospects. General media have less selectivity than direct mail or telephone, and consequently incur more "media waste."

One outgrowth of customer database operations is relationship marketing. It emphasizes building long-term relationships with customers as a competitive weapon. Whether such tactics can shield a financial company from competitive pressures is debatable.

A logical extension of relationship marketing is the lifetime-value-of-a-customer concept. It is used to allocate budgets for customer acquisition. However, the calculations leave out operational and product development effects on the longevity of customer accounts.

Part IV

Managing for Superior Performance

10

Customer Service

Customer service is broadly used by modern business. Most current thinking about service quality arises from businesses such as retailing and manufacturing.

When applied to financial services, goods-related concepts are based on a manufactured analogy. Defects in goods are easily spotted. Attributes of financial services, however, cannot be evaluated with the same objectivity as attributes of goods. Assessments of intangible qualities are necessarily subjective.

Though customer satisfaction programs in the financial sector are commonplace, there is still no generally accepted definition of service quality. The departure of financial services from quality programs in goods-producing industries is evident in discussion of:

- Applications of Total Quality Management (TQM) to financial services
- Diversity of views for assessing customer satisfaction
- A model of customer satisfaction presented in the chapter
- The roles played by core and peripheral services

What Is Customer Service?

Customer service has become the elixir prescribed for business ills in the 1990s. The aim of business has always been to satisfy customers. This idea was first popularized by Sears, Roebuck in the late nineteenth century with its slogan, "Satisfaction guaranteed or your money back." More than 100 years later, this idea still remains a cornerstone of department store policy. The "buyer-is-king" philosophy gradually shifted from retailing to manufacturing and then to other business segments. Customer-orientation has become such a generally accepted way of doing business that it is virtually an article of faith among many—from business journalist to college professors. *The Honomichl Business Report*[1] (1993) notes that the greatest gains in marketing research were achieved by leaders in consumer satisfaction measurement. In 1992, revenue from consumer satisfaction studies rose 128 percent among the top 50 research companies. No other segment of the industry showed such a dramatic increase.

A recent version of a "concern-with-a-customer" approach is "Total Quality Management" or TQM. Ideologically, the rationale was inspired by Japanese successes in auto and electronic industries, though the Japanese find little or no value in the American construct. Nor did the late Edward Deming, an American professor, who initially tutored Japanese businesses in quality control.

As applied to manufacturing, Total Quality Management is thought of as a tool to reduce product defects. "Cost-of-quality" programs usually focus on costs of preventing or correcting production of defective items. One result of this renewed emphasis on quality is the Baldrige National Quality Award program. Judges give customer satisfaction a weight of 30 percent in the overall service quality rating. Financial services companies have been among Baldrige Award winners.

In 1992 AT&T's Universal Credit Card won a Baldrige Award in the service category. This card was introduced in 1990, and today lists more than 10 million account holders in its database. Customer charges amount to more than $20 billion annually.

AT&T's credit policy is often cited as evidence of customer satisfaction. The Universal Card division has no collection department, yet boasts a lower delinquency rate than that of any other credit card issuer. AT&T's telephone representatives arrange payment plans with customers in an amicable way. These results are highly reminiscent of Westinghouse's Hawthorne experiments of more than half-a-century ago. While the Westinghouse experience

---

1   "The Honomichl Business Report," in *Marketing News*, (June 7, 1993).

related to employees, the AT&T results suggest common principles with respect to customers. A firm can gain a lot by treating customers as human beings rather than as robots, or, when put in financial terms, as "revenue units."

Customer satisfaction programs in financial service industries have been used extensively to retain current customers and acquire new ones. Yet there is no generally accepted definition of what constitutes customer service quality, or what creates superior customer satisfaction. The manufacturing dictum of correcting defective items, as applied to services, accepts many subjective judgments as to what constitutes a "defect." Unlike goods, there are few concrete qualities that can be tested and evaluated objectively. Consequently, there are no accepted definitions of customer service.

Many believe that customer service quality is generic, purporting to apply to all businesses. Other views relate quality attributes to specific industries. Some definitions pertain to functions, and rely on tangible measurements, such as handling inquiries, shortening depositor waiting time at banks, expediting ATM usage, and resolving complaints. Other descriptions involve psychological attributes. One author lists cheerfulness, helpfulness, intelligence, and knowledge as vital to quality service. Professors Zeithaml, Parasuraman, and Berry claim reliability, responsiveness, assurance, and empathy as key dimensions of service quality.[2] Other writers regard any improvement in service as an enhancement in service quality, and therefore desirable.

However, without generating cost or value improvements, "Total Quality Management" is just bells and whistles that increase expenses and yield no benefits.

Paul Kahn, who headed AT&T's credit card business during its formative years, claimed that Universal's customer service program reached for "customer delight." But what brings delight to customers? If delight was the object, AT&T would have done better if it forgave all debts. But, then, it would not be in business. Actually,

---

2   Valarie A. Zeithaml, et al., *Delivering Quality Service* (New York: Free Press, 1990).

AT&T's research department developed a list of 108 quality indicators, which are monitored daily. The program is proprietary. Chase Manhattan's Customer Information Service claims to having identified 110 specific attributes of customer satisfaction. If you have more than a hundred possible explanations of what drives customer satisfaction, you have no explanation at all. There is no way of evaluating and weighing all attributes, and relating them to an effective plan of action.

Most studies of customer satisfaction have been done by marketing research firms whose techniques follow precepts of social psychologists. These firms rely on "soft" data, such as feelings and emotions derived from interviews. The *Marketing News 1993 Directory of Customer Satisfaction Measurement Firms* lists 97 companies. The vast majority of these use "qualitative" methods, such as focus groups and interviews with customers. But financial service firms don't need interviews to measure tangible performance, such as returns on investment, interest rates, and sales. Such data are measured routinely. But market research firms in the customer service area concentrate on vague, insubstantial attributes that encounter major conceptual difficulties. Many practitioners see surveys of this type as lacking coherence.

From a review of the literature on the subject, however, some generalizations are evident. Practically everyone would concur with the following paradigms:

- Customer satisfaction is specific to the particular service and to the company. Criteria used to satisfy business customers must be quite different from those used to satisfy retail customers.
- Any acquisition of information in the customer service area must be actionable. If a firm can do nothing about a problem, there is no sense in spending money to study it. Simply prepare yourself to meet the uncontrollable outcome.
- Programs designed to solve problems must compare the cost of action with expected returns from undertaking an action.

These rules are not much help. They are rather vague, and can apply to almost anything. So let's keep these basic elements and try to synthesize customer satisfaction in more detail.

Model of Customer Satisfaction

There are several ways of approaching the problem. One way is the customer-introspective approach. Advocates of this line of action invoke what may be called a "first cause" argument. They insist that since satisfaction emanates from the user of a service, not the vendor, the subject must be studied from the standpoint of the customer. How? Just ask customers their opinions. This method is most common with marketing research companies that conduct interviews asking customers how they feel about a service, what they like about it, and what they don't like. Wisdom, to put it in the vernacular, comes directly from the horses mouth.

The trouble with this method is that horses don't talk. Besides the impossibility of measuring feelings, there remains a question of meaning. What people say isn't necessarily what they do. People may like bank tellers, and say they are highly satisfied with the way their accounts are serviced. But a CD that pays less than 3 percent will have difficulty in keeping its customers when it matures. People may be happy with the personal attention they receive from their credit card issuer. But high annual fees and above-average interest rates are not a prescription for loyalty. A mutual fund that earns low returns usually finds itself with fewer shareholders. No company can employ public relations to correct a defective financial product.

An alternative view of customer satisfaction is to examine customers' actions. When customers favor an equity fund with increasing investments, they give unmistakable evidence of satisfaction. When people refinance their mortgages, does it matter what they tell interviewers about their confidence in the future? In 1992 and 1993 banks did a booming business in mortgage refinancing, even while Michigan State University and the Conference Board reported wavering indexes of consumer confidence.

The customer-extrospective approach infers satisfaction from objective data. It derives conclusions about satisfaction from what customers do. But keeping a close eye on customer behavior is not a direct measure of satisfaction. Customers may continue dealing with a firm because they lack better alternatives. Firms must anticipate new alternatives and future options. Banks that did not foresee the mass exodus from savings to mutual funds lost customers by the droves, no matter how satisfied depositors said they were.

Along which avenue of customer satisfaction should a firm proceed? That answer depends on the nature of the financial product, customer type, and functions of the service.

The Nature of a Financial Product

Customer service is closely related to the nature of a product. A mutual fund or a 401(k) plan may have completely different objectives from those of an insurance policy or a credit card. In the performance of a service, different purposes give rise to different functions.

For example, both mutual funds and insurance companies invest money obtained from customers. If the insurance firm makes bad investments, it undoubtedly will upset its stockholders. Its customers would only be concerned with the rates they pay and how their claims are handled. But if a mutual fund invests unwisely, customers become very unhappy. It's their money that is at risk. In these two cases, investment policy bears a different relationship to customer service, and therefore what makes customers satisfied in one instance does not in the other.

If satisfaction is associated with type of service, we must define the nature of financial services. In fact, we must group these services in accordance with common characteristics. Though a number of formal classification systems are available, they generally follow lines of business, such as banking, insurance, and brokerage. But one business can perform many functions. For example, banks handle deposits and checking accounts, invest customers' money in stocks, bonds, and money markets, administer trusts, underwrite securities, make loans, and act as financial advisors and consultants. Firms in other lines of business conduct an equally large variety of activities. In fact, in today's deregulated environment, banks, insurance companies, and brokerages can offer the same types of financial services.

Regardless of a firm's main line of business, it is the performance of a particular service—what is done and how it is done—that leaves customers satisfied or not. Accordingly, we will classify services in terms of their prime function rather than their line of business. From this point of view, all financial services perform six basic functions: (1) lend money (2) borrow money (3) manage money (4) advise about money (5) facilitate uses of money (6) protect against loss of money. The following table links these prime functions to the major types of financial services.

The functions listed in Table 10–1 are not mutually exclusive. For example, shoppers use credit cards for convenience. But about 70 percent of cardholders maintain outstanding balances, using their cards as lines of credit. Companies that issue credit cards also offer customers a number of benefits not associated with the prime functions listed in Table 10–1.

Table 10-1. Prime Functions of Financial Services

1. Lending money, such as mortgages, home equity loans, business and personal loans.
2. Borrowing money, such as time deposits, certificates of deposits.
3. Managing money, such as mutual funds, trust funds.
4. Advising about money, such as consulting on business and tax matters, evaluating assets, and engaging in estate and portfolio planning.
5. Facilitating uses of money, such as checking, credit cards, debit cards, funds transfers, trading stocks and bonds.
6. Protecting against losses, usually unexpected, such as various types of insurance.

Customer Type

Firms commonly divide their customers into business and retail segments. These two types of markets must be serviced differently, even when the product is the same. As customers, business firms count fewer in number, but account for larger transactions. More people are involved in a transaction, and the decision-making process often requires drawn-out negotiations. These conditions put a premium on personal contact in servicing accounts. Retail markets offer more prospects, but smaller sums per transaction. Services lend themselves better to standardization, and therefore pay less attention to individual accounts. As financial houses conduct business under these conditions, they alter their services accordingly.

Core and Peripheral Services

Financial services can be divided into two types: those carrying out core functions and those performing peripheral functions. A core function is one whose performance is both necessary and sufficient for a company's success. For example, banks lending money secured by property compete on interest charges with other mortgage underwriters. The most important competitive weapon of mutual funds is return on investment. Even funds with relatively high up-front charges or "loads" can compete quite favorably if they succeed in giving investors high returns.

Most financial firms, especially those offering multiple products, perform several core functions at the same time. Banks borrow and lend money in their normal course of business. Insurance companies protect against unexpected losses and lend money collected from premiums. Brokerage firms execute orders for clients and trade on their own accounts.

Other financial firms combine one or more prime functions in servicing the same customer. Chase Manhattan markets life and accident insurance to its credit cardholders. It thus combines two distinct services, facilitating the use of money and protecting against loss. A Chase sales brochure stuffed into a billing envelope portrays

LifePlus, a life insurance offer, as a way "you can protect your Chase credit." The brochure notes that in the event of death, "LifePlus guarantees to pay off the entire outstanding balance on your account, up to $10,000." Central Resource Group, Inc., an integrated financial services company, offers its bank customers one-stop shopping. In addition to the traditional banking services, Central Resource Group includes life insurance and investment services in its product mix. NationsBank runs a program that gives users of either its VISA or MasterCard from 1–6 percent credit on purchases. The credit accumulated by each customer goes into an escrow account earmarked for a retirement annuity through MetLife.

Periphery functions are only weakly or not related to the main line of a business. Examples of peripheral services abound everywhere. Banks run social programs for older depositors, such as one-day shopping trips and cruises to exotic places. They give discounts on hotel rooms and two-meals-for-the-price-of-one at various restaurants. Credit card companies ply customers with heady discounts and "reward programs."

Unlike core services, peripheral ones may or may not be necessary to the conduct of a business. When a service is unnecessary, it is a waste of money. One such program was the ill-fated Air Miles, developed by Loyalty Management Group in 1993. This program offered participants a way of giving their customers bonus points for free travel if they purchased goods of certain vendors. Loyalty Management pitched its program as one encouraging loyalty or repeat business through buyers piling up travel points. While experts are still doing post-mortems on why the program failed, financial services that participated benefitted from neither repeat business nor loyalty. Why should people make extra deposits at a bank or do more buying with their credit cards? Air Miles simply had nothing to do with the conduct of a financial service.

Some peripheral services, though somewhat divorced from a firm's core functions, are nonetheless necessary because competitors offer them. It is true that ATMs extend the period for transacting business to 24 hours, and are cheaper than keeping banks open longer and hiring tellers. Yet many banks find such benefits dubious but still offer ATMs because competitors do. Customers expect them. Likewise, many mutual funds supplement monthly or quarterly statements by maintaining costly toll-free 800 numbers, so that customers can call in for fund quotes, price changes, and outstanding balances in their accounts. Brokerage houses sweep dividends and sales proceeds into money market accounts with checking privileges or into individual bank accounts.

Many peripheral services deemed necessary are in essence a cost of doing business. They do not make a firm more competitive because every rival extends a similar customer service. Though these peripheral services do not help, they can hurt firms that do not offer them. Only if their core services are truly superior to those of competitors can a firm neglect the bells and whistles. But the fact is that companies whose core services rise above the rest usually make good profits, throw off surplus cash, and pile up more than enough "slack" funds to indulge their customers with bells and whistles.

To summarize our model, customer satisfaction depends upon two factors:

1. The nature of a financial service, as defined by the six prime functions listed in Table 10-1.

2. The rendition of services, as related to the prime functions.

This model is visualized in Figure 10–1.

Customer Satisfaction as Competitive Strategy

Customer satisfaction can be a potent competitive strategy, but only when customers are satisfied with the company's core services. This is the basis for gaining a competitive advantage. A firm must demonstrate competence, if not superiority, in accomplishing what its business is meant to do.

This view assumes that customers act in a rational manner, seeking the lowest cost or best returns for their money. Business

Figure 10-1. Model of Customer Satisfaction

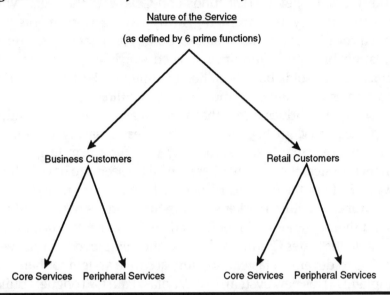

customers certainly buy financial services rationally. Their decisions feature professionalism and systematic analysis. No—financial managers are not devoid of human qualities, nor humane ones. They don't always act in an impersonal manner and deal at arm's length. They accept vendors' invitations to prestigious country clubs and fancy bars and restaurants. They go out of their way to do favors for long-standing friends and cronies. But there are proscribed limits to personal preferences and favoritism. This sort of behavior flourishes when almost any competitor can deliver the same service. But when products differ substantially, economic considerations assume primacy in decision making. Only financial products with a distinct economic advantage translate into a competitive advantage.

Although consumers are not as knowledgeable about financial services as professional managers, retail customers do not buy on a mere whim or sudden impulse. They deliberate. Americans are not frivolous about money, except for the politicians, who make decisions about other people's money. When interest rates shot up in the 1980s, money market funds and CDs were the rage. When rates fell, money fled from niggardly-paying instruments and headed for higher returns in stocks, bonds, and annuities. Mutual funds mushroomed. Annuities showed startling growth. In 1987 financial firms sold about $4 billion of annuities. Forecasts for 1993 placed sales of annuities at more than $16 billion.

Many authorities agree that when markets reach saturation, companies must go beyond basic services to satisfy customers. When market growth slows, the only way for a firm to gain customers is to steal them from other firms. This seems to have become a way of life in the credit card field, where issuers engage in cutthroat forays to build market share. In turn, targets of these attacks defend their positions with enhanced customer service facilities.

Atlantic States Credit Card Association employed Veritas Venture Inc. to develop a faster and more accurate system for handling complaints. This new system, says Veritas' Paul G. Tongue, "builds loyalty, prevents file raiding." Writing in the July 5, 1993 issue of *Marketing News*, Howard Schlossberg praises the services of AT&T Universal Card and the GM card. "Both have distinguished themselves in an over-crowded industry," he writes, "by offering Malcolm Baldrige Award-level service and tangible benefits for consumers."[3]

But what evidence is cited? Schlossberg follows many other writers on business topics which describe a company practice and then cite the company's financial results.

For example, one author describes how Meridian Bank of Pennsylvania built a customer database by selecting the right demographics. The firm then sent out a direct mail package, with "a wide variety of inducements," to recruit signups for its Club 50. The author then tells us that the result of this program was 100,000 new accounts. This kind of writing intimates that favorable financials came directly from the practice in question, in this case, the mail-

---

3   Howard Schlossberg, "GM, AT&T Cards Rise above Competition," *Marketing News*, (July 5, 1993), p. 2.

ings. Did the contents of the offer—the variety of inducements— have anything to do with returns on the mailing?

In the same way, Schlossberg waxes eloquent about AT&T's mediatory collection policy and then quotes its $1 billion-a-month billable charges. In fact, he writes: "such factors as customer delight, continual improvement, and the ability to establish and use customer listening posts have spearheaded one of the most successful credit card introductions ever."[4]

The AT&T card introduction was indeed a highly successful one. But what was responsible for bringing $12 billion in annual charges—accommodating those who were delinquent in their payments and establishing listening posts? Decidedly not! AT&T took a page out of Sears' Discover Card, now a part of Dean, Witter, Discover. AT&T charged no annual fee and one full percentage point less interest than major competitors. Like TV broadcasters, AT&T gave its product away free, hoping to recoup its expenses elsewhere. "Free TV" stations derive revenue from advertisers; AT&T gets its compensation from retailers, and additional revenue from interest on outstanding balances.

Every other successful credit card issuer had the same experience. GM offered its card with no annual fee and huge rebates which could be applied to new vehicle purchases. The Ford-Citibank Card copied the main features of the GM card. Its no-fee card offered 5 percent rebates on purchases, which could be applied—up to $3,500—toward buying or leasing a new car, van, or truck from any Ford division. This rebate, exclusive of any retailer incentives, could also be applied to downpayments. Following GM, Ford combined core services from two different types of business—auto pricing and creditcard rebating.

The possibility of ringing up as much as $3,500 toward the purchase of a car is quite a hefty inducement for price-conscious automobile shoppers. Since Ford's entry into the credit card business, GM has upped the $3,500 limit by allowing cardholders to

---

4   Ibid.

earn an additional 5 percent if they use their cards to pay for goods or services purchased from a select group of customers called "GM Card Partners." This group includes Avis, Marriott, MCI, Time Warner, Mobil, and Continental Airlines.

Other financial services manifested a similar focus on core services or outstanding performance in their delivery. The most successful mutual funds are those which show a consistent record of above-average returns. Appendix 10 shows the 20 leading mutual funds in terms of assets, and their returns.

Most of the top 20 funds are broad-based, emphasizing high returns. Eight are growth and income funds. Another seven are growth and capital appreciation funds. The remainder are equity income or "asset allocation" funds. Interestingly, 16 out of 19 recorded five-year returns above those of the average mutual fund. One fund in the top 20 was not in existence five years ago. Since funds carry different risks, a better comparison is a ranking that includes investment objectives. Using *The Wall Street Journal*'s five-year performance ratings, 14 out of 19 received a rating of B or better, C being average. Annualized returns of these 14 firms were in the top 40 percent for a five-year period. Only one out of 19 yielded below average returns.

But substantial variability exists from year to year. As we would expect, the highest volatility exists in growth and capital appreciation funds. The smallest disparities take place in stock and bond funds. Only six out of the 20 leaders bettered returns of the average mutual stock fund during the most recent 12 months. But 16 out of 20 exceeded returns of the S&P 500. Since assets do not fluctuate in proportion to annual returns, it seems the public, to use Herbert Simon's coined term, "satisfices" rather than maximizes. Most investors do not have information that permits them to make short-term comparisons. Mutuals thus tend to possess characteristics of long-term investments. Yes, J.Q. Public demonstrates a great deal of rationality when investing in mutual funds.

The fastest-growing brokerages for the past decade have been discount houses, which charge lower fees for executing orders.

Similarly, no-load mutual funds have made tremendous gains in market penetration. Their share of market climbed from 37 percent in 1988 to 43 percent by 1993.

This trend is paralleled in retailing, where discounters like Wal-Mart recorded the greatest growth. Even leading brands of packaged goods have suffered the same fate of declining share, unless they compete on price with discounters and private labels.

Banks that coped best with falling interest rates in the early 1990s were those that offered better alternatives to CD holders. Some banks set up "investment advisers" to stanch the flow of money from savings accounts and CDs to Merrill Lynch and Fidelity. Chase aggressively promoted securities counselors at its branches to help risk-averse customers obtain higher returns in stocks and bonds. As of February 1993 more than 100 large banks ran their own in-house mutual funds—banks like Chase, Wells Fargo, Bank of America, U.S. Trust, Mellon Bank, and First Wisconsin. Funds of the two last-named banks have no loads. Many more banks now sell funds of other companies, usually for a front-end sales fee of 4–6 percent. Smaller banks usually offer "hub-and-spoke" or "master-feeder" funds. Both types may carry a bank's name or "private label," but they invest entirely in another fund. The choice might be a proprietary bank fund or an investment company fund.

Banks have also moved actively into annuities, and today are the largest sellers of these investments. Typical annuitants are up-scale empty-nesters who had gravitated toward money market funds and certificates of deposit in the 1980s. A monthly-check-for-life option at a good rate of interest makes for an appealing offer to these conservative depositors. Banks that established annuity programs were able to hold on to their existing clients, yesterday's low-risk CD and money market investors.

A number of banks also started brokerage accounts, either on their own or in cooperation with an outside broker. Banking, investing, and a host of other services are increasingly coalescing under one roof. These so-called "all-in-one accounts" issue integrated statements for the convenience of the customer.

The most successful financial institutions have been those that performed prime functions well. For example, Chase-Manhattan's Vista Capital Growth fund showed a five-year total return of 213 percent as of November, 1992. Its Vista Growth and Income fund returned 295 percent during the same period. Needless to say, Chase could offer skittish depositors a viable alternative to their maturing CDs.

Implementing Service Quality

Proponents of service quality seldom differentiate between core and peripheral functions. They treat the subject as though everything to enhance a service has approximately the same effect. A service is a service is a service. The failure to distinguish between important and less weighty functions is the reason why many discussions of customer satisfaction are couched in vagueness and obtuse generalities. Such discourses lack benchmarks or frames of reference.

But financial services are wide-ranging, and their functions are company-specific. Customer satisfaction means different things to financial managers in different lines of the industry. We can, however, group these customer-satisfying practices into three broad classifications.

1. Zero-defect services

2. People-oriented services.

3. Quality-perceived services.

Let's examine each group separately.

Zero-Defect Services

Zero-defect services emphasize accurate information, up-to-date technology, and skillfully-executed operations. They mimic Japanese practices which highlight error-free information and high precision in carrying out operating tasks.

A zero-defect policy applies to both core and peripheral functions. Bank of America, for example, uses PegaCard as a customer-service system for credit cards. The system automates chargebacks by tracking disputed transactions, adjusting accounts, and generating letters to customers. Resolving complaints quickly may make customers happier, but it brings in no new business. Customers do not compare credit card firms on their complaint-handling ability, and relatively few would leave a provider because of an occasional error.

Credit card processing is a routine activity, a necessary cost of doing business. Computer systems usually contain a relatively small number of errors, though these errors may be costly. Firms often spend more money finding and correcting trivial errors than the amounts of money found to be in error. The main consideration in reducing operational errors is cost, not competitive advantage. Do savings justify the outlay? We do not fumigate a whole house just to kill a few flies, no matter how annoying the flies are.

Companies that combine efficiency with core functions prove tough competitors. For example, Fidelity is said to maintain dominance in managing 401(k) plans because of its extensive information-processing systems. This is a major expense in servicing clients who seek a wide range of products for their defined distribution plans. Not only must a service firm possess sophisticated computer software, but expensive telephone facilities that provide on demand price quotations, account values and balances, and literature fulfillment. These systems also take orders, execute them, transfer money, and exchange assets. Usually the telephone services use interactive voice response to keep costs down. The sheer size of investments in such service facilities restrict the number of firms that can compete in managing 401(k) plans. In that event, competitive advantage arises from a broad product line and heavy investment in necessary technology and communication facilities.

Recently, ATMs have had a technological face-lift. The new machines enable customers to link checking, money-market accounts, credit cards, and installment loans with a single ATM card.

The appeal, says the head of Chase's Better Banking account, is "the power and profitability of getting a full relationship with the customer." But the ATMs did not come about from relationships with customers. Rather, the new machines were an outgrowth of "all-in-one" accounts. The establishment of multiple products gave birth to the more flexible ATM, not the other way around. There is no such thing as a tail wagging a dog.

People-Oriented Services

Many firms define service quality in terms of customer feelings. Many adherents of this approach insist that a company should build into its products such attributes as delight, ecstasy, personality, friendship, fun, and surprise. Many market research firms take this position. For example, Melannie Rus, vice-president of Intersearch Corp., thinks that "emotional hotbuttons" hold the key to customer satisfaction. Chairman Sardi of the Knoll Group claims that though emotion is basic, "there are no predefined guidelines for achieving customer delight."

Many of these prescriptions for customer satisfaction are a bit extreme for a financial service. These concepts are carryovers from nonfinancial fields, such as retailing and travel-related services. Customers usually do not buy financial services the way they buy products driven by style. They do not fall in love with a stock, unless it makes money. Unlike retail goods, financial services are not impulse products.

Nevertheless, handling complaints and servicing customers with pleasantness and respect are a necessary part of doing business today. This aspect is especially germane to business conducted on the premises of the service provider. Executives of the banking industry see customer satisfaction as embodied in actions of tellers, loan officers, and employees who meet face-to-face with the public.

To bring the personal element into customer relations, firms rely on hiring and training. Companies generally have developed programs to deal with the public satisfactorily by careful screening of job applicants and good training of employees. While enhancing the personal element in the performance of a service undoubtedly builds customer satisfaction, every new wrinkle also increases costs. One management issue is the distance a firm must go to meet a "necessary" level of service without wasting money. The so-called "extra mile" may be a costly mile to traverse, and if benefits are marginal, they may not be worth the effort.

A much more serious issue is servicing customers at a distance. As financial firms expand their product mix and geographic markets, they must provide for more extensive communication facilities. For example, Chase Manhattan established a Customer Information Center that handles more than 500,000 inquiries a year. Calls range from queries about stock and mutual fund quotes to information on credit card balances, insurance, travel-related services, and a host of other subjects. Nor is Chase alone in the transformation of traditional banking to broad-based financial services. For example, NationsBank of Charlotte has broken the bonds of in-state banking by exploiting a legal loophole and expanding into Florida, Texas, Georgia, South Carolina, and Tennessee. The giant bank also pushed into mutual funds, stock brokerage, derivatives trading, security underwriting, and fee-based services. Many other banks—such as First Union, Wachovia, and a number of other regionals—are taking the same route and battling mutual funds and financial services giants. To compete with the new rivals, these firms must fight for customers in an expanded territory.

Training service representatives in this area is a much more difficult task than training employees to present a cheerful appearance. Servicing customers with a large menu of financial offerings cannot abide reps with pleasant voices and empty heads. Firms would lose credibility were they to do no better than the IRS, which gives callers misinformation roughly one third of the time. Can private business do better with financial options that have become as complex as tax codes? The personnel problem is compounded by a low educational level in our school system. Admittedly, America has a number of elite colleges and universities that are second to none. But graduates from these institutions are not the people who work at jobs manning telephones. The mainstream of "middling" and lower level schools give diplomas to functional illiterates and students inept at elementary algebra. Can these people be expected to understand complicated financial statements and research reports? Companies that wish to bring Wall Street to Main Street must assume the burden of education, with little help from our august institutions of higher learning. Like the Wizard of Oz, most colleges give diplomas to scarecrows who wish for brains.

Image-Perceived Services

The service-perception philosophy is in some ways similar to the attitudinal point of view. Since services are intangible, they cannot be defined quantitatively. Satisfaction, like beauty, lies in the eye of the customer. That being so, service quality is not an objective thing, but a perceptive one. I think, therefore I am.

Many financial firms that market multiple products regard a favorable image as a strong plus in customer choices. Selling products under a corporate umbrella implies a "trickle down" philosophy. Its underlying assumption is that company images become associated with individual products. If a customer regards the company highly, that reputation is purportedly carried over to all financial services offered. Thus, a favorable image of a firm is assumed to transfer the same impression to the company's mutual funds, brokerage services, credit cards, and various other items in its bag of services.

Marketing under a family logo lowers promotional expenses, since prospects are already familiar with the company. But this advantage is often exaggerated, because financial firms can piggyback promotions with billings and direct mailings. For example, Fidelity sells competitive mutual funds at no charge to the customer. Competitors pay Fidelity an annual fee of .25 percent on the account's net assets.

A drawback of the "trickle down" approach is that dissatisfaction with one product may hurt the company's other services. If all is perception, a bad experience with one product is not easily forgotten or separated from products that perform well.

This phenomenon is similar to what psychologists call a "halo effect." A customer who has one bad experience tends to associate negatives with other company products. Lastly, there is no evidence that attitudes trickle down to a firm's entire group of financial services. In fact, customers often deal with more than one company. The average householder owns an average of 10 credit cards, and a large proportion owns more than one bank card. Investors in mutual funds often own funds in more than one company. Though the "image" concept is intuitively appealing, it has still to prove itself in reality.

Summary

Customer satisfaction is not generic. It is specific to the company and the service it renders.

A service may involve many different functions. But not all functions are of equal value. Importance depends on whether a function is central or peripheral to a service's main purpose. The type of customer also dictates how tasks are carried out. For example, retail markets lend themselves to standardization. Business services concentrate on individual accounts.

Superior performance of core functions yield competitive advantages. Though benefits please customers, they may be a waste of money if they are not closely related to the main purpose of a service.

In some instances, however, peripheral services are deemed necessary to the conduct of business. They are offered by competitors and customers have come to expect them. They thus constitute a cost of doing business.

Implementation of service quality must therefore differentiate between core and peripheral functions. To compete successfully, core functions must be carried out well. Peripheral functions may or may not be necessary.

Appendix 10

Table A10-1. *Twenty Leading Mutual Funds*

Fund	Type	Assets	Returns One	Year	Five	Years
		($mils.)	%	R	%	R
Fidelity Magellan	GRO	24,875	23.8	A	18.2	A
Invest. Co. of Amer.	G&I	16,905	12.2	D	13.7	B
Washington Mutual	G&I	11,142	16.4	B	13.4	B
Vanguard Windsor	G&I	9,761	16.9	B	10.6	E
Income Fd. of Amer.	EQI	7,800	16.1	B	13.2	B
Vanguard Index 500	G&I	7,405	13.4	C	14.0	A
Janus	GRO	7,279	15.0	D	20.0	A
Fidelity Puritan	EQI	6,728	22.2	A	13.6	B
Vanguard Wellington	AA	6,372	14.3	C	12.0	B
Vanguard Windsor II	G&I	6,296	15.7	B	13.7	B
Fidelity Go & Inc.	G&I	5,711	20.7	A	17.3	A
20th Century Ultra	GRO	5,650	39.3	A	24.5	A
Fidelity Eq.-Inc.	EQI	5,628	21.2	A	11.7	C
Dean Witter Div-Gro	G&I	5,565	14.5	C	14.0	A
AIM Weingarten	GRO	5,555	7.4	E	14.9	B
Amer. Mutual	G&I	5,033	15.8	B	12.4	C
20th Century: Sel.	GRO	4,897	16.7	C	13.2	C
20th Century: Gro	GRO	4,789	7.4	E	15.7	B
Fidelity Asset Mgr.	AA	4,672	17.4	B	NS	
Growth Fd. of Amer.	GRO	4,453	16.6	C	13.5	C

Notes

Type of Fund: G&I = growth and income; GRO = growth and capital appreciation funds have been combined under this category; EQI = equity funds; AA = asset allocation funds, which allocate stocks, bonds, and cash in various proportions.

Assets: As of March 31, 1993.

Returns: Percentage gains ended June 30, 1993. Five-year returns are annualized, and assume all distributions are reinvested, but without effects of sales charges.

Ratings: Designated as R. Ratings range from A to E, based on annualized returns of funds with the same investment objectives, as defined by *The Wall Street Journal.*

Source: Based on "Quarterly Report on Mutual Funds," *The Wall Street Journal,* July 6, 1993.

11
Forecasting

Forecasts of financial data are pervasive. They are used in planning, implementing, and monitoring company programs. These forecasts are increasingly computer-based, and involve mathematical abstractions.

Using nontechnical language, this chapter sets forth the main forecasting methods employed by financial services companies. A forecasting method can be used for various purposes while maintaining the same form. From this perspective, this chapter will:

- Explain four popular methods for analyzing and forecasting—time series, correlation and regression, data analysis techniques, and mathematical modeling
- Evaluate forecasts of corporate earnings, which enter importantly into investment decisions
- Discuss problems of "data explosion"

Role of Forecasts

Forecasts are an integral part of financial service operations today. Properly conceived and executed, forecasts help managers accomplish the twin goals of anticipating future events and gauging the effects specific actions may produce. When large databases are employed, computers become a necessary device for deriving forecasts.

For managers of small firms, business plans may be informal and forecasts are implicit. Large companies usually draw up plans with stiff formality, and forecasts are explicit. Either way, most forecasts concern themselves with events external to the company—price movements, customers' orders, interest rates, general economic activity.

In terms of company actions, predictions relate mainly to two streams of revenue—money coming in from sales of financial services and funds flowing from investments.

Many authorities depict business activity as a reaction to the external environment. Business commentators spend an inordinate amount of time analyzing effects of government policy, consumer confidence, general economic conditions, and the outlook in specific markets. But firms do more than react to these external events. They interact with their environments. By anticipating future events, firms endeavor to avoid negative consequences and exploit favorable ones.

Forecasting techniques are the same, regardless of application—marketing or investing. This chapter will therefore examine the major techniques employed by the financial service industry. This approach emphasizes form rather than content; the technique remains constant regardless of content.

The most common forecasting methods are grouped into three categories:

1. time series;

2. methods of association; and

3. and mathematical modelling.

Time Series

A time series is composed of data collected over time. Company sales figures are an example of a time series, whether collected daily, weekly, or monthly. The same is true of government statistics tracking prices, retail sales, production, interest rates, or the host of other data periodically collected by various public agencies.

Financial firms use time series database analyses for a broad spectrum of analytical purposes. One is to forecast economic and business conditions. A popular time series used for these purposes is the federal government's Index of Leading Economic Indicators. This index draws together a number of separate time series, including stock prices, corporate bond yields, industrial prices, and initial unemployment claims. The behavior of these indicators is supposed to precede that of the general economy, thus acting as a harbinger of recession or expansion.

Stock prices are the most widely-used time series for firms concerned with investment markets. Broad stock groupings, such as the Dow Jones and Standard & Poor's indices are used to forecast the general direction of the equities market. Investment firms use sector indices to judge stock movement of various business segments, such as pharmaceuticals, chemicals, and transportation. Individual stock prices guide buying and selling decisions for particular securities.

Time series analysis often seeks to utilize databases to anticipate underlying trends of a stock or a group of stocks. Is a trend up, down, or sideways? Once a trend line is established, securities analysts extrapolate those trends into the future, and use these projections for trading decisions. Is the actual price of the stock higher or lower than its trend line? The trend projection is used as a benchmark to judge whether the price is too high or too low.

Trend lines represent an average of the individual statistics in the series adjusted for long-term movement of the series. The movement includes both direction and velocity.

Variability is another key component of a stock trend line. It measures the extent to which statistics fluctuate from average or typical values. Traders frequently ignore variability because the measure is not convenient to use. For example, the standard deviation is a common statistical measure of variation. But traders often buy and sell securities at discrete prices, not at ranges marked by normal standard deviates.

A time series is represented by continuous data spread over time, such as those statistics illustrated in graphs and charts. There are several basic methods of working with time series. Wall Street, however, prefers "charting" along with standard statistical techniques. "Charting" relies on empirically-based techniques rather than on methods which strictly follow theoretical mathematics.

A time series forecast contains three major weaknesses:

1. Its basic assumption is flawed.

2. It cannot pinpoint turning points.

3. It says nothing about what influences trends and observable fluctuations.

Assumption is flawed.
By extrapolating a trend, or even seasonally adjusting it, we implicitly assume that the future will behave in the same way as the past. It seldom does. As the time span of a projection increases, the greater reality deviates from the forecast. Time series forecasts are better suited for the short run, because fewer substantive changes can occur in the measured time period.

Time series cannot predict turning points.
These points in time designate when the basic trend changes abruptly. For example, in 1987 the Dow Jones Industrial Average dropped by more than 500 points in a day. When changes occur that suddenly, many investors have no choice but to take large losses. By the time they act, assets already have lost a good deal of their value.

Influences are not specified.
An extrapolation of historical data provides no clue as to what makes things change. In securities trading, a time series does not tell us why a trend is up or down. A mathematical projection is only a first step in decision making. It indicates where events are going, the speed of change, and the likely limits. But business managers want to know what factors are associated with change. To search for a better understanding of change, we must proceed from pure mathematical extrapolation to techniques concerned with causality.

A Search for Explanations

A concern with causality permeates practically all marketing and investing decisions. Securities traders and market analysts, for example, commonly regard earnings per share as a strong determinant of stock prices.

Causation means that certain changes bring forth alterations in some other outcome. A cause-and-effect explanation must satisfy three conditions to be valid. These requisites are as follows:

- A strong association must exist between "causal factors" and an outcome. If earnings were unrelated to a stock's price, they could not have exerted any influence. If President Clinton's taxes have no bearing on economic conditions, they cannot cause our economy to veer in one direction or another.
- A causal factor must precede the outcome. An actual or anticipated rise in per-share earnings could not have "caused" a jump in price if it came after the price change.
- No other explanation is possible. Though the first two requirements are present, they are not sufficient to prove a causal relationship. An explanation must be the only possible one. This is why causality can never be proved beyond the shadow of a doubt. It can only be inferred, and then only with qualifications. Other possible "causes" can seldom be dismissed.

Causal factors may include people or organizations, things, and events. For example, analysts using price/earnings ratios implicitly assume that changes in stock prices result from changes in a company's earnings and in the amount of stock issued. Recently, news analysts and business commentators predicted various effects of President Clinton's tax package. Some claimed it would lower interest rates, and thus spur the economy. This view sees stock prices going up. Others think taxes would siphon off business and consumer spending, and thus slow the economy. This scenario anticipates stock prices going down. In either case, however, new Federal taxes are regarded as a causal factor in affecting economic conditions and security prices. "How would you apply these analyses of the tax hike based on the three requisites?"

Recency-Frequency-Purchase Volume

Marketing makes extensive use of association measures, especially to identify logical prospects or "best customers." Many direct marketers of financial services use databases to predict the probability of purchase behavior. A popular method is that of "RFV," that is, recency, frequency, and purchase volume, This method was originally devised by Sears Roebuck in the 1930s. Sears graded all catalog customers on the basis of their RFV scores. The overall score was made up of the following weights: recency 50 percent, frequency 35 percent, and dollar volume 15 percent. This grading system supposes that recency, frequency, and dollar volume have a 50:35:15 ratio in order of importance. Customers with higher scores are, of course, preferred over those with lower ratings.

Over the years, statisticians have criticized the Sears' rating system on many counts. One argument asserts that the weightings lack a theoretical basis, and that the ratios of 50 to 35 to 15 are arbitrary. Another objection is that the system uses the same weights for different products.

The objection also can be applied to financial services. For example, an insurance policy is renewed each year. Its frequency of purchase is once a year, while recency is twelve months. In contrast, credit cards also reflect a yearly renewal, but the frequency and dollar volume of purchases varies. The dollar volume of a credit card also can be calculated on the basis of credit charges and interest on outstanding balances. The weights a credit card issuer would assign cannot be the same as those of an insurance firm.

A third negative concerns the relationship between recency and frequency. At any point in time, a more frequent buyer is likely to be a more recent buyer. If this is true, the recency-frequency factor is assigned an inflated importance weight. Statistical theory holds that it is impossible to assign weights to factors that are highly intercorrelated. The term statisticians use for this linkage is collinearity.

Despite these presumed miscalculations, the RFV customer-scoring system has persisted—and with good reason. It works. Department stores, catalog houses, and mailers have recorded highly successful results when using RFV. Given two customer lists—one of good customers and one of bad ones—solicitation to better buyers will always outpull efforts directed to less-frequent purchasers.

The technique is apparently well-suited to marketing frequently-purchased goods to known customers, but, what about repeat purchases made over long intervals? A number of insurance companies claim to have used RFV designations in soliciting policy renewals and sales for new financial products. But the weightings must be modified in accordance with behavioral patterns in the marketplace.

Correlation and Regression

With the increasing use of computers, intuitive and trial-and-error methods have given way to formal statistical analysis. One of the most popular methods that deals with causality is correlation. Computer software that performs the calculations is readily available, cheaply-priced, and made to fit virtually any PC. Best of all, these computer programs can be bought off the shelf. These can be found in various software directories. The American Marketing Association, headquartered in Chicago, publishes a *Directory of Software.* Although this directory emphasizes marketing, a great deal of the listed software can be applied to many applications other than marketing.

A correlation measures the degree of association between two or more variables. These variables encompass both market activity and consumer behavior.

For example, trading in securities is presumed to be associated with variables such as trends in stock and bond prices, yields, investment alternatives, corporate earnings, and personal assets of investors. Correlation measures range from +1 to –1. A +1 means a perfect positive correlation. If the price of a stock rose in the same proportion as its earnings per share we would have a perfect association between the two variables.

A –1 means a absolutely negative correlation. For example, if a stock index fell in proportion to a rise in interest rates, the correlation would be perfectly negative. Stock prices would move opposite to changes in interest rates. A value of zero means no relationship whatsoever. High correlation values indicate close statistical relationships, which can be positive or negative.

When a close relationship exists between elements, we can forecast one thing from values of other factors, called independent variables. This forecast is made from an estimating formula, known as a regression equation.

Any forecast depends on the variability of related elements. For example, it's easy to forecast daily summer weather conditions in the Sahara, even well in advance. Every day will be hot, sunny, with low humidity and a large diurnal spread. This forecast will be fairly accurate because there is no great change from day to day. Weather forecasts for New York City will be less accurate. The same variables apply to New York as to the Sahara, but New York's weather is more changeable, and hence less predictable.

Unfortunately, buyers' behavior and investment outcomes are like New York's weather—highly variable and not very predictable. For example, commentators often do "Fed watching," and explain daily shifts in the stock market by fluctuations in interest rates. Stocks are said to rise when interest rates fall, and *vice versa*. But several studies failed to demonstrate such relationships. A Prudential Securities study covering more than three years of daily trading recorded stocks rising only 51 percent of the time when yields fell on 30-year Treasury bonds. On days when yields rose, stocks also went up 51 percent of the time—the opposite of what many analysts expected.

Ned Davis Research used 90-day Treasury bills as a benchmark against the behavior of stock prices. Its two-and-a-half year study, beginning in October 1990, revealed that the DJIA gained some 607 points on days when interest rates rose, but only 512 points on days when rates fell.

Then why try to forecast iffy events? There are two reasons. Iffy forecasts might be better than no forecasts. When large amounts of money are at stake, even a small benefit may account for significant sums.

A second value of forecasts is establishing goals that can be checked periodically. If we find that results seemingly depart from projected goals, we can modify our actions. Results are monitored at given intervals, and if off track, firms can take actions to rectify the undesirable deviation.

Increasing computer usage has spawned a number of regression-like programs known under the generic name of "data analysis techniques." The most popular of these are discriminant analysis, clustering, and factor analysis. They are used mainly in marketing, though they have application to economic and financial analysis.

Discriminant Analysis

Discriminant analysis is similar to multiple regression, but the estimated outcomes, called criteria variables, have no metric values. Rather, they represent "nominal" groupings, such as risk-taking and risk-averse customers.

The method compares characteristics of two or more groups. Do these groups differ from each other? And how do we leverage those differences for increased business? A computer generates a series of equations to estimate the probability of any unit belonging to a group.

The experiences of the U.S. Army admirably illustrates how this statistical procedure works. Army processing centers assigned recruits to jobs on the basis of discriminant functions. One recruit might be poor at everything, but is put into the mechanized forces and trained as a mechanic because his aptitude is best for that job. Another recruit qualifies as an excellent mechanic, but is assigned to an electrical training school because he is better suited for electrical work than for fixing motors. The two groups, mechanics and electricians, thus contain personnel who are well-qualified for other jobs. Each group also harbors people who are poorly qualified, but would likely perform even worse elsewhere.

In business, discriminant analysis finds its major use in segmenting databases and markets. For example, a mutual fund might group investors by the investments they are likely to buy—equities, bonds, or money market instruments. Some individuals may have low probabilities of belonging anywhere, while others may fit well in all groups. But every customer falls into one classification, presumably the one with the highest probability of belonging.

As with Army personnel, each group contains misfits and anomalies. One reason is temporal conditions. For example, a person holding a lot of cash does not necessarily make a good prospect for "safe" investments, such as CDs. He or she may just be waiting for the stock market to improve before moving into equities.

The data a firm uses also can cause ambiguity in classifying customers. Did the company ask customers to check off their professed investment objectives on a questionnaire? Are the customers sure about what their objectives are? Did the survey instrument force them to make a choice that was vague and ambiguous? Or were the objectives derived from customers' past investment patterns? Customers' actions are not always consistent with their intentions.

Marketing research companies are the prime users of discriminant analysis for market segmentation. Claritas Corporation, for example, fitted some 37,000 zip code areas into 54 socio-economic segments (see Chapter 5). Since the method places each area in one group, there is no overlap. Each segment is mutually exclusive. But the zip code areas obviously contain varying proportions of people who are much like those in other segments. When firms promote to geodemographic segments, marketers must use judgment in selecting their "target areas." Each area will contain numbers of both desirable and undesirable prospects. Determinations must be made as to cut-off points.

Clustering

As a statistical method, clustering lacks a standard definition or even a useful description. It is actually a statistical umbrella that covers a variety of ways to classify people, objects, and events. Discriminant analysis qualifies as a clustering technique insofar as it concerns itself with categorizing groups.

Firms use clustering primarily to classify customers and prospects. The objective is to create homogeneous groups or data sets. The major stimulus for clustering came in 1963 from two biologists, Sokal and Sneath, who set out plausible rules for creating groups of similar units, and described the properties of clusters. When viewed in a metric context, these properties are as follows:

1. *Density.* A throng of points in relation to areas which contain few or no points. An example is geographic mapping. Suppose your company were to plot a metropolitan area, with each dot made to represent 10,000 persons. The central city would display cluster dots close to each other. As we move away from the center, the dots thin out. Population density decreases.

2. *Dispersion.* The degree of dispersion—or the extent to which units are farther apart—increases with greater distance from the center of the cluster. Consequently, clustering seeks to create groupings that have low dispersion, but are quite distinct from other clusters.

3. *Size.* If the cluster is identified metrically, its size can be measured. For example, Chapter 5, Figure 5–1, depicts segments with round shapes. Here, we can measure radius and

diameter. We also can measure the distance between one segment and another.

Many marketers define segments in psychological terms, such as perceptions of products. For example, we might define financial products in accordance with investors' objectives. When various financial products are purchased to satisfy similar objectives, they are regarded as competitive with one another no matter how different they are as financial instruments. If utility stocks and municipal bonds are purchased for income purposes, they are likely substitutes for each other.

4. *Shape.* The shape of a segment is determined by the arrangement of points.

5. *Separation.* This property describes the degree to which clusters overlap or stand apart. When clusters overlap, segments become indistinct. Financial "all-in-one" accounts basically assume the existence of overlapping segments. Stockholders, bondholders, and money market fundholders are offered the same financial products, as though they constitute a single, homogeneous market.

Factor Analysis

Factor analysis entails a statistical procedure for clustering units that correlate with one another. But a statistical relationship may contain many "independent variables" that correlate with a predicted outcome. The goal of this type of analysis is to factor out elements that do not significantly affect the outcome. For example, the propensity to invest in mutual funds may be related to age, income, education, marital status, occupation, market conditions, interest rates levels, stock market volatility, and a host of other things. In this situation, effective action cannot possibly consider all variables simultaneously. The objective of factor analysis is to simplify this large body of information by reducing the data to a few underlying factors—those that make a difference.

Mathematically, a factor is a linear combination of variables. Factor analysis seeks to choose those combinations that capture the essence of the data set. In mathematical terms, factor analysis extracts one or more factors that account for a large part of correlation values. It thus presents a substantive interpretation of "causal" relationships.

Mathematical Modeling

The ability to manipulate large volumes of data has encouraged the development of mathematical modeling. There are many kinds of models, and they involve a large variety of mathematical techniques. Computer models range from business games and civilian versions of war games to highly complicated programs of artificial intelligence and neural networks. For example, Booz, Allen & Hamilton converted war games played by the Pentagon to "competitive simulation" games which pit corporate competitors against each other. At the other extreme, Fidelity's Disciplined Equity Fund employs neural network technology, mimicking the intricate structure of the human brain, to pick stock.

Specifically, Fidelity's program for Disciplined Equity seeks to determine undervalued stocks relative to their industry norms. The selection must conform to predetermined fundamental and technical standards. Fidelity's program screens thousands of stocks on such criteria as historical earnings, dividend yield, price-to-book value ratio, earnings per share, payout ratio, and financial leverage.

But the computer also uses more subjective data, such as companies' growth potential, current earnings estimates, and stock buying or selling by corporate officers and directors.

Though highly diverse, mathematical models share common traits. One characteristic is an attempt to represent the real world in simplified form. A second common feature is abstraction: models are couched in mathematical equations and formulae. A third trait is that models attempt to incorporate relationships that are decision-relevant.

But even the largest computer cannot recreate every nuance and event-influencing factor. Often, empirical data are not available. In such cases, many models have the option of using managers' assumptions about causes of desired effects. These subjective estimates are justified on grounds that, when trying to simulate some process, managers' experience is better than a know-nothing attitude.

Financial service firms use models for a variety of purposes, such as: instituting customer programs, evaluating credit requests for commercial and retail loans, forecasting economic data and security prices, plotting corporate strategy, and building portfolios with computer-assisted stock selections.

The greatest advantages of mathematical models are:

- providing managers with a greater understanding of a business process, whether it is credit approval or stock selection;
- giving management a systematic way of looking at things and evaluating what it is doing (models allow management to see more clearly how things fit together);
- making ill-defined assumptions more explicit (relationships in investments and markets are expressed with greater clarity); and
- permitting sensitivity analysis, such as answering "what if" questions (this is done by altering presumed relationships programmed into computer memories and observing the "what might be" outcome).

Computers and modeling are not new to financial firms. For several years, more than 80 percent of the banking industry has been using models to score applicants' credit in commercial and consumer loans. A number of brokerage houses, pension fund managers, and mutual funds have used models for a long time to screen securities for desirable attributes, such as low P/E ratios, high yields, good cash flow, above average growth, and continuous dividend increases. Most of these applications relied on the computer's data processing ability to gush out streams of numbers, such as daily reports, bills, spreadsheets, and transaction summaries. The newer models build some judgment into the machines, making them "smart." Among these newer models, the most popular are expert systems, neural networks, and chaos theory.

Expert Systems

Expert systems are an outgrowth of artificial intelligence, which began servicing the business community in the early 1980s. The term "artificial intelligence" is a catchword for a variety of computer techniques, including expert and neural systems. The early systems overpromised benefits, understated costs, and fell into disrepute. Some 20 software houses along Massachusetts' Route 128 filed for bankruptcy when the artificial intelligence they touted produced poor results. But these systems did not disappear; they reemerged in modified forms.

Unlike early artificial intelligence programs, expert systems did not try to replicate the human brain in order to make machines think like humans. But, the expert systems did incorporate decision-making rules taken from experts. In that sense, an expert system is a decision-making technique. The decisions focus on lower-level operating tasks rather than on high-level strategies.

A widespread application of expert systems evaluates credit applicants for loans and mortgages. Credit-scoring models are developed from historical data. Their objective is to distinguish "good risks" from "bad risks" when reviewing information on loan applications. Analysts use discriminant functions or regression analysis to determine in what ways applicants who paid off their loans differ from those whose loans were charged-off. The weights assigned to each characteristic are then fed into the computer.

Most banks that use credit-scoring models set cut-off points that automatically accept or reject a loan request. For example, if the cut-off point is put at 200, credit applicants who meet that criterion are approved. Those scoring less than 200 are summarily rejected. However, the cutoff point is often ambiguous because of institutional rules of conduct. A gap or empty space might exist between the lower boundary of acceptance and the upper level of rejection. In those circumstances, a loan officer would decide whether or not to lend money to people who fall into this no-man's-land of yes-and-no.

Experience indicates that these expert scoring systems lower costs, improve control over credit, and eliminate many time-consuming procedures. For example, before an expert system was installed at American Express, dozens of credit authorizers sat at computers and looked at as many as 16 screens of data for each customer. The credit scoring system did away with all that. Lending institutions also found that the computer-based decisions actually expanded the number of customers, with no increase in delinquency rates.

Neural Networks

Neural networks try to imitate the workings of the human brain. They process information in parallel, like the brain. A simple system contains three layers: one for processing inputs, a "hidden" one to represent concepts with symbolic formulae, and a third one to produce computer outputs.

Unlike expert systems, neural networks do not require a company to specify "if this—do that." The network is supposed to "learn" as it gains experience, and set its own rules.

Studies done by Herbert L. Jensen, an Ernst & Young research fellow at California State University, Fullerton, concluded that neural networks can rate loan applications as accurately as credit scoring systems. However, the neural system expressed a bias toward approving weak loan applications. A neurotic tendency?

Neural networks are increasingly coming into use as forecasting devices in securities markets. Shearson, Lehman, now Lehman Brothers, has been experimenting with a neural network to forecast security trading patterns. This software was developed from historical data that embraced a decade of experience.

Another example is that of Troy Nolan, head of Norad, Inc. He turned from working on military software to creating a neural system for Merrill Lynch. Merrill faced the task of setting daily prices for corporate bonds and other securities.

As we said previously, Fidelity Investments has been in the forefront of applying neural network technology to financial problems. Bradford Lewis, the fund's manager, describes the system as "an index killer," alluding to the S&P 500 Index. The idea is for the fund to outperform the S&P 500.

But Fidelity is not alone among mutual funds. A number of mutual fund companies have already ventured into computer-guided investing, such as Colonial Investment Services, Guardian Investors Services, and Vanguard Group.

Chaos Theory

Chaos theorists have taken their discipline from the staid world of academia to the hectic environment of Wall Street. Financial executives still view these academics with curiosity and distrust, but they are getting a hearing. Whether rightly or wrongly, followers of chaos have thrown out compelling challenges to the conventional portfolio theory of investment, which has dominated financial thinking for more than a quarter of a century.

Contrary to its literal meaning, chaos theory does not postulate a system of hopeless confusion in either the physical universe or on Wall Street. These theorists maintain that social structure, like physical systems, often appears to follow a random pattern. But in reality, social relations adhere to a rigid set of rules that can be understood through "feedback."

Chaos theorists insist that portfolio theory is incorrect. For one thing, portfolio theory holds that markets reflect rational decisions based on information. The chaos school denies a direct causality that links changes in stock prices to changes in information. Rather, the new theory sees market players processing information in an inconsistent manner. Investors act irrationally and haphazardly. Therefore, say chaos proponents, stock prices do not mirror all publicly available data. Markets consequently represent "nonlinear" systems and require nonconventional mathematical constructs to model properly.

Currently, few financial firms have adopted chaos as a method of portfolio management. Even if theories of irrationality and inefficient markets prove valid, a firm must make a giant leap to translate this theory into investment programs. So far, chaotic programmers have not demonstrated a superiority over existing models, and firms won't pour money into untried and unproven methods.

Bull Work or Brain Work?

Today, computer-based forecasts are virtually universal. They are the outgrowth of two irrepressible forces—the enormous increase of information and the startling advances in computer technology. Continually lower costs per unit of output have enabled the computer industry to control the ever-swelling torrents of data. The key question is no longer use or disuse of computers, but what kinds of computer outputs can best guide decisions.

What roles should humans and machines play? To phrase the question in contemporary jargon: How should employees and managers "interface" with computers?

Most of the time computers grind out descriptive data which are used for both planning and control of operations. To assist in drawing up business plans, company research departments have at their disposal huge stores of conventional forecasts, such as industry production trends, sales, prices, inventories, and employment. Although financial analysts are inundated with charts, graphs, and statistical tables, they keep calling for more. Traders must have up-to-the-minute stock and bond prices at their finger-tips or they cannot act. One fund manager might want operating statistics for the leading firms of designated industries so he or she can plot buy-and-sell programs. A second manager might want figures on smaller firms. Yet another may demand all NYSE-listed companies that increased dividends in each of the last 10 years.

Operational control compares various forecasts with actual results. Sales and expenses are matched with "planned" outcomes. A large discrepancy between predictions and actualities indicates a plan gone astray. Computers track investments and relate their values to predetermined targets.

In almost all these situations the computer-generated data are neutral. They have no inherent meaning. They do not suggest what to do. Users give significance to facts and figures. Decisions and prescriptions to action are inferential and subjective. Two analysts may look at the same information and interpret it differently. The computer acts as a lifeless, mindless thing, doing bull work once done by humans. It also performs feats that lie beyond human capacity, not by "thinking" better but by working faster.

As technology develops, computers replace humans, not merely in number-crunching, but also in decision making. The newer applications empower computers with decision capabilities, as in expert systems. For example, credit scoring allows computers to approve or reject applicants. Credit card issuers rely on computers to set credit limits of cardholders. Computer trading programs trigger buying and selling activities on stock exchanges.

Yet these "decisions" are a far cry from those that call for an exercise of more complex judgment. The rules are predetermined and programmed into a machine's circuits. The machine itself has no discretion. It slavishly follows with minute detail the rules laid out by its programmer. In that respect, it can outperform human employees, and at much lower costs.

Recent models, using artificial intelligence techniques, have injected machines with "learning" skills. By comparing results with expectations, the computer modifies the rules in order to achieve predesignated goals. In other words, the computer is free to change the decision rules, but not the prime directives, which are man-made goals.

How have these machine-thinking programs worked? Since they are proprietary, their performance is not open to public scrutiny. But much of the publicity they received is seemingly exaggerated.

For example, in the second quarter of 1992 bonds yielded a total return of 2.9 percent. In contrast, stocks returned only 0.5 percent. Yet Merrill Lynch's neural network apparently failed to predict such results, and Merrill maintained its recommended asset-allocation blend at 30 percent for bonds. Lehman Brothers actually reduced its recommended proportion in bonds from 35–25 percent, materially lowering returns for its asset allocation portfolio. Although the leading brokerage houses all have some sort of computer forecasting system, they differ greatly as to their suggested mix of stocks, bonds, and cash. Table 11–1 shows the recommendations of a select number of brokerage houses, as reported in July 1993 by *The Wall Street Journal*.

On the basis of Table 11–1, Prudential was bearish on bonds, while A.G. Edwards called the turn correctly. Kemper apparently liked neither stocks nor bonds, and increased its horde of cash. Lehman Brothers was bullish on stocks—the wrong call. Merrill kept its middle-of-the-road course. It is at once obvious that the computer models of all brokerage houses cannot be right.

Table 11-1. Recommended Asset-Allocation Blend of Select Brokerage Houses (as of June 30, 1993)

Firm	Stocks	Bonds	Cash
	(%)	(%)	(%)
A. G. Edwards	55	40	5
Goldman Sachs	60	35	5
Kemper	50	20	30
Lehman Bros.	75	25	0
Merrill Lynch	55	30	15
Paine Webber	73	26	1
Prudential	70	10	20
Raymond James	60	20	20
Salomon Brothers	45	30	25

Many large brokerage houses and mutual funds, loaded with computers worth billions of dollars, have failed to achieve above-average performance. For the last five-year period, professional managers under performed the S&P 500 Index. In July of 1992 IBM's stock sold for more than $100 a share. By the end of the year IBM's value sank to about $50 per share. Yet 12 out of 31 analysts reportedly issued "buy" recommendations on IBM as late as September. Only three analysts had a "sell," even in December when IBM announced it could no longer support its dividend. In six months, a veritable American institution saw its market value fall by an astonishing $28 billion, and Wall Street forecasts gave nary a hint of the catastrophic event.

Fidelity's Disciplined Equity Fund probably received more publicity than any other fund with respect to its neural network system. Several articles have highlighted the fund's performance, which since 1991 has bettered the S&P 500 Index by comfortable margins.

Yes, Disciplined Equity, a growth fund, performed well. But in a rising stock market, most growth funds outperformed the S&P 500. Morningstar's newsletter of March 1993, *5-Star Investor*, notes that "nobody's diversified stock funds measure up to Fidelity's." The article attributes Fidelity's superiority to larger economies of scale, an outstanding research department, and strong management. Morningstar is a research firm that rates and evaluates funds.

So let's compare Disciplined Equity and Stock Selector with other equity growth stocks in Fidelity's portfolio. Both Disciplined and Stock Selector are managed by Malcolm Lewis, with a big assist from the neural network.

As Table 11–2 shows, every Fidelity growth fund except one outdid Disciplined Equity and Stock Selector. Since these other funds ostensibly did not rely on a neural network to make stock selections, computer-made decisions did not translate into a competitive advantage.

Even the strongest proponents of artificial intelligence models view them with apprehension. Fidelity's Brad Lewis attributes his

Table 11-2. Total Returns of Fidelity Growth Funds

Fund	6 Months	1 Year	3 Years
Dis. Eq.	5.9%	15.7	15.0%
Stock Sel	8.0	21.3	NS
Blue Chip	12.7	25.8	19.8
Contra	13.9	28.2	25.2
Destiny I	13.1	23.9	18.6
Destiny II	12.8	23.3	19.4
Exch	2.4	9.9	9.9
Gro Co	8.1	27.7	17.0
Magin	15.6	23.8	16.9
Trend	9.7	29.1	15.3

Note: Three-year returns are annualized.

Source: Based on "Mutual Funds Quarterly Report," *The Wall Street Journal* (July 6, 1993), p. R12.

funds' above-average returns to his model's selections, but does not hesitate to override its "dumb" decisions. In Stock Selector's Semi-annual Report, ended April 30, 1993, Lewis tells about his veto of the computer's tobacco stock picks. Though cheap on a historical basis, Lewis writes, these stocks "can go lower if tobacco products are hit with taxes to fund a health-care program. So I'm not buying them." His decisions to buy gold stocks and hold healthcare stocks also went against his computer's "advice," but made money.

Despite PR hyperbole, managers generally do not trust computers to change investment rules that matter. Fidelity's Disciplined Equity Fund employs its computer to screen 2,000 stocks on 115 variables to identify undervalued securities. A task of such magnitude goes beyond human capabilities. It calls for fast and extensive processing. But the two funds using the neural network then fall back on Fidelity's bottom-up approach to investing. Teams of research analysts visit companies that have passed the screening criteria, talk to their managements, and evaluate their prospects. Only after studying those reports do fund managers choose what they deem the most attractive investments.

Computers do the bull work. They screen out possible buying situations. Computers propose. Human managers do the brain work; they dispose.

Forecasts of Expected Corporate Earnings

Regardless of the investment model in use, expected corporate earnings form a basic component of stock-picking decisions. Securities analysts compose the main source of bottom-line forecasts, the consensus of which has become a virtual proxy of market expectations. Empirical research strongly supports the dominance of "consensus forecasts." In general, numerous studies show securities analysts' predictions as superior to those based on time series. But how good are they?

Both academic and industry researchers have studied this subject extensively for almost two decades. Though explanations vary, virtually all studies agree on one central theme: consensus forecasts leave much to be desired.

A recent study by David Dreman, chairman of Dreman Value Management, in collaboration with Michael Berry, a professor at James Madison University, provided more documentation of incredible forecasting. Dreman reported the research findings in an article entitled "Chronically Clouded Crystal Balls," published in the October 11, 1993 issue of *Forbes*. The Dreman-Berry study sampled more than 67,000 quarterly estimates of stock on the New York and American exchanges. To avoid distortions of extreme deviations, the authors used a minimum of six forecasts per company. The minimum base for more widely-followed companies was twenty-plus forecasts.

According to Dreman, forecasts less than three months old missed their quarterly targets by an average of 40 percent. Some 57 percent of these quarterly consensus estimates deviated from reported earnings by more than 10 percent, and a little less than half by more than 15 percent. Dreman calls such forecasts "utterly undependable."

If short-term forecasts are of such poor quality, what can we say about long-term expectations? Many stocks are bought on the basis of expected earnings which are to emerge far in the future. For example, Value Line projects companies' bottom-line prospects three-to-five years out. Mutual funds, which account for the lion's share of securities trading, constantly sing the praises of investing for the long haul. However, many funds "turn over" their portfolios at a high rate. Yet recommendations for long-term investments hardly inspire confidence when they rest on flimsy foundations. Dremon writes that when using forecasts for long-term investments, "chances of being right are not much higher than winning a lottery."

Another recent study by Lucy F. Ackert, a professor at Wilfred Laurier University, Ontario, and William C. Hunter, a vice-president of the Federal Reserve Bank of Atlanta, evaluated 3,864 estimates of securities analysts. This study was reported as Working Paper 93-9 (August 1993) by the Federal Reserve Bank of Atlanta.

The authors examined earnings forecasts from the standpoint of "rational expectations." In a technical context, a forecast must meet two criteria to pass the test of economic rationality:

1. Forecast errors must have a mean of zero. As compared with reported earnings, overstated and understated forecasts must average out so as to offset each other. That is, pluses and minuses from actual earnings must net out at zero. This property, known as "orthogonality," implies an unbiased estimate.

2. Forecast errors must be uncorrelated with the values of all other variables. This property, known as the lack of a serial correlation, implies that forecast errors are not related to past values of the information set.

Ackert and Hunter are more charitable than other writers toward securities analysts. These two authors argue that since firms monitor and revise earnings, the constant updating produces forecasts that "converge toward rational expectations." But firms that trade in securities might find the unadjusted forecasting errors quite costly. They may have no time to act on the revision. They can incur substantial losses to remedy a mistake, especially if the value of a security drops precipitously. Revising forecasts might reduce losses, but it cannot prevent them.

Except for the matter of revisions, the Ackert-Hunter study is consistent with the findings of other research:

- Forecasts depart substantially from actual results.
- Forecasts display a tendency to overstate subsequent reported earnings.
- Forecasts reveal a "herding" instinct among securities analysts. Their releases look like those of other analysts, even when the information on hand supports a contrary forecast. If analysts are wrong, they don't want to stand alone in the spotlight.

Regardless of the reasons for poor forecasts, commentators have proposed a number of remedies. Those that enjoy the most currency are contrarianism, value investing, and risk adjustment. These corrective measures are not mutually exclusive.

David Dreman argues that a contrarian approach to investing can turn analysts' follies into opportunities.[1] But there is no conclusive proof that contrarians make superior stock selections. If half the forecasts fall outside of acceptable limits, the contrarian cannot know which half is correct. To use an old cliche, a glass half full is also a glass half empty.

Value investing is a conservative approach, relying on continuous revisions. This strategy focuses on monitoring reported earnings to detect forecasting errors. Since Wall Street usually overreacts to earnings that deviate from forecasts, value investors look for "beaten down" stocks, especially those with low price-earnings ratios. Several computer programs screen "undervalued" stocks of companies in the same industry. This approach takes advantage of

---

1   David Dreman, "Chronically Clouded Crystal Balls," *Forbes* (October 11, 1993), p. 178.

---

forecasts that understate earnings; it anticipates "undervalued" stocks to make above-average gains when actual earnings exceed forecasts. Value investing contains subjective judgments as to what constitutes an "undervalued" stock.

The risk-adjustment approach commonly uses volatility of consensus forecasts as a measure of "risk." Anticipated gains are then gauged against the potential risks of achieving them. A risk-adjusted performance is intuitively appealing. It rests on two basic assumptions. First, the idea assumes that forecasting variability is a true measure of risk. In reality, it is only a proxy for risk. Second, the degree of acceptable risk remains a subjective decision, the correctness of which cannot be verified. Critics argue that only real performance, not risk-adjusted performance, describes the contribution to a bottom line. Though risk-adjusted methods may lead to better results, they still fall short of optimality.

Fractured Models

Why haven't computers, with immense knowledge-storing capacity and even "learning" skills, failed to best the puny human brain? Is it a plot hatched by vested interests? Do humans willfully sabotage the handiwork of a seemingly superior entity and engage in a nefarious cover-up? Wrong!

Regardless of their huge memories, no computer can embrace all of reality. Models only simulate reality by sets of abstractions, and, in doing so, create a reality of their own. This new reality, encapsulated in a closed system, is guided by its own rules of logic. Events in this artificially-created universe invariably digress from those in the larger world that models are supposed to represent.

Here's why:

Faulty assumptions.
In constructing a model, the first step is to specify the underlying assumptions about causal relationships. An assumption is an assertion which, more often than not, cannot be verified in advance. Yet such judgments must be made, because they form the support upon

which every model rests. They carry the model's postulates about the essence of reality.

The category of assumptions that is most troublesome in economic model-building relates to the environment. These assumptions circumscribe the mathematical abstractions. For example, how do market forces influence behavior of what you want to predict? In what ways do government actions affect business outcomes? When these economic or political forces act otherwise than assumed, they can cause large distortions from reality, and bring into question the validity of the model itself.

Relevant factors are omitted.

For example, Fidelity's computer recommendation to buy tobacco stocks was based on a mathematical deviation from some "norm" or trend line. The model had no way of factoring in a political possibility. Nor can the choice of individual stocks account for competitive action, or other possible events which have not yet occurred.

Models often generalize from the part to the whole. For example, a model might say that a reduction in price will result in an increase in sales. But if competitive firms do the same thing, the price cutter will not benefit.

Generalizations from a part to the whole are often referred to as the "fallacy of composition." This reasoning process holds that events influencing the part are analogous to those affecting the whole. They may not be.

Irrelevant factors are included.

In cases where experience is sparse, or hard facts are not available, executives' opinions are fed into estimating equations. If their assessments are wrong, computers grind out decisions by assumption.

Another way irrelevant factors find their way into models is when events of the whole are generalized to the part. Errors of this type are often referred to as the fallacy of division. For example, the NAFTA treaty expands trade between Mexico and the United States. Would U.S. textile mills also witness an expansion of sales? Many mills would find their competitive positions worse off competing with cheap labor south of the border. In that event, the assumptions about the beneficial effects of the treaty would not be valid for a particular company.

Factors have wrong values.
Flawed statistics are fed into the model. Figures by both government and private sources contain errors. For example, the price-earnings ratio is generally regarded as a key determinant in the price of a stock. Yet, projected earnings are themselves subject to many vagaries. Table 11–3 shows 1993 earnings estimates made at the beginning of the year for a select number of large companies. The figures, collected by Zacks Investment Research, were reported in *The Wall Street Journal,* January 18, 1993.

Industry estimates are also highly variable. Figures compiled by Institutional Brokers Estimate System in December, 1992 showed consensus estimates of share earnings for 1993 in complete disarray. They varied by 22 percent for the fuel industry, but by 70 percent for the steel and airlines industries.

Updating forecasts in the financial service industry, like restructuring in corporate America, has become a major preoccupation in business. In both instances, the terms that describe the

Table 11-3. Estimates of 1993 Earnings per Share

Company	Low	Consensus	High
ALCOA	$3.70	$5.00	$9.00
Caterpillar	1.00	2.20	4.50
Ford	1.40	2.85	4.50
Georgia Pacific	0.90	2.10	4.00
Phelps Dodge	1.70	4.50	6.50
UAL	(3.00)	5.88	12.00

Source: Based on a report in *TheWall Street Journal* (January 18, 1993).

activities are euphemisms for corrections of past mistakes. When garbage goes into models, garbage comes out.

Relationships among factors are wrong.

Variables can be incorrectly linked for various reasons, ranging from errors in data to incorrect assumptions about what impels events. For example, marketing research has consistently shown that high ratings on "satisfaction" are related to customer loyalty. But does customer satisfaction produce customer loyalty? Both loyalty and satisfaction with respect to a mutual fund may be caused by good returns on investment. A fund which yields good returns usually has satisfied customers who are not about to redeem their shares. Figure 11–1 diagrams the two views on loyalty-satisfaction relationships.

Computer models hold ever-larger quantities of data. The mere increase of information, however, does not make predictions more accurate. On the contrary, size and complexity make Murphy's Law more likely; more things are apt to go wrong.

Then why create mindless giants as keepers of our knowledge? As information capabilities expand, financial service firms take on more functions. Trading securities worldwide, for example, neces-

Figure 11–1. Assumed Loyalty and Satisfaction Relationships

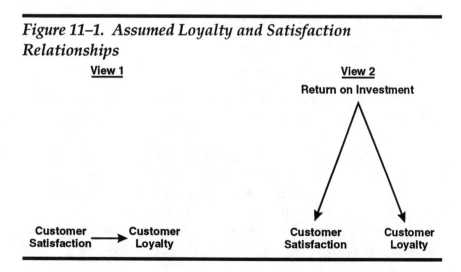

sitates vastly more information that must be available instantly. If information holds opportunities, computer systems are the only means of preventing this tidal wave of data from engulfing us. Computer systems enable us to reduce data and extract only those parts relevant for efficient operation. It is impossible to do that job manually. From this standpoint, computer modeling represents an investment the outlays of which should be judged against expected returns.

Computer systems also reduce operating costs. Even if a mechanical system does not improve decisions, it can still replace wage labor with slave labor. Computers do not agitate for wage increases, halt work for coffee-breaks and lunch, and take vacations. They don't complain about petty slights and ill-mannered behavior of supervisors. They do exactly what they are told to do. They have much to commend them, even if they do not think like humans. On the other hand, managers should not attempt to remake human beings so that they think like computers.

Summary

The four most popular methods of forecasting are:

1. time series,

2. correlation and regression,

3. data analysis techniques, and

4. mathematical modelling.

Time series techniques are basically extrapolations of past data, such as "charting" stock prices and projecting economic and business trends.

Correlation analysis relies on association to formulate predictive equations, called regression equations.

Data analysis techniques are used primarily in marketing, as in segmenting markets and customer databases.

Mathematical models are of various kinds: expert systems, artificial intelligence, neural networks, and systems using chaos theory. Their major applications are evaluating credit applications and securities.

As more and more information becomes available, computers become all the more necessary to handle the vast amounts of data. But firms are confronted with problems of data overload.

Appendix 11

Table A11-1. Leading Twenty Banks Worldwide

Bank	Country	Assets*	Profits*
Sumitomo Bank	Japan	575,842	196
Fuji Bank	Japan	564,977	541
Sakura Bank	Japan	556,212	539
Dai-ichi Bank	Japan	554,168	439
Sanwa Bank	Japan	552,161	887
Mitsubishi Bank	Japan	483,841	700
Industrial Bank of Japan	Japan	413,563	382
Long-Term Credit Bank of Japan	Japan	317,213	218
Tokai Bank	Japan	313,591	236
Deutsche Bank	Germany	311,643	1,128
BNP	France	291,775	403
Asahi Bank	Japan	281,985	337
Bank of Tokyo	Japan	271,707	353
HSBC Holdings	Britain	266,236	1,907
Societe Generale	France	264,235	608
ABN AMRO Holdings	Netherlands	257,871	847
Barclays Bank	Britain	229,853	722
National Westminster Bank	Britain	223,607	300
Citicorp	U.S.	217,000**	722
Paribas	France	208,969	165

*In US$ millions.

*Based on 1991 data.

Note: Assets and profits are for 1992 fiscal year, except for Japanese banks which are based on the latest figures reported before May 31, 1993. All after-tax earnings are translated at currency exchange rates as of May 31, 1993.

Source: Based on "The Business Week Global 1000," Business Week (July 12, 1993).

12
Toward the 21st Century

Though difficult to discern, the seeds of the future lie imbedded in the present. What major trends can we expect will emerge by the 21st century?

This chapter identifies three major trends that will drive change:

- The expansion of financial services firms into diverse lines of business (this implies a diversification of their product mix)
- The continued globalization of commercial services
- Increasing computerization, which will become more necessary to handling information and competing in a broader marketplace

All three megatrends will revolve around concerted efforts to reduce transaction costs.

The Pace of Change

Practically every business operation anticipates change. When a specific event in the industry occurs, logical reactions occur. This is certainly true of the financial service industry. What will the industry look like in the 21st century?

If the past is any indication, we can expect change to proceed at a snail's pace. For example, ATMs were introduced more than a quarter-century ago. Yet, even today, a sizable portion of older customers do not use them. Banks will only realize the full benefits of this technology as new generations of depositors, more familiar with computers, replace their parents and grandparents. So, change will be evolutionary, with newer and older ways of doing things existing side by side for many years as the world rolls on in a slow, muddle-headed manner. But eventually, a time comes when the old becomes obsolete, and eventually ceases to exist.

What drives such changes? Three interrelated trends will shape the future course of the financial service industry. These megatrends are: financial department stores; increasing globalization of financial services; and an expanding volume of information handled electronically. Each of these trends poses major challenges to financial services companies, which in turn prompt corporate actions.

The major long-term issues deal essentially with asset allocation. Exploiting these issues raises a number of questions, such as:

- What are the best ways to employ company resources?
- Given available resources, what is the most advantageous product mix?
- How can we gain a competitive advantage?

There is no single answer to these questions. Problems and solutions are in part company-specific, since each firm markets a different product mix and commands varying resources. But management response to long-term change seems to revolve around a single strong, unifying force—the reduction of transaction costs.

Financial Department Stores

The United States is a mature economy, an economy driven by consumer demand. The consumer segment accounts for the lion's share of gross domestic product. One characteristic of economic maturity is slow growth. Over the past two decades, our real growth has been less than most industrial countries and substantially below that of emerging nations.

How then will financial firms grow in a business environment of creeping expansion? One way is by expanding into different lines of business. This approach works best when a firm uses "asset synergy" or "economies of scope," two or more activities using the same assets. A firm embarks on a new venture that is closely related to an existing business. This type of expansion describes an old strategy. At the turn of the century, department stores were built on that very principle. Different merchandising lines were simply put together under one roof, sharing the same facilities, same fixed costs, and same management. Each business addition came at low incremental cost. This lesson from the past has now gripped the financial field.

American Express used its existing businesses as the foundation to establish various ventures. For example, the AmEx travel business drew its sustenance from its Traveler's Cheques. With acceptance of its Traveler's Cheques worldwide, issuance of credit cards was the next logical step. Businesses that accepted AmEx's cheques quickly accepted the credit cards.

When AmEx built up a large customer database of cardholders, the firm launched magazines catering to travel and entertainment, with titles such as *Travel & Leisure* and *Food & Wine*.

Its credit card base of customers also encouraged the establishment of a direct marketing group. Monthly statements are stuffed with flyers for luggage, jewelry, clothes, and electronics. Merchandisers at AmEx use cardholder purchase information to plan their assortments and promotions. By the beginning of the 1990s, direct sales were running close to $600 million a year.

In 1987 American Express introduced Optima, a credit card designed to compete directly with bank cards. Optima was offered to existing cardholders who had a good payment record.

Because AmEx marketed only to its own customers, its introductory costs were low—only a fraction of the money spent by Sears when launching the Discover card. For example, Sears reported losses of more than $200 million before reaching a break-even point. In contrast, Optima contributed profits almost immediately.

Synergy worked for AmEx. But the marketing program restricted Optima only to current AmEx cardholders, and so limited Optima's market share. As compared with the 36 million credit cards issued by Sears, AmEx garnered only one-tenth that figure.

Though synergy is useful, it cannot by itself produce a major market presence. If you want to be a big player, you must be willing to ante up big bucks.

Following a retailing strategy, Sears in the 1980s acquired Dean, Witter and Century 21. Already owning Allstate Insurance, the idea was a "one-stop shopping" mart which offered both goods and financial services. At a single location Sears would repair cars, service air conditioners, and sell apparel, appliances, insurance, securities, and real estate. Sears' strategy was analogous to the conventional wisdom of joining diverse goods and services under one management, with stores selling these assortments at each location.

Recession and the real estate collapse in 1990 forced Sears to retreat from its strategy of retailing both goods and financial services. But many financial institutions have been honing that strategy for many years, broadening their range of services. They pushed into many new lines of business by emphasizing existing skills and facilities.

For example, Merrill Lynch is the largest brokerage firm in the United States. It used it core business to penetrate almost every part of the financial services industry in an aggressive expansion program.

With its stock and bond trading know-how, Merrill employed its large financial resources to become the second largest mutual-fund manager in the nation. As of June 1993, Merrill managed more than $110 billion in fund assets. In addition, the firm oversees more than $71 billion in individual retirement funds. That total exceeds the combined amount managed by the 100 leading banks. Merrill Lynch is also the largest manager of money market funds, which offers customers check-writing and credit card options.

From its core operations in brokerage, Merrill also branched out into investment banking. Instead of just trading securities, the firm began underwriting them. Today, Merrill stands as the nation's largest securities underwriter. It is involved in bringing to market almost 20 percent of all new stocks and bonds issued in the United

States. Merrill's Interfunding unit loaned $1 billion to small businesses, though this business is now winding down.

Merrill's other banking and nonbrokerage businesses include a $13 billion insurance line, making it the 24th largest insurer. The firm makes loans to individuals, such as mortgages, home equity, and mortgage refinancings. In other instances, the company allows holders of cash management and brokerage accounts to borrow against their assets held by the firm.

Is Merrill Lynch really a brokerage firm? Though executives may still regard securities trading as its core business, commissions accounted for only 27 percent of its total revenue. The remaining 73 percent comes from fees and non-trading activities. In the true sense of the word, Merrill Lynch is a highly diversified financial company, providing both banking and nonbanking services.

Like retailers who melded various product lines into one-place shopping emporiums, Merrill Lynch represents a financial services counterpart. The product mix displays a hybrid of brokerage, banking, insurance, and real estate operations.

Another outstanding example of employing a core business to expand product lines is that of Fidelity Investments. Like Merrill Lynch, Fidelity's main business remains mutual fund sponsorship and management. With more than six million customers and some 200 funds, Fidelity stands above other funds like a giant in a land of pygmies.

As a company, however, Fidelity encompasses more than a narrow mutual funds niche.

Insofar as Fidelity doesn't take deposits and make loans, it does not legally qualify as a bank. But the firm engages in banking as well as in brokerage. Fidelity's money market funds pay interest to depositors, called fundholders. The firm offers checking privileges, issues VISA credit cards, and fills ATM networks. Except for the fact that money held in funds does not bear the stamp of a government guarantee, differences between bank deposits and money market holdings are mainly superficial.

Fidelity Investments runs a large discount brokerage operation that is *second* only to Charles Schwab in trading volume. In addition to handling diversified securities instruments, Fidelity's brokerage unit sells the mutual funds of other financial houses.

Fidelity is now a market leader in managing pension funds, particularly the "defined contribution" type. Its enormous investment in information technology allows it to process its own proxy solicitations, amounting to more than 30,000 ballots. Its software program, called Proxy Edge, is currently being offered to other firms, putting Fidelity in the data processing business.

Other large mutual fund companies have taken the same diversification route as Fidelity. George M. Salem, banking analyst at Prudential Securities, describes mutual funds as "the bank deposits of the 1990s."

As mutual funds carry out banking functions, banks have moved into mutual funds, insurance, annuities, and brokerage. Because earnings from investment management have become increasingly important as a source of bank income, banks are becoming less dependent upon lending.

The idea of "traditional banking" today is virtually an anachronism. A wide array of financial products, including investments in equities, bonds, and collateralized mortgage obligations are as common as deposits, checking, and auto loans. Only firms with limited resources now pursue a course of single-line products and niche markets.

Banks strive to develop a cornucopia of products to meet almost all financial needs of customers. In that process, they join together market segments and often disregard them entirely. There are few meaningful distinctions among holders of equities, bonds, CDs, and money market accounts. Money flows are determined largely by perceived risk and expected returns. Offers of multiple products by the same firm blur market segments, and obscure traditional definitions of business lines such as banking, insurance, and brokerage.

Globalization

The trend toward globalization of financial services was strongly spurred by better growth prospects in many overseas economies. Over the last two decades the United States has lagged behind most industrialized nations in economic expansion. The demand for capital is especially large in high-growth areas which promise larger returns than mature, slow-growth regions. As financial markets develop in countries with rapidly expanding economies, these nations attract more investments from areas of capital surpluses.

Capital flows over national borders as easily as goods. From 1980 to 1990, U.S. transactions in foreign securities increased at a compound annual rate of 30.4 percent. However, cross-border investments are not all one-way. Foreign investments in America also have grown during the 1980s, but at a rate of 17 percent. Net U.S. purchases of foreign securities in 1992 set a record of $48.6 billion, having increased by $3.6 billion from the 1991 record year. It is estimated that more than 10 percent of American portfolios are invested in foreign securities.

At the beginning of 1991, foreign branches of U.S. banks held total assets approximating $557 billion. U.S. affiliates of finance, insurance, and real estate firms accounted for capital expenditures of approximately $2.9 trillion in 1992. This figure stood at $552 billion in 1983, representing an increase of more than 400 percent in a decade. The greatest gain was registered in Europe, where American capital grew from $199 million to $1,741 billion. Asia and the Pacific rim was next with $544 million, having increased from a mere $62 million in 1983.

American investments flowed most heavily into major markets, such as Canada in North America, United Kingdom in Europe, and Japan in the Orient. Yet the movement of American funds abroad was impressive, considering that investors face greater risks when they stray from the environment of their national borders.

Investments outside the United States are normally denominated in foreign currencies, which are generally more volatile than dollars. Though many U.S. companies engage in "transaction hedg-ing," they cannot protect themselves completely against uncertainty in currency exchange rates. Rules abroad for auditing and financial reporting are not as demanding as are U.S. standards. Information about foreign companies lacks the detail or reliability of data re-ported on American firms. Political systems, legal climates, and business customs impose additional risks on Americans going abroad. The dangers and pitfalls of foreign investments, however, do not set up prohibitive barriers that exclude American firms from seeking the rewards of higher growth.

Globalization of financial services has increased competition both here and abroad. American credit cards took on an interna-tional flavor, gaining acceptance throughout the world. While U.S. banks penetrated distant markets, foreign banks established strong footholds in the United States. Japanese banks in particular fun-nelled large portions of their bloated export surpluses into global investments. Despite a sharp recession at home, Japanese banks in 1992 accounted for a staggering $2 trillion in international loans. They made 16 percent of all commercial and industrial loans in the United States, and a whopping 35 percent in California.

Business Alliances

As financial firms expand their products, both at home and abroad, few have the money, manpower, or expertise to pursue every new line of business. Joint ventures have always been common in secu-rities underwriting and in real estate, where either risk or capital requirements are too large for a firm to go it alone. In these cases, a number of firms would pool risks and capital for a particular endeavor and go their separate ways when the job was finished. Today, however, cooperative projects have proliferated to almost every type of venture, and are more enduring than the stand-alone job.

On the domestic scene, joint ventures between banks and non-banks are common in "co-branding" credit cards, such as those sponsored by GM, Ford, H&R Block, K-Mart, AARP, and a host of other organizations. In most instances, banks issue cards tied to organizations and businesses because these nonbanks have ready access to markets. In turn, the bank contributes its expertise in operating a credit card company.

Lately, many banks have entered into partnerships with brokerage houses to offer customer services for trading in securities. The brokerage contributes its trading know-how, while the bank sets up accounts which transfer money electronically when securities are bought and sold. These accounts usually have check-writing options.

On the foreign scene, financial services offer what Harvard's Michael Porter considers "multidomestic" products. Such services are best rendered when providers maintain a physical presence in the market. Foreign banks, for example, must operate in the United States if they wish to serve American clients. Likewise, American banks must set up offices in foreign nations to do business there. Most of these services cannot be exported from a home base.

Building a physical presence outside the United States is facilitated enormously by joint venturing with a partner from the host country. A foreign partner, with a standing in the community and access to markets, offers a benefit that cannot be underestimated. Among the principal benefits brought by a foreign partner are familiarity with home markets and distribution outlets, particularly in non-English speaking lands.

A number of governments, mainly in Latin America and Asia, have imposed various restrictions and "performance" standards on foreign firms. With memories of Western colonialism still lingering, some developing nations make it mandatory for a foreign firm to take on a native partner. They also limit the proportion of stock a foreigner can own, in order to prevent foreign control of economic resources. Our southern neighbor, Mexico, has in place legal barriers to majority control of Mexican firms by foreign corporations, even though Mexico badly wants infusions of capital. In other instances, governments restrict the number of foreign firms by a confusing web of arcane laws and numbing regulations.

Even a global powerhouse such as Japan presents a hostile climate for non-Japanese financial firms to do business in that country. The entry of financial services into foreign markets often must be aided by loose alliances, joint ventures, or mergers and acquisitions.

Why should American firms seek to enter markets where they operate at a disadvantage and where their investments may be in jeopardy? While financial markets in many Asian and Latin American countries are barely developed, their economic growth has been dramatic and expansion in manufacturing and trade result in the need for new capital and financial expertise not available from their native financial institutions. Emerging economies require financial services such as insurance, pension plan management, payroll processing, and short-term credit. Capital in underdeveloped nations is always in short supply, and their governments are usually looking for help in financing large-scale projects, such as building highways, bridges, and power-generating plants. Many of these economies have a burgeoning growing middle class with new wealth and an increasing need for financial services.

Mexico admirably illustrates the reciprocal relationship of rapid economic development and financial services. The insurance industry is a case in point. In 1992 Mexico's insurance premiums grew more than 20 percent, amounting to $5 billion. Yet, insurance remains a small, undeveloped industry. The country itself still lacks an "insurance culture." When an earthquake hit Mexico City in 1985 only 15 percent of the buildings were insured. Despite the impressive growth of the country's middle class, the average Mexican spends only $31 annually on insurance. Less than 2 percent of the population carries life insurance. Only one-fourth of automobile owners have car insurance, despite the high incidence of auto accidents in Mexico. Even professionals, such as doctors and lawyers, are unlikely to have liability insurance.

In order to "get in on the ground floor," a number of foreign insurance companies have begun operations in Mexico. Aetna International recently bought a 30 percent share of Seguros Monterrey, satisfied that its $100 million outlay of "patient capital" will eventually yield good returns. Metropolitan Life, acting with Banco Santander of Spain, acquired a 49 percent share of Seguros Genesis, Mexico's ninth-largest life insurance company. Analysts project Mexico's insurance industry to grow some 900 percent within the next 10 years.

Mexico is not merely underinsured; it is "underbanked." Privatization began only in 1991, and bank competition is still sparse. With passage of the North American Free Trade Agreement (NAFTA), U.S. banks are now allowed to open subsidiaries in Mexico. Among major U.S. banks planning to establish branches south of the border are Chemical Bank, Chase Manhattan, J.P. Morgan, Bankers Trust, and Midland Bank. Citibank, which ran branches in Mexico since the 1930s, plans to add its operations. Twenty-one and one half of the banks moving into Mexico are expected to concentrate on areas where they enjoy competitive advantages, such as mergers and acquisitions, foreign exchange transactions, and securities trading. Most will bypass consumer services.

Though NAFTA creates equal operating conditions for both American and Mexican banks, it does not do away with limits on volume. U.S. banks must limit their individual market shares to 1.5 percent of the banking system's total assets. The combined share of all U.S. banks is set at 8.0 percent for 1994, and rises gradually thereafter to 15 percent by 1999. With its financial sector projected to expand at a 10 percent to 15 percent annual rate for the next several years, Mexico should afford American banks plenty of room to grow.

In another part of the world, China represents the prime attraction among emerging markets. This sleeping giant has finally awakened from centuries of rural slumber, and now promises to become one of the world's largest economies by the end of this decade.

Although U.S. diplomatic relations cooled since the Tiananmen "massacre," American business activity keeps ballooning. United States' 1993 investments in China are estimated at $5 billion.

Many of our financial firms have invested in Asian companies that operate in China. Hong Kong's Hang Seng Index, which lists a number of mainland outfits, has become the center for Chinese investments. The United States' financial inroads into China should be further encouraged by the Chinese government's proposed reforms of its banking institutions.

When a company goes into a market which is expanding at a supernormal rate, its competitive strategy targets rapid market penetration. Boston Consulting Group has long maintained that market shares acquired early yield compounded returns. For example, if analysts are correct about Mexico, current insurance premiums of $5 billion will grow to $50 billion in 10 years. If a company could gain just 1 percent of that market today, its premiums would amount to $50 million. If this same company could maintain that measly 1 percent share of the market, its premiums would mount to $500 million in 10 years. And the ideal time to build a business is in the early growth stage, when customers are first coming into the market. Increasing business is extremely difficult and more expensive to get when the market approaches saturation and increases of new customers slow to a trickle.

Information Handling

As financial markets expand both here and abroad, there is an ever-greater need for information. Banks and lending agencies must process greater quantities of loan information. Growing customer databases mean more internal processing. Large banks, insurers, and mutual funds, which must process the small transactions made by millions of customers, spend money lavishly to handle mountains of data. Every year these companies upgrade their abilities to store, analyze, and retrieve the information contained in their internal databases and information transmitted from the outside.

More number-crunching power might keep up with the constantly growing volume of information. But, the solution to the information deluge is not buying more powerful and faster machines. What and how information is processed remain the keys to information handling. Financial firms serve as information-users and information-providers, and those that can gain greater efficiency will also gain a competitive advantage. Assuming that the right tasks are implemented, information programs will increasingly become the launching pads for all financial services.

The most effective programs will hinge on two aspects of information handling.

- Customer involvement.
- Replacing print with electronic media.

Customer Involvement

Financial firms copied the department store approach to broaden their customer base. Now, they need to copy retailers' self-service systems. Self-service, a frequent euphemism for no service, lets customers do their own searching, comparing, and selecting of merchandise. Greater customer involvement has the potential of significantly lowering costs by reducing human labor. The store just puts a checkout counter at the exit to ring up sales. In like manner, financial firms already have customers transacting business with no help from behind-the-counter personnel. ATMs have for a long time symbolized the do-it-yourself approach in financial services.

One aspect of consumer involvement relates to what is called electronic interactive media. Most of these services are in the exploratory stage, though interactive media has been in existence in some forms since the late 1970s. The oldest and largest ongoing service is Prodigy, a joint venture of IBM and Sears. Having begun development work in 1982, Prodigy introduced the service to PC owners in 1988. The service was initially intended as a device with which consumers could electronically shop, bank, and transmit and receive information. The emphasis, however, was on shopping. As it turned out, neither shopping nor banking from one's home captured much consumer enthusiasm. Instead, the most popular usage of Prodigy is electronic mail and the acquisition of information.

Though Prodigy claims about two million subscribers, and has spent about $1 billion, it has yet to show any profits. Reaching a break-even point has been pushed to 1995 from 1993, and many observers doubt that the flow of red ink will stop even then.

The second largest interactive service is CompuServe, a unit of H&R Block, Inc. The system claims some one million subscribers and is oriented toward financial data and information. It has been profitable since 1981, but whether it has yielded adequate returns on investment is doubtful.

More recent interactive systems are either small-scale operations or still in the planning stage. These systems have expanded transmission methods to include telephones and television in addition to computers. At the end of 1992, Prodigy began exploring how television can enhance usage of its services.

A recent entry into the electronic interactive field is America Online, an outgrowth of Quantum Computer Services. This Virginia-based company has only 180,000 subscribers. Its services are customized to local markets and to special consumer groups.

Typifying this segmentation strategy is a deal made with SeniorNet, an organization that promotes computer usage by senior citizens. America Online receives a commission for each member who signs up. In turn, America Online installs special features of interest to older people, such as information on healthcare and sex.

A somewhat hybrid electronic-print service is that of the *Atlanta Journal and Constitution*. This service, called FaxTicker, offers fax messages on demand. Subscribers can call up a stock in which they are interested and receive a fax report in seconds.

A number of new entrants into the electronic interactive field are now on the horizon. The most prominent are AT&T and a proposed venture of Lotus and Philips Electronics NV. Both projects combine phones and computer capabilities.

AT&T's SmartPhone program, announced at the end of 1991 (but not available then), uses a touchscreen input device. The Lotus-Philips project is similar to the AT&T proposal, but is apt to use standard PC chips and software, with inputting done from a keyboard. This venture will use technology developed for Citibank's Enhanced Telephone project. The system employs a telephone with a video screen to perform banking tasks at home. The Lotus-Philips venture will initially target the financial service market, such as home-banking, bill-paying, and on-line information services. Plans are to eventually move into the home-shopping area.

Multimedia services combining communications, computers, and video technologies are still in experimental stages. These services are presently dominated by telephone companies and cable systems. But, a large number of contenders loom on the multimedia horizon. Among them are equipment manufacturers, software houses, and entertainment companies. For example, in January 1993, media giant Time Warner announced plans to build an "electronic superhighway" to deliver a variety of services on demand. According to company spokespersons, the system will begin operating in the suburbs of Orlando, Florida in 1994. Other significant multimedia plans in the works are those of First Cities, a group of eleven cooperating companies which include Apple Computer, Tandem Computers, and U.S. West; a Hewlett-Packard-TV Answer, Inc. alliance that visualizes a network of stations tied by satellite; and Tele-Communications, Inc. that plans to provide a 500-or-more channel system. Companies such as IBM, AT&T, and a number of regional phone companies are not far behind in planning a brave new world of multimedia delivery.

A cable-computer system is visualized by Continental Cablevision, one of America's largest cable operators. It moved onto the information highway in August 1992 by connecting with Internet, a system that services some 20 million users in more than 50 countries. This link allows Continental to bring electronic information to homes and businesses via cable. When accessing Internet's databases, the cable company's customers can hook their PCs directly to the cable system while bypassing telephone lines altogether.

Despite technical innovations, success will depend on the demand factors of a mass market. Are customer's willing to pay an estimated cost of $70 to $100 a month? Some projects failed because customers were unwilling to pay more. In the meantime, Continental hedged its bets with a modest plan to do its first hookups in Cambridge, Massachusetts, where many of its subscribers are professors and students at Harvard University and the Massachusetts Institute of Technology.

An even more formidable barrier for Continental, as well as for other cable companies, is access to capital. Experts estimate that the cable industry will require $20 billion to $43 billion to upgrade its existing physical structure. Cable companies that wish to participate in the race down the interactive multimedia highway will need huge amounts of long-term capital. One potential source is the Baby Bells, which have both deep pockets and vested interests to enter into alliances with capital-seeking cable systems.

Interactive media is still an embryonic business. Financial services will probably comprise only a part of a much larger package that contains shopping, learning, and entertainment. The long period of trial and error in interactive media has so far been mostly error: costly failures and a seemingly unending stream of development dollars. This emerging industry is still characterized as a technology seeking markets. As such, the final shape of interactive media remains shrouded in uncertainty.

Servicing Customers Electronically

Interactive media focuses on new revenue-producing activities. Customers perform existing functions, such as hooking up to stock exchanges via computers or "smart" phones.

More common in the financial service industry are electronic technologies that cut costs not only by replacing workers with computers, but also replacing the printed word with video messages. Customers often participate, doing a portion of the task formerly done by an employee. But the goal aims at cost reduction, not customer satisfaction. However, cost reduction and customer satisfaction are not mutually exclusive.

The greatest assaults on the costs of labor and materials have been most effective so far in intercorporate businesses. One form of automation in financial services is electronic data interchange (EDI). This process transmits standardized messages from computer to computer. The predesignated formats distinguish EDI from the free-form messages of electronic mail. EDI's standardized formats permit companies to transact business with each other in a paperless environment.

Another version of an automated communication system is electronic funds transfer (EFT). Though EFT can be considered a form of EDI, the industry regards EFT as a stand-alone technology. EFT systems were in existence for several decades. In the 1970s checking account information was transmitted from offices where checks were posted and processed. Gradually the system evolved into an interbank clearing and settlement system. Technological advances have generated increasingly more sophisticated EFT features, enabling banks to handle transactions of automated teller machines, point-of-sales, and debit cards.

EDI/EFT eliminate not only paper, but a number of manual processing steps. Among the potential benefits are:

- Electronic transmission of funds and financial information reduces personnel in customer support activities.
- Payment periods shorten when funds are automatically transmitted from buyer to seller.
- Real-time banking improves cash management and ties customers more closely to a bank.

Publishers were among the first to realize that electronic media are capable of reducing gigantic piles of paper—paper that breeds armies of employees and costs millions of dollars. The promise of a paperless society has yet to be fulfilled for publishers, but it seems within the reach of financial firms.

It is true that EDI/EFT have hardly begun to reduce labor and materials in financial services. But these systems are only a beginning. Image processing is another emerging technology that promises further assaults on the paper trail. This technology digitizes documents and delivers their pictures from department to department and from company to company.

None of these electronic systems is cheap. The installation of an image processing system, for example, is estimated to run between $350,000 and $1 million. It is also obvious that only the large financial houses will be able to afford extensive electronic systems. But as these systems penetrate the market, service and cost benefits filter down from larger to smaller firms, pressuring the laggards to adopt the new information technologies. Smaller firms can compete in this new technological environment by joining a network managed by a large bank or specialized processor. The diffusion of this technology also may lead to banks expanding their client services to accounts receivable, accounts payable, and checking account reconciliation.

Reorganization

As markets and technologies change, companies must reorganize their way of doing things. They must rearrange their work force and reassign tasks to take full advantage of the efficiencies promised by new technologies. An office that uses word processing programs the same way it used typewriters is not exploiting a computer's capability to its advantage.

Advances in computer technology are clearly moving away from mainframes toward PCs and desktops hooked up to a network. The Chase Information Exchange system, called CIX for short, offers some glimpse of this electronic world of tomorrow.

In late 1991, the CIX system went on-line. This system took several years to develop and cost $1.8 million. It was designed in-house in conjunction with several computer specialist firms. Essentially, the system integrated data from a variety of internal and external sources. All CIX information can now be presented in a standard format on desktop computers.

For example, an account manager can input conversations with clients. In turn, a salesperson or researcher can access the document, sharing the same information for investment analysis and customer support activities. Michael Dacey, executive vice-president at Chase Manhattan, characterized CIX goals as follows: "We wanted information self-sufficiency at the desktop (level)."[1]

However, the system is still in its developmental phases, and will probably not be fully operational for several years. CIX operates in three different desktop modes: Microsoft's DOS, IBM's OS/2, and Unix. These three modes do not form a completely "open system." That is, some Chase products operate on one system but not on another.

The move from mainframes to desktops provides a greater amount of information to more decentralized locations. This implies that the new software must be extremely simple to use. For example, customer service personnel cannot be expected to master complex instructions written in "computerese." Decentralization of information also demands that employees be knowledgeable of various operations relating to the data. This requires more careful recruiting and more extensive training of personnel. Companies like Chase operate on a worldwide scale, and so must integrate information on a global network.

Is the Chase prototype a harbinger of financial service operations in the years to come? Perhaps. As new technologies compete on information delivery, there is no telling which system will emerge as dominant. But one thing is certain: financial services will center on information. They already do.

Summary

Three major trends, evident now, will change the face of the industry by the 21st century. These are: expansion into other lines of business, globalization of financial services, and greater reliance on computers to handle the ever-growing masses of information.

Many of our financial services operate in mature business environments where growth is slow. In order to grow, financial

---

1   Quoted in Rosemary Hamilton, "Chase Banks on 'Info' Access," *Computer World* (January 27, 1992), p. 6.

houses must seek lines of business which are in growth stages. As this process evolves, a company's product mix expands. The area of competition expands, as banks, insurance companies, brokerage houses, and mutual funds offer similar financial products.

More rapid growth rates abroad give impetus to more globalization of financial services. Higher risks do not appear as major obstacles to American firms seeking the rewards of higher growth.

As firms expand their product lines and markets, they must handle more information. Advances in electronic technology offer a way of coping with greater demands for information handling. Among the emerging technologies with promise are interactive media, electronic data interchange (EDI), electronic funds transfer (EFT), and image processing.

Appendix 12

Table A12-1. Fifteen Largest Insurance Companies Worldwide

Company	Country	Assets*	Profits*
Internationale Netherlander	Netherlands	181,367	939
Union des Assurance de Paris	France	127,186	201
GAN	France	116,282**	75
Allianz Holding	Germany	113,451**	239*
Aetna Life & Casualty	U.S.	89,930	(5)
Prudential	Britain	82,057	440
American International Gp.	U.S.	79,839	1,625
Equitable	U.S.	78,869	(32)
CIGNA	U.S.	66,740**	337
Tokyo Marine & Fire	Japan	62,307	191
AGF	France	58,281**	278
Travelers	U.S.	53,600	(104)
Aegon	Netherlands	46,975	509
Zurich Vers.	Switzerland	46,973**	303*
American General	U.S.	39,740	533

*In US$ millions.

**Based on 1991 data.

Note: Assets and profits are for 1992 fiscal year, except where indicated by an asterisk. After-tax earnings translated at currency exchange rates of May 31, 1993.

Source: Based on "The Business Week Global 1000," Business Week (July 12, 1993).

Table A12-2. 15 Leading Financial Services Firms Worldwide

Company	Country	Assets*	Profits*
Fannie Mae	U.S.	181,000	1,649
American Express	U.S.	175,800	436
Mitsubishi Trust & Bkg	Japan	175,012	258**
Sumitomo Trust & Bkg	Japan	162,952	232**
Salomon	U.S.	159,500	550
Mitsui Trust & Bkg	Japan	142,098	92**
Yasuda Trust & Bkg	Japan	109,185	80**
Merrill Lynch	U.S.	107,020	952
Tokyo Trust & Bkg	Japan	83,590	169
Morgan Stanley	U.S.	80,353	510**
Nomura Securities	Japan	71,707	271
Nippon Shinpan	Japan	67,759	35
Orient	Japan	65,481	44**
Daiwa Securities	Japan	53,832	(401)
Sallie Mae	U.S.	46,620	394

*In US$ millions

**Based on 1993 data reported before May 31, 1993.

Note: Assets and profits are for 1992 fiscal year, except where indicated by an asterisk. Earnings are translated at currency exchange rates of May 31, 1993.

Source: Base on "The Business Week Global 1000," *Business Week* (July 12, 1993).

Index

About the Authors

William S. Sachs is a former business professor. He formerly taught at Eastern New Mexico University. He is both an economist and specialist in marketing. He has written extensively on product development, research methods, computer modeling and product distribution. He is the author of six books, including *Direct Marketing*, Second Edition (Macmillian, 1992).

Dr. Sachs has held management positions with the Advertising Research Foundation, a major advertising agency that is now a division of Saatchi & Saatchi. Among his clients were major financial institutions, including Chase Manhattan, Citicorp, GE, and ITT.

Frank Elston is a Professor of Finance at Eastern New Mexico University. His background includes a Doctor of Jurisprudence from Emory University and a Ph.D. from the University of Virginia. He has done extensive research and consulting in the capital markets.